Timelock

Other books by Ralph Keyes

WE, THE LONELY PEOPLE
IS THERE LIFE AFTER HIGH SCHOOL?
THE HEIGHT OF YOUR LIFE
CHANCING IT

Timelock

How Life Got
So Hectic
and What You
Can Do About It

RALPH KEYES

HarperCollins*Publishers*

FIRST EDITION

Designed by Alma Orenstein

Library of Congress Cataloging-in-Publication Data
Keyes, Ralph.
   Timelock : how life got so hectic and what you can do about it /
Ralph Keyes. — 1st ed.
      p. cm.
   Includes index.
   ISBN 0-06-016576-6
   1. Time management—United States.   2. Time—Social aspects—United
States.   3. Stress management—United States.   I. Title.
HN90.T5K49   1991
640'.43—dc20   90-55926

91 92 93 94 95 CC/HC 10 9 8 7 6 5 4 3 2 1

For my sister NICKY,
who has always helped me.

Contents

Acknowledgments

I would like to acknowledge help from the following people: Freda Abrams, Irwin Abrams, Lee Aiges, Peggy Anderson, Judith Appelbaum, Jane Applegate, Bruce Beans, Peter Caranicas, Susan Carpenter, Bill Coulson, Gay Courter, Philip Courter, Cathy Crimmins, Al DeLeon, David Diamond, Larry Dossey, Philomene D'Ursin, Emma Edmunds, Richard Farson, David Fletcher, Janet Fletcher, Pat Gershwin, Dick Goldberg, Phil Goldberg, Reba Gordon, Rick Gross, Jonellen Heckler, Lou Heckler, John Herrmann, Barbara Holland, Bob Inman, Gene Keyes, Nicky Keyes, Scott Keyes, Steve Keyes, Lynn Keyser, Margaret King, Gloria Klaiman, Leslie Kolkmeier, Art Kover, Herb Kurtz, Mae Kurtz, Donald Lee, Janis Lee, Barbara Leff, Robert Levine, Kathy Louv, Richard Louv, Bernie Lynam, Marilyn Machlowitz, Tom Maeder, Roland Marchand, Jeffrey Meikle, Scot Morris, Mike Mulligan, Jeanne Murtha, Bette Nadler, Wolfgang Nadler, Tia O'Brien, Bill Phillips, Gladys Phillips, Martie Proffitt, Nick Proffitt, Kathryn Ritter-Smith, John Robbins, Sue Robbins, Judith Sills, Robert Ellis Smith, Eileen Spinner, Anne Stillwell, Bill Stillwell, Marta Vogel, Robin Warshaw, Sheila Weinstein, and Jean Zimmerman.

Staffs of the following libraries were unusually helpful to me in doing my research: Swarthmore Public Library; Swarthmore College Library; Greene County (Ohio) District Library, Yellow Springs Branch; Antioch College Library.

My editor, Hugh Van Dusen, has been supportive throughout this project. John Boswell, my agent, was diligent in tending to its birth. As ever, my wife Muriel has been my best source of help and support.

Author's Note

When I began researching *Timelock,* the 1980s were waning. As I finished writing it, the 1990s were under way. In the process America's social context changed dramatically. New economic realities made life more hectic than ever. A triple whammy of global competition, domestic recession, and a downsized workforce increased pressure to *produce.* At the same time incomes stabilized, or even declined. The need to make ends meet is the most common explanation for time stress. Those ends were beginning to feel farther and farther apart. Until recently we worked long hours to get ahead. Now the struggle became to keep up. In either case the result was a feeling that time was scarcer than ever, and the pace of life faster.

This feeling will persist as the 1990s take shape. It's a sign of the times that so many consumers prefer merchants who promise not to make them wait: one-hour photo developers, jiffy auto lubricators, and pizza makers who guarantee delivery in less than half an hour. "The impact of perceived time scarcity extends to all types of retailers," noted Leonard Berry, director of the Center for Retailing Studies at Texas A&M. "In the 1990s, a store that wastes people's time will be committing competitive suicide."

For all of this, I suspect that we will cope with time stress better in the years to come than we did during those preceding. For one thing we have more experience in juggling demands on our time. We've also learned that some balls must be dropped—and left on the floor—if we're to come to terms with time's pressure. Many who thought they could have it all and do it all are wondering what reward is worth the hectic pace necessary to pursue this impossible dream. That doesn't mean we will return to an earlier era of office daddies and coffee-klatch moms. Working couples are here to stay. However, as I detail in *Timelock*'s conclusion, the shape of society is gradually changing to accommodate the needs of time-pressed families.

A combination of new flexibility in the workplace and realism at home will allow tomorrow's families to function better timewise than did those in our recent past. Tougher times themselves could also ease hectic schedules. As *Timelock* explores, there is a paradoxical connection between too much income and too little time. Leaner living will force us to slow down, take stock, and select more carefully: what we buy, how we live, the ways we choose to spend our time. In the process we may develop better alternatives to the frantic pursuit of *more*. Learning to make do with less could pay a substantial bonus of a commodity hard to find at any price: time.

Everyone written about in this book is an actual person. There are no made-up or composite characters. To protect their privacy, the identity of some of those who are discussed has been disguised. Except where noted in the text, such people are identified by a first name only.

The Rise of Timelock

Desperately Seeking Time

On the twenty-third floor of a corporation's headquarters in downtown Chicago, a 35-year-old executive named Alicia described how she tried to combine family and career. Of medium height, with wavy auburn hair, Alicia wore a gray-on-black maternity dress. Her 4-year-old, Matthew, had been born one week before she completed her MBA finals. His sibling was due in five months. Because commuting from her home in Waukegan took up to two hours each way, Alicia's alarm was set for 5:30 A.M. On a typical morning she showered, woke up Matt, then popped a frozen waffle or Pop Tart in the microwave for him to eat while watching a video. Alicia then put a coat over his pajamas, picked up the bag of clothes and toys she'd packed for him, and took Matt to her sister Julie who lived fifteen minutes away.

Sometimes Julie was still in bed when they arrived. If she was, Matt crawled into bed with his aunt. Alicia tried to spend five more minutes with him before dashing out to catch the 7:20 train to Chicago. Between 5 and 5:30 P.M. she reversed the process, picking up Matt two hours later. By the time they got home at 8 P.M. or so, Alicia had about enough energy to take a bath and crawl into bed. Matt and her husband Bob (a commodities trader with as long a commute as hers, but different hours) were usually there waiting for her, snacking on apples or spooning cereal from a bowl. Some nights they'd order pizza. Or get takeout from McDonald's. Then they all would lie around in bed watching television, looking at books, reading stories to one another. Alicia usually fell asleep first. Sometimes when her alarm went off the next morning Matt would be sleeping beside her. Other mornings he'd be back in his own bed. This was their normal weekday schedule.

"We don't eat dinner very often," said Alicia. "We shoot for Friday night dinner together, even if it's at Taco Bell. Then we eat all our weekend meals together.

"Every second of the waking day is used up," she continued, her words streaming out. "I don't even have time to get to church. I'd like to be more active in the community. There's not too much private time. If so, an hour here or an hour there. Plus doing all the errands. You have to be really flexible. Not worry about certain things not getting done. Like cleaning the house."

Does it ever feel like too much?

"Absolutely."

What suffers from the schedule she and her husband keep?

"Well, the bathroom hasn't been cleaned in two months," said Alicia with a rueful smile. "The microwave didn't work for a while after it caught fire making popcorn. I thought I would die. I don't think I could live without the microwave. Or the answering machine. Or my sister. Probably my sister is the one thing I couldn't live without."

How do you feel about the amount of time your son spends with her?

"It means when I'm here I can be totally here. I don't worry about Matthew while I'm at work. But sometimes when I get home he says he misses his aunt."

Does that get to you?

Without hesitating Alicia punched her chest. *"Right* to the heart."

Is Alicia's case out of the ordinary? Hardly. She speaks for many. Specifics may vary, but the theme is always the same: Time is scarce and getting scarcer. Few of those interviewed for this book saw time as a congenial presence in their lives. "My enemy," is what more than one subject called it. Others barely used words at all. Upon hearing that I was studying time pressure and the pace of life they simply clutched their stomachs and moaned.

When I asked a group of lawyers in New York whether time was an issue for them, Harold, 55, immediately snapped, "It's no longer an issue. There is none."

"Time is the only issue for me," said Victor, a 60-year-old veteran of thirty-five years in a corporation's legal division. "It's the most precious commodity I've got and I don't have enough of it. It used to be money. Now it's time."

"There are at least a hundred things to think about at any one time," concurred his colleague Brent, a 38-year-old father of four, "but you've only got one brain working. The only time you can spend lots of time on anything is either by artificially shutting out people who are trying to get at you or doing things in private time later. I have a young family, and when the kids all go to sleep things are calm and I can go back to work. It's really about the only time I can spend more than five minutes on anything knowing that I won't be distracted.

"When I got home last night, all my kids were in bed and my wife was asleep on the couch."

When traffic grows so congested that it can no longer move, engineers say it's reached a state of "gridlock." Many of us are in a state of "time-lock." Timelock is the condition that occurs when claims on our time have grown so demanding that we feel it's impossible to wring one more second out of a crowded calendar. As one Minneapolis businesswoman put it, "You prioritize, list your 'musts,' then you can't even get to your musts." Almost 60% of 443 subjects who filled out my questionnaire about time said that their lives had grown busier during the past year.* More than half agreed with the statement "There aren't enough hours in the day to do everything I have to do." Another 31% concurred that "on the whole I have just about enough time to do what I have to do." In other words, 85% felt that they had virtually no "spare" time. As compared with ten years ago, 60% said they had less leisure time today.

Other surveys have found the same thing. In 1985 a majority of subjects told Roper's pollsters that they had far too little leisure time. Ten years earlier most had said that they had about the right amount. A Louis Harris survey reported that between 1973 and 1987 the average American's free time had shrunk from 26.2 hours a week to 16.6 hours a week. Although the accuracy of Harris's numbers has been questioned, that's almost beside the point. His findings attracted a good deal of attention because they struck such a common chord. In Harris's words, "Time may have become the most precious commodity in the land."

The Time Crunch

Two words come up more than any others in contemporary discussions of time: "never enough." This phrase is the slogan of the time-pressed. On my questionnaire I asked the subjects—who came from many walks and stages of life—to jot down whatever words first came to mind when they thought about time. Their responses were revealing. Although those polled lived all over the country, it was as if they had been jammed together in a crowded classroom copying off each other's papers. "Never enough" or "not enough" was written down more than any other single phrase—by nearly a third of those who filled out the form. Well over half wrote some variation on the time scarcity theme. "Desperately seeking hours and blocks for many projects that I don't know how or when will get done,"

*A self-scoring version of this quiz is included as an Appendix.

scribbled a 42-year-old female hospital administrator. "Too many things to do, not enough time," said a 31-year-old male transportation planner. "Can't do what's important to me."

Some streams of consciousness about time were almost poetic:

> never enough
> time always
> accounted for
>
> never enough
> always rushed
> can't slow down
>
> not enough
> rush
> when?
> now
> want
>
> leisure
> speed
> regret
>
> pressure
> intrusion
> precious
> quiet

Other free associations about time included:

Which kid needs to be driven where?
Sorry I'm late.
Is it that time already?
It's what day?
Help!
I need sleep.
A few more minutes of sleep.
If only I had four more hours a day.
Too much to bear, sleepless nights, headaches, tension.
Pressure, pressure, pressure.
Unmanageable.
More valuable than money. The currency of the '90s (and I'm broke).
Babysitters rule the world.

"I had to go through twelve babysitters to get here tonight," reported Marilyn, a 40-year-old working mother of two during a focus group on time pressure held outside New York (one of sixteen conducted around the country for this book). After a successful career as a computer programmer Marilyn had reduced her hours to spend more time at home. Even so, time was tight. "I grew up on Donna Reed, unfortunately, as a lot of us did," she said. "I love to cook but I don't have the time to do as much as I'd like to. Dinnertime is hectic. It gets crazy at that hour. There's a lot of screaming and yelling. Even on my days off it's hectic, maybe because I'm trying to catch up on all the things I couldn't do the rest of the days. I bought a microwave just to heat up meals but now I have to admit I'm baking potatoes in it, which I was totally opposed to."

During a focus group held near Dayton, Ohio, Susan, a 35-year-old freelance copywriter and mother of two, compared her life to "riding a wave: jump on your surfboard at six in the morning, wash up on the beach at ten that night." Like Alicia, Susan didn't know how she'd cope without a microwave oven and takeout pizza. Yet her own mother—a schoolteacher who had far fewer conveniences—also seemed to have more time. "I can remember my mother having time to hang clothes on the line, bake pies," Susan recalled. "Theoretically I should have that time too, but I feel I have less."

"The sign of the times is that all our mothers used to bake brownies," agreed Sandy, a Boston supermarket supervisor. "There is a microwave brownie mix and in six minutes you can have brownies. My son and I love it. I think they're comparable to the others. He wouldn't know. He once said, 'Mom, what's apple pie?' "

DayRunner Syndrome

What is going on? Wasn't modern technology supposed to provide less work and more leisure by now? Just the opposite seems to have happened. Two centuries since the first apple parer began saving time in America's kitchens and nearly four decades since the introduction of computers to its offices we're more beleaguered than ever by demands on our time. A poll of nonvoters in the 1990 Congressional elections found that the most common excuse—given by 30% of those questioned—was lack of time. The usual explanation given for taking a pet to the pound is that its owner no longer has time to care for it. Appointment calendars that used to begin at 8 A.M. and end at 6 P.M. now start at 7 A.M. and end at 7:30 P.M. In the age of timelock such time-organizing tools have come to feel indispensable for many. This is the DayRunner Syndrome. "I live on an appointment schedule book," said Jed, a 60-year-old Dallas psychologist. "My life revolves around that. I'm self-employed. My wife and I do a lot of work together, and that's very time-demanding, highly scheduled, and highly structured. It seems like there's never enough time." Nancy, a San Diego nurse who was raising a learning-impaired 5-year-old by herself, said she spent so much time with date book in hand that she'd taken to calling it her "brains." "I never go anywhere without my 'brains,'" Nancy commented during a focus group. "My little red book has to go with us so we can make sure that everybody's on track. Otherwise we miss stuff. It's like everything has to be put together with Super Glue, and even then it doesn't stick."

Time warriors on the front lines—single parents and two-career couples—find that balancing their hectic schedules requires huge appointment calendars on the kitchen wall and message pads by every phone. Those who feel caught in time's pincers develop a ravenous hunger for any and all means to squeeze more productivity out of each available minute. Timelocked consumers crave fast service: overnight package delivery, eyeglasses made in an hour, lunch served in less than five minutes.

When Gail, a working mother in New York, was asked whether she appreciated the advent of three-minute microwaveable meals, she replied, "Even three minutes is too long for me." Her family's meals usually consisted of Wheat Chex, simple salads, or takeout. "It's not just making it," Gail said of their dinner scheduling problems. "It's when do you have time to eat it? We eat in shifts. At least I always eat with Megan (her 1-year-old). My husband is usually late. Occasionally I make us something quick. That's it. Dinners have really suffered around here. Also breakfasts and lunches."

Despite being armed with datebooks, microwaved meals, and one-hour loans, most of us feel that we have less time than ever. In an attempt to squeeze some into our schedules we typically engage in an endless search for the perfect time organizer; buy any and all gadgets that promise to save a few minutes; perfect the art of doing two, three, or more things at once; give up activities such as napping or reading novels as luxuries from the past; try to do everything just a little bit faster; and wonder why none of these steps seems to ease time's crushing pressure. On balance, most of the attempts we make to master time don't succeed. They simply add to the pressure. The ongoing theme of this book will be just that: *The harder we try to control time, the more time controls us.* Why should that be?

Chapters to come will explore different aspects of this paradox. Key questions to be considered include: "How did life get so fast-paced and hectic?" "What toll is timelock exacting on our bodies, spirits, and family life?" and, most importantly, "What can be done about it?" These questions will provide the focus for *Timelock*'s sections: first exploring the *rise* of timelock; then its *causes,* its *impact* on our bodies and spirit; and, finally, *alternatives* for those who wish to avoid becoming timelock's victims.

To gather information, I've conducted individual and group interviews throughout the country to supplement data collected from questionnaires. I also talked with a wide range of experts on different aspects of today's time pressures and scoured libraries for material going back well into the last century to put this topic into perspective. From telegraphy in the 1840s to facsimile transmission today, one innovation after another has responded to our demands for a faster tempo, then speeded it up some more. Labor-saving devices eased the drudgery of our lives but added to their expense. Being able to pay for a standard middle-class life-style has grown increasingly more expensive and time-consuming. Two paychecks can feel essential to do so. As a result, our sense that time is growing short has been exaggerated, not alleviated. To keep up, we step it up. The results are all around us.

Fast Forward

We all feel life's quickening pace. How could we miss it? Graphologists see its impact in the scrawl of modern handwriting. A Delaware court reporter said witnesses now speak twenty to forty words a minute faster on the average than they did in the 1950s. During two decades of writing for magazines, I've watched the preferred length of articles halve, even quarter. Declining newspaper readership has led to shorter news articles with lots of graphics, designed more for scanning than reading. On television news the length of sound bites is down. In movies the tempo is up. "Everybody has learned to live faster lives," explained Kingston Trio member Bob Shane after they up-tempoed old standards for a comeback tour. "We moved up the pace."

It's as if life had been put on fast forward. After time's scarcity, subjects of this study most often pointed to its accelerating pace as a source of stress. "Time flies," wrote several. "Too fast," said others, or "too hectic," "too much hurry," "always rushing," and "always on the go." Two-thirds of those who filled out my questionnaire said that during a typical day they felt rushed constantly or often. Another 30% said they sometimes felt that way.

It's become a commonplace to observe that *speed* of transactions is crucial in today's economy. (As we'll see, this conclusion has a longer history than we usually realize.) Methods of production, distribution, and marketing that deliver products faster than competitors do gain crucial market advantage. A mushrooming commerce sells time over product. The Bank of New York boasts a "60 Minute Loan," one "designed to keep pace with a hurry-up world." Compaq claims that their computers are "dizzyingly, blindingly fast." Toshiba says that with their portable computer in hand, "you're fully armed for today's fast-paced business world."

More than any other pollster, the Roper Organization has studied the specifics of what one Roper executive calls our "society on the go." This ongoing market study polls 2000 consumers throughout the country ten times a year. Roper has been tracking the time shortage trend since their current survey began in 1973, and has noted its impact since the mid-1980s in particular. "Our studies clearly show that people feel they have less and less time," reported Tom Miller, editor of Roper's *Public Pulse.* "They have the impression that they have less hours and days than they used to."

In his seventeenth-floor Manhattan office, surrounded by computer printouts, Miller said that in recent years Roper has found a steady rise of interest in goods and services that promise to save time. These range from takeout food through automatic bank machines to VCRs (which subjects say they particularly like because watching taped movies takes so much less time than seeing them in theaters). Those polled report spending less time browsing in stores than they used to, having fewer hobbies and a declining number of "personal interests" overall. "Instead of mentioning six or seven interests they'll mention three or four," said Miller. "This suggests that people feel this time pressure, the increasing lack of time."

Miller made a direct connection between such findings and those that show rising levels of stress. In 1987, some 42% of Roper's sample said they felt stress and tension at the end of the day. Two years later, 47% said they felt that way—a statistically significant increase. More women than men reported feeling tense by day's end, working women in particular. Other high-stress groups included executives and parents of children under 18, particularly those who are part of a two-income household.

"Few researchers would need to examine the diary data to know that working parents are under severe time pressure," agreed University of Maryland sociologist John Robinson. For nearly three decades Robinson has studied how Americans use time by having them fill out detailed activity diaries. In his latest survey (based on material gathered between 1985 and 1987), the sociologist found that nearly one-third of a representative group of Americans said they always felt rushed. This was up from 28% who said the same thing in 1975 and 25% in 1965. Robinson found that over 40% of women aged 18–44 now said they always feel rushed. The highest figure for rushing—52%—was recorded for women who work 50 or more hours a week. Only 40% of the men who work such a schedule reported feeling that pressed for time, probably because they do less parenting and house-work. On the other hand fathers of preschoolers recorded the sharpest drop in free time in their diaries, down ten hours a week since 1975 (compared with a four-hour weekly loss by mothers of preschoolers). In general Americans aged 36–50 had the least free time, while those aged 51–64 reported the greatest gain of leisure since 1965, probably due to the empty nest syndrome.

Because of this range of findings, John Robinson takes a more measured approach to the time shortage issue. Unlike nearly every other student of this topic, he questions whether work weeks actually are getting longer as leisure time shrinks. In the time diaries he's been studying since 1965, Robinson has found no evidence that free time is declining across the board. Older subjects, unmarried ones, and those who are less affluent even record a modest rise in free time. And, although hours spent at work have stayed steady in recent years, the amount of working time used for personal chores and errands has gone up. On balance, said Robinson, with the exception of beleaguered groups such as baby boomers in general and working parents in particular, free time is actually up slightly, not down.

But that's a big exception. As Roper's Tom Miller emphasized, time pressure is felt most acutely in the 35- to 44-year-old "baby boom" group that is our largest demographic cohort. Even as they grow older, Miller thinks this bulge group will continue to feel pressed for time. In addition, he said, whether or not our overall pool of free time is actually shrinking, most subjects *feel* that it is and consistently report this feeling to pollsters. Eventually such prophecies become self-fulfilling. Or as Miller puts it, "Attitudes predict reality."

This is why he, like many, is sure that time scarcity will be one of the great social issues of the nineties. Yet little serious inquiry has been made about the origins and impact of this problem, to say nothing of ways to avoid becoming its victim. How did life get so busy, its pace so fast and furious? Is the pressure of time self-inflicted, or has it been imposed on us? Is timelock a uniquely American phenomenon or one that's more global? What price are we paying for the demanding pace of our lives? Are there practical ways to seek relief from time's pressure short of fleeing to Tahiti?

Time-Phobes and Time-Philes

Everyone does not respond to pace and pressure in the same way, of course. Some don't mind it at all. A minority of those filling out my form said that they actually enjoyed the brisk tempo of modern life, and that they preferred a crowded calendar to one without enough written on it. "If I didn't want pressure, I'd be a Maytag repairman," noted a 34-year-old ad copywriter on his questionnaire. "I like it and it motivates me." "I like pressure and a fast pace at work," agreed a male research scientist of 42. "They make me more productive." "I love stress and time deadlines," concurred a 23-year-old female television news producer. "That's when I'm at my best. I get bored when things slow down."

In the Fort Myers, Florida, focus group, debate was lively about whether today's time pressures had to be so toxic. "I feel a great pleasure

in time," said Harris, a 40-year-old self-employed management consultant.
"I like to meet and beat deadlines. I like the feeling of having some of the
things in my life on a schedule and I like to be able to get them completed
in that time. It's not pressure for me. It's very pleasant, the using of time
and the manipulating of time."

Rachel, who had recently resumed her teaching career, had the group
in stitches as she described her approach to coping with pace and pressure
while raising three children. "I'll tell you how I do it," Rachel said. "The
surface has to be clean. Everything else gets thrown in the closet. And if
you happen to open the closet and it all falls out, that's your problem. I really
hate to cook, so I cook meals in the microwave because it's fast. Get it over
with quickly. Why bother washing dishes when you can use paper plates?
I'm the only one in this whole area that serves on paper plates. I am not
upset about it. People know it. I set the table. I throw it out. I don't feel
like I have to be a perfect wife, or a perfect mother. I don't feel like I have
to do everything perfectly. I guess that doesn't put too much pressure on
me. Time doesn't bother me at all."

Rachel admittedly had enjoyed the luxury of raising her children without
having to work for income. But since resuming her teaching career to help
pay for their upcoming college tuitions, she didn't feel worse off timewise.
"I think my kids had more of a problem dealing with the fact that I went
back to work full-time than I did," said Rachel. "They would say to me,
'Where's my shirt?'

" 'In the dirty laundry.'

" 'Why didn't you wash it?'

" 'Well why didn't *you* wash it?'

"Going back to work hasn't been that big of an adjustment. You have
to roll with the punches. Life just doesn't hassle me as far as time. There
are other things in my life that are much more important to me than time.
My attitude is, 'If it doesn't get done today it will get done tomorrow.' "

Rachel was among a minority who felt relaxed about time. More typical
was Cal, a father of three young daughters with a working wife. Cal described in vivid terms the pressure he felt from time. "It may take me two
or three days to read the paper," he told the Fort Myers group. "I'll see
a front page that I like but it's not news anymore when I get to it." Cal
owned a small castings business that he'd started soon after getting married
ten years before, at age 30. Until then he'd had a lot of time to himself. After
the first of his daughters was born in 1982, personal time became a memory.
Cal admitted that it took a long time—three or four years after their oldest
child was born—before he could go for days at a time without resenting his
loss of free time. Only after realizing how much he enjoyed the company
of his family and needed the security of a stable business could he accept
the fact that leisure time was part of his past (and, he hoped, his future)

but couldn't be part of his present. "I finally made some peace," Cal concluded, "when I realized that someday, maybe, when I'm 65 I will have more time. But right now, because the business and the children are my first priorities, I've written off personal time."

Cal's wife, Wendy, a successful television producer, was 28 when they were married. Trying to balance that career with raising three children hadn't been easy. "I'm saying to myself there may be something wrong with all this churn, churn, churn," said Wendy, "but there's also something equally wrong when it stops dead at age 65 as it seemed to for my parents. I wish there were more integration. Couldn't we just be busy until we're 85 and not be so frantic in our younger years? Couldn't there be more of a meld? My ideal would be if you could be moderately busy. If society could recognize for the time you're raising small children that that needs to be an emphasis for you and didn't cut you off. Because if you're not working while you're raising small children, you've cut yourself off of all of those years. When you try to jump back in again at age 45 or 50 you might as well forget it. Couldn't society come to some recognition that there are phases and ways to time this so that you're not, as my mother is, desperate for something to do at age 72, and me begging for two minutes?"

Wendy spoke for many. Timelock is a symptom of the times. In the next section I'll try to put the rise of timelock in context. It's easy to imagine that time as we conceive of it—as a sequence of seconds, minutes, and hours beleaguering our lives—is so natural and so universal that nothing can be done to change that conception. This simply is not the case. "Time," as we use that term, is a modern concept that still makes little sense in much of the world. Before we can begin to understand the role time pressure has come to play in our lives, we must first look at the invention of time itself. Because time, in the modern sense, is not just an invention, but a fairly recent one at that.

2

A Brief History
of Timekeeping

> The clock, not the steam-engine, is the key-machine of the modern
> industrial age.
>
> —LEWIS MUMFORD

The first thing many of us do while on vacation is remove our watch. It's amazing how much lighter this can make us feel. Shaking off the clutches of time isn't that easy, of course. For the first few days we're likely to glance at our bare wrist repeatedly, look about for the closest clock, or ask any watch-wearing person in the vicinity, "Could you tell me what time it is?"

If the vacation goes well, we soon stop asking that question. The answer doesn't matter. There is no innate need to know what time it is. To the contrary. As a good vacation of reasonable length reminds us, our bodies are happier when they *don't* know what time it is. At least not what time the clock records. Bodies keep their own time. They tell us when it's time to sleep, to wake up, to eat, and make love. On the rare occasions when we're able to live according to our body's time, it lets us know how grateful it is in no uncertain terms. It relaxes.

Organic Timekeeping

Left to their own devices, our bodies keep a remarkably varied schedule. When we eat, sleep, and work is directly related to the influence of season, sunlight, and inner body clocks. In 1989 a 27-year-old woman named Stefania Follini spent four months in an underground cave near Carlsbad, New Mexico, as part of a research project on the effects of isolation. Without time cues of any kind, Follini's body quickly developed its own schedule. Sometimes Follini stayed up twelve hours and slept for five.

14

Other days the ratio was seventeen to seven. On occasion she stayed awake for twenty-five hours, then slept half that amount. There were times when she had extended bursts of energy. Other days Follini just took it easy. Variety characterized her schedule, not uniformity. When she emerged from her isolation chamber after four months underground, Follini thought she'd only been gone for two.

For most of human history, body time was the only time human beings kept. Until quite recently there was simply no need to "tell time" in the modern, precise sense. Measurement of time was by the position of the sun or duration of events. Primitive units of time were based either on the position of the sun or how long it took to complete a given task. To the Masai of Kenya, the hour before sunrise was known as "the blood-red period," or "the time when the sun decorates the sky." In Uganda, Baganda women tilling gardens called early morning "first pipe," midmorning "second pipe" (the periods when they stopped to smoke). In Madagascar, "a rice-cooking," was roughly half an hour, "the frying of a locust" a few seconds. In England the same amount of time was called a "pissing while."

This might be called "organic timekeeping"; measuring time by one's body, the sun, and events. Even in an age of precisely calibrated microseconds there is still a tendency to tell time this way. My 10-year-old son once popped a piece of Bubble Yum in his mouth, then asked if he could play video games "until my gum loses its flavor." Before I bought a chronograph to measure my running to the second, I gauged it by laps around a track, or a certain route around town. When my wife Muriel and I review our history together, points of reference have little to do with clocks or calendars as such. Saying that something happened "in 1967," or "during the winter of '75" doesn't help us as much as saying "that happened just after we left college," or "around the time of that big windstorm in San Diego." We all tell our life's time by major markers such as "when Kennedy was shot," or "just after we got married." Individual markers are usually based on milestone events such as first love, leaving home, getting married, buying a house, and having children. Measuring time this way integrates it with our lives. Time told by important events has texture, and resonance. The associations are rich. Gauging time by the calendar or clock is sterile. The names of months and days, or the numbers on a watch mean nothing without a context. All they are is precise.

Telling time by events is imprecise. But for most societies throughout history this means was accurate enough, and synchronized with a way of life that had no need for uniform units of time. When shown a watch or clock, "primitive" people typically find it interesting, but little more than a curiosity of no obvious value. To this day many of the world's people don't even have a word for "time" as such. They don't distinguish this concept from related activities. Among the Nuer of Nigeria, anthropologist E. E.

Evans-Pritchard found that time was gauged primarily by cow-keeping chores. "At milking," was a common demarcation. So was "when the calves come home." According to Evans-Pritchard the Nuer had no way to "speak of time as though it were something actual, which passes, can be wasted, can be saved, and so forth. I do not think that they ever experience the same feeling of fighting against time or of having to coordinate activities with an abstract passage of time, because their points of reference are mainly the activities themselves, which are generally of a leisurely nature."

Soft Time

This was true of our own ancestors. The pace of pre-industrial life was dictated by the elements. Before clocks came on the scene, time had a softer, more flexible texture. One sought evidence of the time in shadow movement. When the sun wasn't out, stomachs took over as time's next best indicator. "Your belly chimes," said an old English proverb, "it's time to go to dinner." At night it was futile to try to determine the time unless one was an accomplished stargazer willing to step outside into the cold blackness. Nor was there much point in trying to get any work done by the flicker of a candle, particularly as one's eyesight declined with age. During long winter nights most residents of northern latitudes simply resigned themselves to having no idea what time it was.

Think of this as soft time. Soft time is the antithesis of the uniform, precisely measured kind. It is vague, changes with seasons, and is measured primarily by what one is doing. Until recently this is the only kind of time humans were capable of recording. Not that it mattered. Ignorance of the exact time was a real nonproblem until the last couple of centuries. Most pre-industrial people lived off the land. They were more concerned about seasons than time of day. Other than determining the proper moment to sow seeds, slaughter hogs, and harvest crops, they had no pressing need to know what time it was. The right "time" to do things was when conditions were optimal. Being at the mercy of the elements—droughts, blizzards, winds, darkness—promoted a fatalistic attitude toward time's passage. In a general way our ancestors realized that time was running out. (The Roman poet Ovid portrayed "tyme fleeting like a brooke.") But they were not surrounded by calendars and clocks to keep reminding them of this fact. An intimate tie exists between time measurement and time pressure. It's hard to feel pressed for time when you're not sure exactly what time it is. Ignorance of time encourages a leisurely pace and a less-than-full schedule. How can you even create a schedule if you can't distinguish one hour from another?

Before the industrial revolution there was no lane but the slow lane.

Without clocks people worked until a job was done, not until a timepiece told them to stop. Life was filled with uncontrollable interruptions: rain, sunset, the lameness of an ox. On such occasions there was little to do but take a break. This made for a fuzzy distinction between work and leisure. Even during periods of extended work, the day was filled with pauses. Long mealtimes and after-meal naps were not the taboo then that they are now. In addition to 52 Sundays a year there were as many as 115 holidays honoring saints in medieval Europe. Long, hard days of harvesting crops usually culminated in the year's biggest festival. Our ancestors did not equate *hard* work with *constant* work as we so often do. Like Stefania Follini in her cave, their work usually consisted of bursts of intense activity followed by periods of respite. This irregular rhythm was in tune with our body's own clocks. British historian E. P. Thompson thinks the fact that this rhythm still characterizes students, the self-employed, farmers, and others suggests that it is the way most of us *would* work if we controlled our own schedule.

The Key Machine

The beginning of the end for soft time came with the development of timekeepers. The world's first "clock" probably consisted of a peasant's mark on the ground to measure shadows. Sundials formalized this method long before the birth of Christ. By recording the movement of shadows, sundials made it possible to measure time in abstract units, independent of associated activities. By doing so they implied that time has a life of its own. With the use of sundials our smallest unit of measurable time was reduced from the day to the hour.

Not everyone was thrilled by this development. Over two thousand years ago the Roman playwright Plautus moaned:

> The Gods confound the man who first found out
> How to distinguish hours! Confound him, too,
> Who in this place set up a sundial,
> To cut and hack my days so wretchedly
> Into small pieces! When I was a boy,
> My belly was my sundial—one surer,
> Truer, and more exact than any of them.
> This dial told me when 'twas proper time
> To go to dinner, when I ought to eat;
> But nowadays, why even when I have,
> I can't fall to unless the sun gives leave.

Despite the modern tone of this lament, it would be some centuries before precisely measured time began to rule our days. The saving grace of sundials was that they were so unreliable. These early clocks gave only an approximate reading of time. The length of their hours varied with the season. Clouds and sunset shut them down altogether. Sundials were hardly the basis for a modern society based on carefully measured units of time. "Water clocks"—timekeeping devices that recorded time's passage with falling water—were the most accurate of early timekeepers. But they required elaborate mechanisms and only worked when the temperature was above freezing. Hourglasses measured time's passing with a fair degree of accuracy, but had to be turned regularly. In some medieval monasteries an unlucky monk had to keep track of time throughout the night so that his brothers could be roused for prayer or work.

The dearth of dependable timekeepers made it hard to coordinate activities. When two or more people needed to gather at a specific time, dawn was the best time to do so. Agreeing on any other time was problematic. This is why so many important occasions in history took place at first light: battles, meetings, public hangings. Historian Marc Bloch describes one medieval episode in which a duel was scheduled to take place in a French village at sunup. Only one duelist showed up. According to protocol he waited until "none" (as noon was then known), then departed. The man asked that his adversary's cowardice be recorded. The only problem was that there was no way to confirm that it was actually midday when the single duelist left the scene. A court was convened to consider this matter. After examining the sun, consulting with clerics, and debating among themselves, the court concluded that noon indeed had passed before the man departed. His victory was put on record.

Bloch calls this episode symptomatic of "a vast indifference to time" which characterized medieval life. Not only were there no dependable, accurate, and agreed-upon means to measure time, there was not even a consensus about what was being measured. Before the mid-eighteenth century, Europe was filled with competing calendars. Countries, provinces, even neighboring villages used different means of telling time. In some settings midnight was considered the base hour, in others noon, or else sunrise, or sunset. Even after the invention of mechanical clocks, travelers had to reset their clocks repeatedly as they passed from one location to another.

A large part of the history of Western timekeeping has had to do with the struggle to develop uniform and precise forms of measurement. The day and the year are pretty much in nature's hands. No one argues with her. But they've argued about almost everything else. In pre-Renaissance Europe the length of hours varied with the season. Summer's hours were longer during the day and shorter at night. During the winter it was just the opposite. Not until the birth of mechanical timepieces did Western time start to be measured in units of equal duration: first hours, then minutes, and finally seconds.

Hard Time

Today we take uniform time units for granted. But when the mechanical clocks which made them possible first appeared they were considered revolutionary. Such clocks made their debut in Europe during the late thirteenth or early fourteenth century (no one is sure exactly when). Once they appeared, we at last had the means to measure time whether or not the sun shone, water froze, or a monk fell asleep and forgot to turn the hourglass.

The technology to do this existed long before clocks were actually invented. Only when enough people had a pressing need to measure time precisely did some unknown genius put the pieces together into the first mechanical timekeeper. "No one could have stumbled on it or dreamed it up," noted Harvard historian David Landes. "But someone, or rather some people, wanted very much to track the time—not merely to know it but to use it. Where and how did so strange, so *unnatural* a need develop?"

When mechanical clocks first appeared, most Europeans tilled the soil, worked on water, or kept house, blissfully ignorant of what time it was. But two groups had a pressing need for accurate time: merchants, and church-men. Monks in particular lived a rigidly scheduled life in thousands of monasteries where they were summoned to work or pray according to the time told by sundials and hourglasses. This is why the medieval clergy took to mechanical clocks like children to candy. With clocks to toll bells, not only would monks get a better night's sleep but the faithful could be summoned to prayers more faithfully. Such clocks began to appear on belfries through-out late medieval Europe, and caught the public's fancy. In time it was a poor European village indeed that had no "clock tower" to ring the hours. As the Town Council of Lyon concluded in 1481, their community was in urgent need of "a great clock whose strokes could be heard by all citizens in all parts of the town. If such a clock were to be made, more merchants would come to the fairs, the citizens would be very consoled, cheerful and happy and would live a more orderly life . . ."

Early mechanical clocks were greeted as liberators. Like Ukrainian peasants throwing flowers on invading Nazis, late medieval Europeans had no premonition of the price they would pay for this liberation. All they knew was that now they were free of the sun, the moon, and the seasons when it came to telling time. They had taken charge of their own time. A prestigi-ous new class of time emerged: time "of the clock," or "o'clock." Clocks became attractive ornaments in paintings. Poems were written to celebrate their invention. One medieval Frenchman put his tribute to tune:

> The clock is, when you think about it,
> A very beautiful and remarkable instrument,
> And it's also pleasant and useful,
> Because night and day it tells us the hours
> By the subtlety of its mechanism
> Even when there is no sun.
> Hence all the more reason to prize one's machine,
> Because other instruments can't do this
> However artfully and precisely they may be made.
> Hence do we hold him for valiant and wise
> Who first invented this device
> And with his knowledge undertook and made
> A thing so noble and of such great price.

A few cranks begged to disagree. Soon after the bells of a nearby clock began disturbing his sleep a Welshman complained, "Woe to the black-faced clock . . . that awoke me! May its head, its tongue, its pair of ropes and its wheels moulder; likewise its weights of heavy balls, its orifices, its hammer, its duck's quacking as if anticipating day, and its ever restless works. This turbulent clock clacks ridiculous sounds, like a drunken cobbler . . . The yelping of a dog echoed in a pan! The ceaseless chatter of a cloister! A gloomy mill grinding away the night!"

If digital beeps are the melody of the post-industrial era and a clock's tick that of the industrial, the regular ringing of bells was the late Middle Ages' theme song. This sound accustomed those who heard it to begin thinking in terms of uniform hours. Merchants were already thinking along these lines. Their need to notarize contracts, time loans, and plan trading trips reminded them every day of how valuable accurate time measurement can be. The more precisely time could be measured, the more money they stood to make. This new awareness of time's value was central to the Renaissance mentality. To early-day entrepreneurs, time was a commodity to be saved, sold, or rented. In contrast to the medieval way of life they were repealing, time did not feel plentiful to the new merchants of the Renaissance. To them it felt rare and precious. Others picked up the beat. Scholars of the Renaissance began to portray time as highly perishable, much like fish, or butter. To such men time was too precious to fritter away in mere leisure, or idle chit-chat. Tracts began to appear on how to manage time better by sleeping less, creating schedules, and doing more than one thing at a time.

Petrarch epitomized this frame of mind. During his lifetime, the mid-fourteenth century Italian poet was consumed with a need to "restore the ruins of lost time." Determined not to waste a waking moment, Petrarch limited his sleep to six hours a night. Every hour of his day was accounted for. In hopes of making the most of his dwindling supply of time, Petrarch read while having his hair cut, being shaved, or riding a horse. The poet saw his best hope for salvation in vigilant attention to the danger of wasting even a second. To relax was to risk catastrophe. Like so many Renaissance men, Petrarch imagined himself, as he put it, in a "war with time . . ."

Here was cut the Faustian deal that plagues us to this day. After taking charge of our own schedules, we began struggling desperately to bring time to heel. When time was in the hands of Nature and the Lord, there was no need to hurry, or be overly busy. Now there was every need. We began to keep hard time: rigid, uniform hours and minutes, measured by gears and wheels. We've been keeping it ever since. Once time was in our own hands, it was up to us to manage it wisely, schedule it efficiently, and step up the pace to make sure that none was wasted.

It probably is no coincidence that the word "speed" (originally spelled "spede") appeared in English soon after clocks began tolling the hours. Clocks reminded us at least twenty-four times a day that time was slipping away. Better to get a move on. Lest anyone miss this point, the casing of some early clocks, called *memento mori,* were shaped like skulls. In the seventeenth century an Italian poet noted a new sensibility that the increasingly common clocks were encouraging:

> Noble machine with toothed wheels
> Lacerates the day and divides it in hours . . .
> Speeds on the course of the fleeing century.
> And to make it open up,
> Knocks every hour at the tomb.

Clock Shock

The beat of modern life was under way and it sounded suspiciously like that of a metronome. The tempo of our lives gradually fell in step with the clock's regular pulse. This rhythm became the key organizing force of daily life. In its overall impact, the clock proved far more important as a tool for coordinating activity than for telling time as such. Mechanical clocks made it possible for workers to gather at regular times to work for a given number of hours. Without a dependable means to synchronize the activity of many workers, factories could not have been organized. Getting employees to accept time discipline was another matter. Still tuned more to the clocks of their bodies than to the mechanical kind, they were not enthusiastic about being rung to work at sunup and rung home at sundown (or later). For decades workers resisted clock discipline. When given a choice, early industrial employees typically chose time off over an increase in wages. The bane of employers was workers who put in just enough time to meet their needs. It took a combination of fines, bonuses, coercion, and—most successfully— the inculcation of a new "work ethic" to get across the idea that life's tempo should be based on that of the clock.

No people embraced this idea with greater enthusiasm than did Americans. It could hardly be otherwise. This land was settled at the same time that clocks were becoming a commonplace. Ships would not have been able to bring so many settlers to the New World without accurate timekeeping to aid navigation. Many of the settlers they brought were tight-lipped Protestants sympathetic to the idea that time is too precious to waste.

Devotion to work was one of the most basic ways in which the New World contrasted itself with the Old. Benjamin Franklin delighted in tweaking European correspondents by reporting that unlike societies that could afford idlers, in America the only idle beings were hogs awaiting slaughter. When Franklin founded *Poor Richard's Almanack* in 1733, the proper use of time was one of his main themes. Franklin promoted ceaseless industry and a frugal use of time in the most unctuous tones. "Lost time is never found again," Poor Richard advised his readers. "The Devil makes work for idle hands." His most famous maxim of all was, of course, "Time is money." This maxim first appeared in Franklin's 1748 essay "Advice to a Young Tradesman":

> Remember that *time* is money. He that can earn ten shillings a day by his labour, and goes abroad, or sits idle, one half of that day, though he spends but sixpence during his diversion or idleness, ought not to reckon *that* the only expense; he has really spent, or rather thrown away, five shillings besides . . .
>
> The sound of your hammer at five in the morning, or nine at night, heard by a creditor, makes him easy six months longer; but, if he see you at a billiard table, or hears voice at a tavern, when you should be at work, he sends for his money the next day . . .
>
> In short, the way to wealth, if you desire it, is as plain as the way to market. It depends chiefly on two words, *industry* and *frugality;* that is waste neither *time* nor *money,* but make the best use of both.

Once time could be measured accurately, its units became a marketable commodity. Workers no longer sold their skills; they sold their *time.* Piece workers became hourly workers. In England, some factory owners recorded their workers' time to the minute. Needless to say, those used to setting their own pace were none too happy about this new system. For those running it, the key was to break employees' preference for nature's rhythms and teach them those of the clock. Workers were encouraged to accept time discipline by the threat of starvation. The church pitched in by equating clock values with moral virtue. Clergymen preached sermons on the sinfulness of wasting time, and the virtue of saving it. One English minister in 1755 railed against "that slothful spending the Morning in Bed," which he imagined was common among the poor. The solution? An earlier start to the work day. "The necessity of early rising," suggested this minister, "would reduce the poor to a necessity of going to Bed betime; and thereby prevent the Danger of Midnight revels."

Schools picked up the refrain. The scheduling of educational activities grew increasingly strict and precise, meant as much to teach children time discipline as to convey information. In the words of one historian, "Putting little children to work at school for very long hours at very dull subjects was seen as a positive virtue, for it made them 'habituated, not to say naturalized, to labour and fatigue.'"

Thus was born the beat to which we still march. Work was no longer to be done in bursts followed by leisure. Now it would be steady; clocked in, clocked out. The working day would be long, and six or seven days of the week. Holidays grew scarce (it helped that Protestants didn't recognize all those saints). Festivals were shortened, toned down, or eliminated altogether. Extended mealtimes became a thing of the past. So did naps. New values were born: efficiency, haste, being on time. "Men began timing activities that, in the absence of clocks, they had never thought of timing," noted historian Carlo Cipolla of the post-clock world. "People became very conscious of time, and, in the long run, punctuality became at the very same time a need, a virtue and an obsession." By the Victorian era, calling someone "regular as clockwork" was a supreme compliment. The English upper classes developed a time fetish. There were proper times to work, get dressed, eat, and visit others. Only those who could afford a good timepiece could keep track of such elaborate scheduling. This was much of the point. Clocks and watches were major status symbols of this era. Like computers today, they represented power, precision, and modernity.

As long as employers were the only ones who owned timepieces, employees had to take their word for what time it was. It was not unheard of for work clocks to be set forward at the beginning of the day, sped up during mealtimes, and put back at the day's end. As David Landes has noted, once the price of timepieces began to fall, buying one became an act of self-defense for many workers. In the process time went from being a public commodity to being a private one. The owner of a watch became responsible for his or her own time; for being regular, prompt, and punctual.

By now clock discipline is so internalized that we take its values for granted. We assume that our attitude toward time is at least "natural," to say nothing of ethical. A tardy person is seen as disorganized and rude. Those with a knack for leisure are suspected of being lazy. Time has value. It ought not to be squandered. Spending time wisely is virtuous. Wasting it is immoral. And the more we can pack into our time, the faster we can make it go—the more living we will get out of our lives. To products of a timelocked culture this seems self-evident. Only when we leave that culture do we realize that our attitude toward time makes sense only to ourselves.

THE TIME TRAVELER

Robert Levine's first inkling that Brazilian time was not the same as North American time came on his first day as a visiting psychology professor in that country. On his way to teach a 10 A.M. class Levine asked a passerby the time. He was told it was 9:05. After strolling around campus for half an hour he passed a clock. It read 10:20. Levine broke into a sprint for his classroom. Arriving there in a sweat, he found the room empty. Levine stepped into the hallway and asked a group of students what time it was. One said 9:45. Another said 9:43. A third thought it was 9:55. The clock in a nearby office read 3:15. "I had learned my first lesson about Brazilians," he later reported. "Their timepieces are consistently inaccurate. And nobody minds."

The same indifference to time which made his students habitually late to class also allowed them to linger afterward. When Levine's first class was supposed to end, few students left. Half an hour later several were still there continuing the class discussion. "Apparently," he concluded, "for many of my students, staying late was simply of no more importance than arriving late in the first place."

During his year at Brazil's federal university in Niterói (across the bay from Rio de Janeiro) Levine was repeatedly confounded by the local attitude toward time. Appointments to meet at a specific time turned out to be a general framework, give or take an hour. Clocks throughout Niterói—including those in banks—recorded a crazy quilt of different times. (When Levine asked Brazilian friends if there was a number he might call for the correct time, they first looked puzzled, then laughed at the very idea.) He thought this might have something to do with the casual attitude toward time in Brazil. If clocks aren't synchronized, how do you determine lateness? Or promptness? Or anything in between?

Levine's initial reaction was to write Brazilians off as hopelessly lax about time. But the psychologist in him was intrigued. What lay beneath this attitude? Why were his students and colleagues so casual about the hands and numbers of clocks when he was so obsessed by them?

Levine spent much of the next year studying this issue. His research confirmed that a typical Brazilian college student defined "being late" for lunch with a friend as nearly twice as long as did his American counterpart (thirty-four minutes vs. nineteen). But the Brazilians also thought someone would have to show up a full hour before a scheduled appointment to be considered "early" (compared with half an hour among Americans). Thus their approach to time was not just flexible when it came to lateness, but flexible, period. Delving deeper, Levine found that Brazilians he interviewed didn't consider tardiness a sign of rudeness any more than they considered promptness evidence of hustle. To the contrary. They perceived someone who was consistently late as a more successful person than one who was punctual. The Brazilians also thought that such a person was more likely to be relaxed, happy, and likable. Punctual people were considered nervous, unsuccessful, and not terribly appealing. Unlike Americans, however, Brazilians did not consider time attitudes very important one way or the other in how they assessed each other.

This study led Levine to undertake the research that became the focus of his career: exploring how concepts of time reflect, and mold, national character. As with Brazilians, he found that most of the nationality groups he studied (the Japanese being a notable exception) were far less time obsessed than Americans. In countries ranging from Indonesia to Italy Levine found watches less common, clocks less accurate, the pace of walking slower, and the amount of time taken to conduct a routine transaction (buying stamps at the post office) longer. He discovered that an emphasis on being punctual went hand in glove with a faster pace of life. Japan, for example, had the most accurate clocks of any country he studied, the fastest walking speed, and quickest post office transactions. The United States was close behind, followed by Taiwan, England, Italy, and Indonesia.

THE PACE OF LIFE IN SIX COUNTRIES

	Accuracy of Bank Clocks	Walking Speed	Post Office Speed
Japan	1	1	1
United States	2	3	2
England	4	2	3
Italy	5	4	6
Taiwan	3	5	4
Indonesia	6	6	5

Three years after leaving Brazil, Levine spent a sabbatical year studying attitudes toward time in the Far East. His major insights proved to be about himself, and the cultural attitudes he represented. On the plane taking him from San Francisco to Tokyo, Levine at first felt elated about being so free of plans, schedules or time. "My joy lasted nearly 45 seconds," he later reported. "Then the terror: What in the world would I do for a whole semester without a schedule or plans?" How did he cope? Levine made schedules and plans. Within days after arriving in Tokyo he had developed a routine that filled his hours, and made one day like another. "You could have set a clock by my activities," Levine recalled. " 'What time is it,' you ask? 'Bob's reading his book in the park, so it must be 10 o'clock.' "

It took time for Robert Levine to break the grip of clocks on his daily life. In the process he became aware of a fundamental difference in concepts of time that he saw illustrated repeatedly: the difference between "clock time," in which activities begin and end according to the hands of a timepiece, and "event time," which is gauged by how long an activity takes, and how much time "feels" right to devote to that activity. In a small village in India, for example, Levine was invited to tea. Inside the hut were several men carving camels from wood. They stopped to join him. None seemed especially hurried. "It wasn't a question of how long it took," he recalled. "Carving a camel would take as long as it took. They carved, stopping to drink their tea, then carved some more until the job got done."

For those who took as long as necessary to complete a task, living on a clock-determined schedule would feel as alien as living without clocks would feel to us. One key difference was that they did not make the same connection that we do between time and money. "Here," noted the bearded, lanky psychologist during a conversation in his office at the University of California in Fresno, "we take the most ambiguous, amorphous, subjective concept—time—and translate it into the most objective, specific measure we know—money." He picked up a small tape recorder. "I could tell you literally how much of my time is worth that. It's worth twenty-eight minutes, fourteen seconds."

By contrast with such a means of reckoning time, during most of his sabbatical Levine had to adapt to a way of life in which the time on a clock or even the date on a calendar had very little bearing on daily routines. For example, if one does not regard time as money, there is little point in doing more than one thing at a time. Nor did clock-casual people see much reason to schedule activities or to fill their time with as many tasks as possible. What was the point? In country after country Levine had some variation on this basic dialogue:

Native: You Americans. You're always running around. "Time is money."

Levine: But we have a finite amount of time. We don't want to squander it. If you don't use it, you lose it.

Native: That's the whole point. You lose it by hurrying.

The longer he traveled, the more difficulty Levine had holding up his end of that debate.

One Friday afternoon in Solo, Indonesia, he went to buy stamps at the main post office, only to find the employees outside playing volleyball. Business hours, Levine was told, were over. When he returned two days later, the clerk proved more interested in discussing his relatives in America than the business at hand. Would Levine like to meet his uncle in Cincinnati? Which did he like better, California or the United States? Five people behind him in line waited patiently. Far from being perturbed, they seemed interested in the conversation.

Levine's own changing attitude toward time crystallized during a train trip from Rangoon to Mandalay in Burma. This trip took twenty-five hours—from 8 A.M. one morning until 9 A.M. the next. All "gringos" showed up on time and got seats. Many Burmese didn't and had to stand. But they didn't seem to mind. Most were smiling, and seemed to be enjoying the ride. The fact that the train was late arriving at its destination didn't seem to faze them. "At that moment," Levine recalled, "it dawned on me that it's really not just how fast people move and the pace of their life but the *quality* of their life. That's what it's really all about."

In one setting after another he began to see a clear correlation between a relaxed pace of life and the enjoyment people seemed to be getting from their lives. The fewer automobiles there were around, the more relaxed a country's people seemed to be. Levine envied them that part of their life. At the same time he was painfully aware of how mutual the envy was. Especially when it came to car ownership, he realized, "Most of them would trade their life for mine in a minute."

After his year's pilgrimage Levine returned to Fresno so steeped in the immediate that he had trouble focusing on the future or the past. He had come to believe that dwelling too much on the future (especially by overscheduling time) makes it hard to appreciate what one is doing in the present. As tasks arose throughout the day, he tried to ask himself continually, "Is this something I *have* to do? Is it really essential? If not essential, do I *want* to do it?" The answer was usually "no."

Levine tried to translate lessons from his travels into his life back home. He paid attention whenever an old stutter recurred as a tipoff that he was moving too fast. To temper the pace of his life he decided to stay in central California, in the opposite of a fast-paced metropolis. Whenever possible he walked, or rode a bike. "There are certain things I'll *only* do by bicycle," explained the 44-year-old psychologist. "I don't allow myself to think 'I've only got fifteen minutes, I'd better drive.' I *make* myself ride a bike. 'That's a bike trip,' I tell myself."

Levine has continued to study time attitudes, both here and abroad. In recent years he's noted how much more conscious of time digital watches have made Americans. Every hour throughout the day on campus he's reminded of the time by a chorus of beeps emanating from students' watches. When Levine asked one student what time it was, the young man

looked at his watch and replied "Three-twelve and eighteen seconds."
He's tried to imagine how the people he met on his Asian trip would
respond to such a report. For them the idea of synchronizing their activities so precisely with a little machine on their wrists would seem as
preposterous as not knowing what time it was would seem to us.

"North Americans are prime examples of clock-dominated people,"
he concluded. "Our watches tell us when it's time to begin work, time
to begin play, time to eat, and time to go to sleep. We commonly talk
about it being 'too early to go to sleep,' or 'not yet dinnertime,' or 'too
late to take a nap' or 'eat a snack.' The hour of the clock, rather than
the signal from our body, usually dictates when it is appropriate to begin
and when to stop . . . The high value that we assign punctuality and the
God-like power that we give our clocks and schedules are no more
normal than the more flexible approach taken by Brazilians. If, in fact,
normalcy is defined by adherence to the norm, we would have to con-
clude that our own views are relatively abnormal. We are a deviant
minority within the world context."

3

The American Tempo

The sense of hurry seems inborn in the American.

—JAMES TRUSLOW ADAMS

In the early 1830s, a Frenchman named Michael Chevalier spent two years touring the United States of America. His major impression was that Americans were an unusually *active* people. "If movement and the quick succession of sensations constitute life," Chevalier observed, "here one lives a hundred fold more than elsewhere; all here is circulation, motion, and boiling agitation." The American, he continued,

> is devoured with a passion for movement, he cannot stay in one place; he must go and come, he must stretch his limbs and keep his muscles in play. When his feet are not in motion, his fingers must be in action; he must be whittling a piece of wood, cutting the back of his chair, or notching the edge of the table, or his jaws must be at work grinding tobacco. Whether it be that continual competition has given him the habit, or that he has an exaggerated estimate of the value of time, or that the unsettled state of everything around him keeps his nervous system in a state of perpetual agitation . . .—he always has something to do, he is always in a terrible hurry.

Chevalier was not the only visitor to note the fast and furious pace of American life. When Francis Grund, an Austrian, landed on our shores in 1837, he found that "the United States present certainly the most animated picture of universal bustle and activity of any country in the world. Such a thing as rest or quiescence does not even enter the mind of an American." Then, as now, New York struck foreign observers as being unusually fast paced. The Englishman Frederick Marryat characterized a typical merchant in Manhattan as one who "always walks as if he had a good dinner before him, and a bailiff behind him."

Visitors from abroad were fascinated by our eating habits. They giggled over signs reading "Out For Lunch—Back in Five Minutes," and marveled at how much food Americans could shovel into their mouths in brief periods of time. "Gobble, gulp and go," was the way one tourist characterized our approach to food. A mid-century cartoonist spoofed an American restaurant menu which consisted of "short cake," "hasty pudding," "gobble pie" and "rapid transit steak."

Nikolaus Lenau, a German observer in the 1830s, gave this description of the dining room in his Ohio hotel: "A long table, fifty chairs on either side . . . food, mostly meats, covers the whole table. The dinner-bell resounds, and a hundred Americans plunge in; no one looks at another, no one says a word, each one plunges upon his own plate, devours what he can with great speed, then jumps up, turns the chair over, and hastens away to earn dollars."

This approach to consuming food simply reflected a broader urge to keep moving. Americans are a hustle-bustle people and always have been. From early in our history we have claimed an inalienable right to be in a hurry. "In this country," observed Michael Chevalier, "fifteen years is an age."

Like so many who have observed our ways, Chevalier was quick to add that this very pace underlay America's vitality. Because of their extraordinary energy and devotion to work, the Frenchman foresaw great success in business for Americans. But business of a certain sort. "He is fit for all sorts of work, except those which require a careful slowness," Chevalier concluded. "Those fill him with horror. It is his idea of hell. 'We are born in haste,' says an American writer. 'We take our education on the run; we marry on the wing; we make a fortune at a stroke and lose it in the same manner, to make and lose it again ten times over in the twinkling of an eye. Our body is a locomotive going at the rate of twenty-five miles an hour; our soul, a high pressure engine; our life is like a shooting star, and death overtakes us at last like a flash of lightning.' "

An engineer and economist, Chevalier came here to study our transportation network. He later served in the French government. In 1840 Chevalier's reflections on American life were published. He had seen the future, and it looked like the United States of America. From his perspective as an engineer, he thought our passion for steam locomotion would be far more important than any political movement in setting a tone for America's future, and that of the world. Chevalier also saw American ingenuity promoting a revolutionary new approach to industry based on mass production and labor-saving machinery. With a chronic labor shortage and zeal to get ahead, Americans were always looking for ways to save time and effort. At Monticello Thomas Jefferson devised gadgets that opened doors automatically and brought his wine up from the cellar. From its inception, the U.S. Patent Office was inundated with inventions calculated to speed and ease

American life. When Swedish novelist Fredrika Bremer visited the Patent Office in mid-century, she noted that of the 12,000–15,000 machines on record there (many of them displayed in miniature models), most "were for the acceleration of speed, and for the saving of time and labor." Bremer later visited a boys' school during a period of free drawing. Hoping to see what inspired them, the writer walked up and down the schoolroom's rows peeking at the pupils' slates. What most featured, she observed, were "smoking steam-engines or steam-boats, all in movement."

Full Steam Ahead

Steam locomotion was in perfect harmony with the American tempo. Averaging 12 to 15 miles an hour, steamboats doubled the fastest speed attainable by stage. An appalling rate of deaths and injuries resulting from strained boilers seemed a small price to pay for this time saver. "They would sail on a steamer built of Lucifer matches if it would go faster," observed Ralph Waldo Emerson of his countrymen.

On land, America's steam-powered locomotives were renowned for their ingenious design, capacity for speed, and tendency to run off the rails. When he toured this country in the late 1830s, Frederick Marryat marveled at how much carnage we were willing to endure in order to make time. Captain Marryat—an English military officer and the author of *Mr. Midshipman Easy*—described a harrowing derailment that caused nearly a hundred casualties on the Utica line in New York. One man lay beside the tracks with his leg so badly broken that a bone stuck through his trousers. Hovering over him were his wife and sister, themselves bleeding from wounds. This was their dialogue:

> "Oh! My dear, dear, Isaac, what can be done with your leg?"
>
> "What will become of my leg! What's to become of my business, I should like to know?"
>
> "Oh! Dear brother, don't think about your business now; think of getting cured."
>
> "Think of getting cured—I must think how the bills are to be met, and I not there to take them up. They will be presented as sure as I lie here."
>
> "Oh! Never mind the bills, dear husband—think of your precious leg."
>
> "Not mind the bills! But I must mind the bills—my credit will be ruined."
>
> "Not when they know what has happened, brother. Oh! Dear, dear—that leg, that leg."
>
> "Damn the leg; what's to become of my business?"

With that, reported Marryat, the man fell back groaning in pain. The Englishman thought this episode perfectly typified both the rampant commercial spirit of Americans, and their compulsion to make haste no matter the danger. "It can only be accounted for by the insatiate pursuit of gain," he concluded of this attitude, "among a people who consider that time is money, and who are blinded by their eagerness in the race for it . . ."

No means of transportation suited this race better than trains. By speeding the flow of merchandise—including passengers—railroads did more than any other invention of their time to accelerate the pace of American life. Doubling or tripling previous attainable speeds, early trains reduced travel times by two-thirds or more. In the process they transformed our relationship with the visual environment. On foot, atop a horse, or even in a stagecoach, the landscape was visible in detail. From a railroad car, this same world rushed past in a visual waterfall. Such a view was unnerving to those used to observing the cardinal in the bush, smoke curling from a chimney, or a farmer reaching down to lift stones from his furrowed ground. "The very permanence of matter seems compromised," worried Emerson after an early train trip, "& oaks, fields, hills, hitherto esteemed symbols of stability do absolutely dance by you."

Early passengers compared the sensation of train travel to being shot from a gun. Concern was widespread about whether the human organism could adapt to speeds of 20 miles an hour or more. It could, and did. The way we adapted was by detaching ourselves from our surroundings. Unlike the coach rider's constant engagement with the landscape and fellow passengers, noted German immigrant Francis Lieber, the American rail traveler "thinks of nothing else but the place of his destination, for the very reason that he is moving so quickly . . . There is no common conversation, no rondolaugh, nothing but a dead calm, interrupted from time to time, only by some passenger pulling out his watch and uttering a sound of impatience . . ."

The Birth of Punctuality

Railroads didn't just enhance our awareness of time; they transformed our temporal attitudes. As long as travel was slow, difficult, and unpredictable, there was little need for accurate travel schedules. Now there was every need. Timetables, more dependable timekeepers, and greater attention to time on the part of trainmen and passengers alike became necessary. "Have not men improved somewhat in punctuality since the railroad was invented?" asked Thoreau. "Do they not talk and think faster in the depot than they did in the stagecoach?" But such progress came at a price. In one particularly gruesome 1853 crash, two trains on a single track ran into each other head on while rounding a blind curve near Pawtucket, Rhode Island. Fourteen people lost their lives. An investigation revealed that one train's conductor had made a fatal miscalculation because his watch was slow. He reportedly had borrowed this watch from his milkman. The public outcry following this catastrophe fueled a growing demand for more accurate timepieces and better scheduling of trains.

For train schedules to be synchronized effectively, however, another invention had to become widespread: the telegraph. Before electronic pulses began racing information through wires, messages could be sent no faster than the fastest available form of transportation, or by carrier pigeon. Telegraphy provided a whole new form of communication: one that was virtually instantaneous. Its impact on post-Civil War America was like that of fax machines and computers today. Storekeepers could now place orders instantly with distant wholesalers, making possible an enormous expansion of retail trade. The ability to convey financial information quickly accelerated the pace of business transactions. Up-to-date stock news began to be printed in newspapers. So were yesterday's sports scores. Fredrika Bremer said she'd even heard of marriage proposals being tapped out on telegraph keys.

To the railroads' relief, telegraphy also made it possible to synchronize distant timepieces. But this task was complicated by the fact that keeping time was considered a local prerogative, much like hiring teachers and installing sewers. A guide published in 1881 listed eighty-seven different "time zones" served by trains in the United States and Canada. To make matters worse, time differences were not uniform; they did not vary by a predictable number of minutes or hours. This anarchy of time helped keep the era's tempo in check. When clocks don't agree, there's a limit to how fast life's tempo can become.

This would never do for a rapidly industrializing society. Only when everyone agreed on the time could we hope to do business on a modern scale. After much squabbling about which system to adopt, the nation's railroads agreed that on November 18, 1883, the United States would be divided into four standard time zones. Within a year every American line except for two small ones outside Pittsburgh adopted standard time. So did many industries, stock exchanges, and streetcar lines. Not everyone was thrilled about having to keep time by the railroad's clock. A writer in the *Indianapolis Daily Sentinel* complained that all 55 million Americans now "must eat, sleep and work as well as travel by railroad time . . . The sun is no longer to boss the job . . . People will have to marry by railroad time . . . Ministers will be required to preach by railroad time . . . Banks will open and close by railroad time; notes will be paid or protested by railroad time." Some municipalities defiantly continued to set their own clocks. Cincinnati, Ohio, and Bangor, Maine, were particularly determined to keep time local. Such opposition didn't last long. Bangor fell in step with railroad time in 1887, Cincinnati by 1890. In 1918 Congress made standard time the law of the land, ratifying what was by then largely a *fait accompli.*

Once American clocks agreed with one another, keeping track of the time became a national passion. A new phrase—"on time"—entered our discourse. Accurate, mass-produced clocks cluttered America's parlors, and dollar watches filled our pockets. With affordable time available to almost any citizen, punctuality virtually became a civic duty. Side-effects of this development were noted. "The perfection of clocks and the invention of watches have something to do with modern nervousness," wrote Dr. George Beard in 1881, "since they compel us to be on time, and excite the habit of looking to the exact moment, so as not to be late for trains or appointments."

Beard saw nervous exhaustion as the scourge of late nineteenth-century Americans. According to his diagnosis, the capacity of our nervous systems for "sustained work and worry" had not kept pace with demands being placed upon them. Beard thought that this was due in no small part to the spread of dependable timekeepers. "Before the general use of these instruments of precision in time," he argued, "there was a wider margin for all appointments; a longer period was required and prepared for, especially in traveling—coaches of the olden period were not expected to start like steamers or trains, on the instant—men judged of the time by probabilities, by looking at the sun, and needed not, as a rule to be nervous about the loss of a moment, and had incomparably fewer experiences wherein a delay of a few moments might destroy the hopes of a lifetime. A nervous man cannot take out his watch and look at it when the time for an appointment or train is near, without affecting his pulse ... We are under constant strain, mostly unconscious, oftentimes in sleeping as well as in waking hours, to get somewhere or do something at some definite moment."

Despite Beard's warnings, the lives of Americans grew more time-bound than ever. Wind-up alarm clocks—introduced by Seth Thomas in 1876—improved punctuality but reduced sleep. Soon after that Thomas Edison administered the coup de grace to darkness by perfecting incandescent light bulbs. At the same time improved central heating made us less dependent on seasonal tempos. The combined effect of such advances was to reduce our dependence on nature's pace and make it possible to create our own. The less we relied on sunlight and weather to organize our day, the more we relied on clocks. "Efficiency" became an obsession, as big a concept in its day as "productivity" a century later. Time management experts armed with stopwatches invaded the workplace searching for the least time-consuming way to do each task. According to Frederick Winslow Taylor (who pioneered this method), every worker was to have the exact amount of time necessary to do each job, "but not a single unnecessary second."

In the 1890s time clocks began to appear on American factory walls. Few workers cheered this advance, or the role clocks in general began to play at work. Although early timekeepers were lionized in poems, paintings, and plays, such tributes disappeared during the late nineteenth century. More common was this type of observation by a turn-of-century garment worker and poet named Morris Rosenfeld:

> The Clock in the workshop—it rests not a moment; . . .
> The maddening pendulum urges me forward
> To labor and still labor on
> The tick of the clock is the boss in his anger.
> The face of the clock has the eyes of the foe.
> The clock—I shudder—Dost hear how it draws me?
> It calls me "Machine" and it cries [to] me "Sew"!

Efficiency Hits Home

Clocks were not the only tool in the efficiency experts' repertoire. Phones were another. In an early ad for itself called "The Efficient Minute," AT&T reviewed other sources of working speed, then said, "But the Bell Telephone is quickest of all. It is *instantaneous.* No weeks or days or minutes wasted in waiting for somebody to go and come; no waiting for an answer. It is the most effective agency for making minutes more useful, more efficient . . . The Bell Telephone has placed a new and higher value upon the minute—for everybody."

Through tools such as telephones, the tempo of the workplace began to influence what came to be known as "domestic science." Household chores which once were done to the task could now be done to the clock. Recipes used to advise "cook until done," or "bake it well." Now they gave directions in precise numbers of minutes. New technology pitched in to make food preparation more efficient. Before the turn of the century a cookstove and perhaps an eggbeater were the only appliances found in most American kitchens. Now a new implement joined them: a can opener, the better to take advantage of Campbell's newly canned soups, Van Camp's pork and beans, and Franco-American's plum pudding. Such convenience foods didn't only come in cans. Boxed cereals, which were originally developed to make breakfast a lighter, more easily prepared meal, had the incidental effect of speeding up that meal's tempo. So did the newly invented tea bag, and soluble coffee. Food consumption took less time than ever. This was no small blessing for the rapidly expanding force of workers hurrying off to office or factory. There, "lunch wagons" sold sandwiches outside factory gates. A wide range of restaurants, including lunch counters, soda fountains, and automats served fast midday meals to office workers (including a new contingent of "typewriter girls"). One turn-of-century

Chicago magazine marveled at the range of alternatives that city offered workers in search of a quick bite:

> Innumerable restaurants of the hurly-burly kind invite the mobs from offices for the noon-hour lunch. An army of waiters resists the invasion, and there is strenuous action for a space. The all-important consideration is economy of time, and the business of a meal is transacted with barbarous brevity—by a sort of short-hand system of jabs and slashes, punctuated by swallowing. Of this class many are known as cafeterias, or, in the parlance of the impolite, "grab joints," where heaven helps those who help themselves. Men and women hugging roast beef to their bosoms and balancing a toppling armful of dishes rushes to and fro, on a perilous and exciting exploration for seats.

As the nineteenth century drew to a close, accelerating life's pace became a near-obsession among Americans. To us it seemed to represent New World dynamism. "The old nations of the earth creep on at a snail's pace," observed industrialist Andrew Carnegie, "the Republic thunders past with the rush of the express." At the country's helm, Teddy Roosevelt set a hyperactive tone, smartly rapping idle knuckles as he praised "the strenuous life." Waltzes succumbed to the faster beat of ragtime, which in turn gave way to jazz (whose name itself may have originated in the Creole term "jas," meaning to speed up). Vigorous new sports such as football and basketball were played to the clock. Bicycling—which doubled the speed available to most individuals—became a national craze. In 1895 the first organized automobile race covered 55 miles from Chicago to Evanston. Six years later Henry Ford won his first auto race at a speed just under 45 miles an hour and a Florida train set a record by traveling 120 miles an hour. "Breaking records has become a fashion," worried a magazine writer at the time, "and it is always speed rather than excellence that is the test . . . Speed, hurry, rush—doubtless they are effective as commerce accelerators, but they are death to esthetics. We have ceased to write letters, we propose marriage by wire and hold the wire until we hear the answering coo . . . Life to us takes on the guise of scenery passed through on a fast express. Houses, humans, cows, sheep, flash by in confusion. We get impressions rather than clear views. Even our friendships, our loves, and our hates are misty, indistinct affairs, that come and go and become dreams . . ."

Speed Lust

A major study of post–World War I trends commissioned by the federal government called life's quickening pace a sign of the times. The researchers concluded that new forms of communication and transportation lay at the heart of this pace, especially the automobile. By the late 1920s more than 25 million automobiles were registered in this country, more than one car for every five people. If Americans had shown a passion for steam locomotion, they demonstrated a positive lust for internal combustion. "Step on it!" replaced "Full steam ahead" as the best way to go. Cars married the American hunger for independence and love of convenience to its lust for speed. With automobiles at their command American families took longer vacations at greater distances. The leisurely stroll after church gave way to brisk Sunday drives. Teenagers spent more time away from home. The car dug a chasm of tempo between the generations. One mother in Muncie, Indiana, fretted that the only thing her 18-year-old seemed interested in was getting "a Studebaker so he can go 75 miles an hour." During a discussion about frustrations teenagers felt with their parents, a Muncie high school student observed, "Ours is a speedy world and they're old."

One of the earliest discoveries moviemakers made was how thrilled American audiences were by portrayals of speed. Vehicles rushing right at the camera—trains, cars, even airplanes—were a thrilling innovation in early moviemaking. The enormous popularity of moving pictures and their emphasis on rapid movement had more than a little to do with the feeling that life was moving faster. This was what impressed theater impresario Samuel Rothafel after he returned from a period away to create New York's Roxy Theater in 1926. The main change Rothafel noticed was that "life had speeded up tremendously. I soon found that to hold people's interest the first requisite was speed, the second requisite was speed, and the third requisite was still more speed!"

This meant that there was no longer time for slow, solemn overtures. Now even the opening music had to be up-tempo. It also meant that an environment had to be created using "style, color, change, light, brevity, contrast, sweep—all with a reasonable amount of motion" to create a sensation of movement. Rothafel's advice to other businessmen? Create their own up-tempo environment, one that "synchronized with the speed of American life as it is being lived all over the broad land today."

Throughout the 1920s, businessmen were advised to get in step with the new pace of life. Lamenting that no single word portrayed the relationship between time and money, one construction company president used charts and diagrams to make sure that his employees never lost sight of the fact that "the quicker we could do a job, the more chance we would have of making a profit . . ." Advice on how to squeeze more activity into less time became a staple of business magazines. One suggested cutting an inch off the front legs of an office chair intended for visitors. "The caller then cannot help slipping forward on the seat," explained this article. "A set of muscles gets tired—though the visitor does not know why he is uncomfortable. He may not even realize that he is uncomfortable; but his unconscious mind realizes it, and tells him it is time to be moving along!"

The Jazzed Age

Businessmen weren't the only ones to take account of life's accelerating tempo. Writers such as Ernest Hemingway, William Carlos Williams, and John Dos Passos developed a terse, staccato style in tune with the beat of the times. Following the introduction of New York's *Daily News* in 1919, smaller-sized papers that could be scanned on subways and trolley cars grew popular. Such tabloids were the *USA Today* of their era: heavy on visuals, light on text. Following their lead, magazines began to feature shorter, more briskly written articles. *Liberty* even included the estimated article reading times for readers who didn't want to waste a second. *Sales Tales* (a monthly for sales personnel) ran a regular feature called "One Minute Messages."

According to one 1927 adman, "quick" was the word of the hour: "quick lunches at soda fountains . . . quick cooking recipies. . . quick tabloid newspapers . . . quick news summaries . . . quicker novels . . . quick-drying furniture paint . . . quick-smoking cigarettes . . ." Prerolled cigarettes were perfectly suited to those who no longer had time to fiddle with a pipe or enjoy a leisurely cigar. As compared with pipes or cigars, they could be lit in a jiffy, even while driving a car. Cigarettes were in tune with the Jazz Age, a sign of "the rapider pace of civilization," observed a 1925 *New York Times* editorial. One reason for their postwar popularity was that doughboys had found cigarettes easier to smoke between barrages. Wristwatches were also popular at the battlefront; faster and easier to read than the pocket kind. Veterans brought that popularity home. Wearing rather than carrying a watch made it possible to tell the time more quickly and more often. Safety razors were another time-saver given a lift by the war. During that conflict the U.S. Army bought this new convenience from Gillette by the millions. After the armistice razor blades stayed popular as straight razors and leisurely barber shaves were thrown in the dustbin of history. Whether or not they actually eased time's pressure, such conveniences changed the texture of American life. "They did not save much time," noted historian Jeffrey Meikle of the many conveniences Americans began to enjoy after

World War I, "but they created a feeling of increased tempo."

Advertisers were acutely aware that postwar Americans equated speed with the good, the new, and the modern. In one revealing 1922 ad, DuPont portrayed a reverent-looking chemical engineer standing before a speeding train and soaring airplane. "He Has Helped Pack Hours Into Minutes," proclaimed the ad's headline. "The war with Time is as old as time itself . . ." read its text, "yet the most glorious victories have come in the past century . . . the century that has seen the entrance of the Chemical Engineer into the world's industries. It is he who has helped make your minutes as long as your great-grandfather's hours. It is *he* who, working miracles with metals, has made possible the wonders of today's time-saving transportation . . . the mile-a-minute locomotive, the cross-country truck, the racing motor and now, the promises of the sky's highways."

Such ad copy both reflected and contributed to the dizzying pace of the 1920s. Certainly it reflected the way admen felt. Most led hectic lives themselves. They lived in cities, or commuted on packed trains to deadline-driven work settings. Admen felt themselves to be on society's cutting edge. One 1920s copywriter sketched a portrait of "a typical citizen of this restless republic." As historian Roland Marchand has pointed out, this "typical citizen" bears a suspicious resemblance to the prototypical adman of that era.

> Whang! Bang! Clangety-clang! Talk about the tempo of today—John Smith knows it well. Day after day it shirs continuously in his brain, his blood, his very soul.
>
> Yanked out of bed by an alarm clock, John speeds through his shave, bolts his breakfast in eight minutes, and scurries for a train or the street car. On the way to work his roving eye scans, one after the other, the sport page, the comic strips . . . and the delectable details of the latest moonshine murder.
>
> From eight to twelve, humped over a desk in a skyscraper, he wrestles with his job to the accompaniment of thumping typewriters, jingling telephones and all the incessant tattoo of twentieth century commerce. One hour off for a quick lunch, a couple of cigarettes, and a glamorous glance at the cuties mincing down the boulevard. Jangling drudgery again from one until five. Then out on the surging streets once more.
>
> Clang, clatter, rattle and roar! Honk! Honk! Honk! Every crossing jammed with traffic! Pavements fairly humming with the jostling crowds! A tingling sense of adventure and romance in the very air! Speed-desire-excitement . . . !"

Then as now, admen took pride in their demanding schedules. They valued speed. And this value was communicated through taste-setting ads of that period. Among several collected by Boston University's Cecelia

Tichi is one picturing a big racing car beside a small adding machine. "Record-breaking speed" is promised for the latter. A postwar shaving brush touted itself as "the speedy brush." To tout its canned pineapple, one company—apropos of what it wasn't clear—featured a photograph of its assembly line workers captioned, "Speed . . . speed . . . split-second speed . . ."

Shop Till You Drop

As the range of products exploded after World War I, advertising became an increasingly important source of guidance for consumers. Americans were buying more and more things that they used to make, everything from blouses to mayonnaise to stepladders. This development is recent enough that some old-timers still call such products "store-bought," "off-the-shelf," or "ready-made." Presumably one saved time by getting bread from a baker rather than baking it, and smoking prerolled cigarettes instead of rolling them. But buying products created its own pressure. Time and effort are required to master consumption skills. Is one vacuum cleaner better than another? Where should I take my car for service? What toaster toasts best? Which cereal ought my family to be eating? One 1928 writer in the *Ladies' Home Journal* lamented that progress in manufacturing foods had so outpaced "the art of selecting and using them that [the homemaker] is often bewildered and discouraged with the choices offered." An advertising man observed that 1920s consumers had more purchasing decisions to make on a regular basis than many factory purchasing agents did before the war.

Advertisers offered shoppers a hand with such decisions. Then as now, time-saving was a key selling point. Quick Quaker Oats, for example, billed itself as "the most quickly prepared of all hot breakfasts." Such promises had a receptive audience. Families were finding that not just breakfast but all meals were falling victim to new time pressures. In Muncie, sociologists Robert and Helen Lynd noticed a marked decline of families eating together during the 1920s. Just a generation before, they said, midwestern meals had been considered a time of family reunion. But with so many women holding jobs, and with more organized leisure activities and a greater number of civic affairs competing for family members' attention, that tradition was on the decline. "I ate only seven meals at home all last week," complained one Muncie father, "and three of those were on Sunday. It's getting so a fellow has to make a date with his family to see them."

America's homes began to reflect life's new tempo. Traditionally one's home had been considered a tranquil refuge from the stress and strain of the workaday world. Increasingly they became part of that world, at least in spirit. Children's feeding, toilet training, and sleeping were scheduled by clocks and calendars. A *Woman's Home Companion* article proposed scheduling all household chores on a businesslike basis, using one sheet of paper for each day of the week. Rearranging kitchen equipment to reduce movement grew popular. An efficiency expert advised America's housewives that by doing this they could reduce the number of steps required to bake a cake from 281 to 45. A new generation of appliances—electric toasters, washing machines, refrigerators—promised to make housework more efficient yet. According to historian Siegfried Giedion, more household conveniences came to be seen as necessities during the 1920s than in the entire preceding century. With the help of such appliances we no longer were at the mercy of the sun and the seasons to do our daily chores. Now they could be scheduled at our convenience, with a substantial saving of time and energy. In theory, modern labor-savers took a load off Americans' shoulders in the 1920s. In fact we seemed more harried than ever. One observer described many of her friends as leading "A life that is always on the jump, that keeps a wild eye on the clock . . ." It even became fashionable to appear pressed for time. As a contemporary writer put it, Jazz Age Americans had become "time snobs."

Turning It Up a Notch

One would imagine that America's lust for speed came to a screeching halt at the Depression's wall. One would be wrong. After the stock market crashed in 1929 our passion to get a move on barely skipped a beat. All that changed was the rationale. During the 1920s an accelerated tempo was seen as the key to America's prosperity. After the crash, stepping up the pace was widely thought to be our best hope for kick-starting the economy. "Today, speed is the cry of our era," proclaimed Norman Bel Geddes in 1932, "and greater speed one of the goals of tomorrow."

Industrial designers such as Bel Geddes rushed to find ways to make the world at least *look* on the move. "Streamlining" was the result. Locomotives began to resemble inverted rocket ships. Passenger airplanes flaunted sensuous new curves. So did trendsetting cars. For a time during the 1930s everything from tricycles to pencil sharpeners boasted the rounded corners and forward thrust of a dynamic world in motion. Farmers could even buy a streamlined manure spreader. In most cases streamlining made little aerodynamic sense. But that was beside the point. What mattered was giving shape to the dreams of an era in desperate need of some. "Speed!" noted an article on streamlining at the time, "the very word has become a synonym for progress . . ."

Swing music quickened heartbeats during the 1930s, leading one psychologist to warn about its hypnotic beat, "cunningly devised to a faster tempo than 72 bars to the minute—faster than the human pulse." Dances such as the Lambeth Walk, the Big Apple, and finally the jitterbug kept pace with music's tempo. So, in his way, did Dale Carnegie, whose wildly successful *How to Win Friends and Influence People* told readers how to make friends in a hurry. *Life* magazine introduced a picture-based format better suited to scanning than reading. *Reader's Digest* condensed articles onto small pages handy for reading on train, trolley, or at the lunch counter. Lunch-wise, the success story of the era was White Castle. The owners of this chain of tiny hamburger stands perfected a food-delivery method that could get customers on and off their stools in twelve minutes flat. New convenience foods set speed records of their own. In 1937 Kraft's boxed macaroni and cheese made its debut, promising "a meal for 4 in 9 minutes." Five-minute Cream of Wheat soon followed, along with Chef Boy-Ar-Dee's canned pasta and Lay's Potato Chips. In response to the new gastronomic mood, Irma Rombauer published *Streamlined Cooking* in 1939, for "the hurry-up cook."

For some, even hurry-up cooking took too long. With the introduction of Nescafé on the eve of World War II, Nestlé gave new meaning to the term "instant." Although it improved on previous versions, this soluble coffee was still a pale imitation of the real thing. (Instant coffee ranked 342nd among food preferences of World War II GIs, just ahead of fried cabbage.) But Nescafé's success had little to do with its quality. In the guise of a breakfast drink, Nestlé was actually selling time, convenience, and independence. Brewing a pot of coffee assumes that enough people are around with time to finish the whole pot. Instant coffee could not only be prepared quickly, but one cup at a time. Nescafé was ideally suited to an increasingly hurried people leading ever more fragmented lives. As Nestlé later noted about their introduction of Nescafé on the eve of World War II, "Already at that date it was simple to predict that as the years advanced, so the tempo of everyday life would become increasingly greater and that more and more preference would be given to the use of food which could be prepared quickly."

The new gastronomy had its price. "Our modern 'eat-and-run' way of living is hard on digestion," conceded a cigarette ad at the time. "Hence unusual interest attaches to the following fact: that smoking Camels has been found to have a marked beneficial effect on aiding digestive action." Another ad advised the busy housewife (shown relaxing beside her vacuum cleaner, cigarette in hand) that, "All day, you probably go without a real let-up . . . household duties, social activities, each with its own contributions to nervous tension. So, when you feel yourself getting jumpy or irritable, just ease up and smoke a Camel."

The mood of the times was receptive to any and all means to cope, particularly such new labor-savers as automatic toasters, roasters, mixers, blenders, and stand-alone steam irons. At the 1939 New York World's Fair, Westinghouse put the home of the future on display: one dominated by electronic appliances. To prove their efficacy, a "Mrs. Drudge" regularly conducted a wash-off with "Mrs. Modern," doing dishes by hand in competition with her rival's dishwasher. (Like the Harlem Globetrotters, Mrs. Modern always won.) Swinging above Westinghouse's pavilion was a huge round pendulum with an hourglass design set inside. Along the rim of the pendulum was imprinted: ELECTRICITY SAVES TIME.

The theme of this fair was "The World of Tomorrow." At its opening, President Franklin D. Roosevelt assured the crowd that they were about to get a glimpse of the future. He wasn't too far off. Raymond Loewy's "Rocketport" took fairgoers' breath away with its simulation of space travel. Henry Dreyfuss's "Democracity" looked like a model for tidy planned suburbs of the future. "Futurama," Norman Bel Geddes's preview of city life in 1960, dazzled spectators with 50,000 streamlined little vehicles speeding along soaring elevated highways. A huge, electronic map highlighted a proposed interstate highway system. Facsimile transmission of documents was demonstrated at the fair. The promise of atomic power was discussed, and television's prospects. Might it replace radio? RCA President David Sarnoff was bullish on this point. Not only did Sarnoff foresee a television in most future living rooms, he also thought that recent advances in microwave transmission made it possible to imagine "motorists in separate cars talking to each other as they speed along the highway."

On the eve of World War II, a new world of ease and leisure seemed in view. That world would have to wait for the war to end, of course. But once it did, Americans quickly resumed their passionate pursuit of a life that was modern, convenient, and faster paced than ever.

McSPEED

In Urbana, Illinois, a watchmaker did business for a time in a very un-watchmakerlike building. Now it's a storage area for the Chinese restaurant next door. This little building stands at the convergence of five major roads. Its frontspiece consists of four large panes of glass that tilt outward. The building's roof rises gradually from back to front, as if about to soar into space. Its tile siding is painted gray and white. To me this building looks incomplete. What it lacks is two large yellow arches abutting the sides of the structure. For years it had those arches, in the early 1960s when my friends and I came here for lunch from the next town over during high school.

We'd pile into Mike Mulligan's '55 Chevy and roar off to this odd building with its yellow arches, red and white tile siding and neon sign announcing how many millions of hamburgers they'd sold. The restaurant had a limited menu, but I always got the same thing anyway: cheese-burger, fries, and an orange soda. The fries were skinny, and had a nice crunch. I didn't care for the two pickles in each hamburger and always plucked them out. The bill came to less than half a dollar. At this price we could afford to skip our paid-up cafeteria meal back at school. And it was served fast enough that we could drive to Urbana, order, get our food, wolf it down, and be back in time for Social Studies.

This hamburger stand was an early McDonald's franchise. My friends and I were unwitting pioneers in a social revolution. That revolution had started soon after the war, when Richard and Maurice McDonald de-cided that their San Bernardino drive-in had no future. Carhops serving teenagers in cars took too much time. Customers weren't turning over fast enough. "We had entered the age of jet propulsion," recalled Richard McDonald, now retired in his native New Hampshire, "and we were still using a 'horse and buggy' system. Everyone seemed to be in a hurry and did not want to have to wade through a large menu. They wanted to eat quickly and get on their way."

In the fall of 1948 the McDonald brothers took drastic action. They closed their restaurant for three months and completely revamped its procedures. First the McDonalds fired all twenty carhops. Then they gutted their restaurant's interior. After that they invented a whole new food delivery system. Based on an analysis of three years of sales slips, fare was limited to the nine most popular items, headed by hamburgers. Uniform 1.6-ounce patties were to be fried on a huge grill. With the help of a machinist the McDonald brothers designed a pistol-like tool to squirt condiments onto twenty-four buns at a time as they circulated on a big, steel lazy susan (also of their own making). Washable utensils were replaced with disposable ones. Prices were halved. With so few items on their new menu the McDonalds could prepare everything in advance to serve walk-up customers thirty seconds after they placed an order.

Assembly line hamburger preparation was not revolutionary. White Castle pioneered this approach (a fact that McDonald's tacitly recognized in their first slogan: "Buy 'em by the bag;" White Castle had urged "Buy 'em by the sack.") What *was* original about McDonald's "Speedee Service System" was its invitation for customers not to sit down—to drive up, get out of their car, order their food, receive it in less than a minute, then eat in their car, on their car, or wherever else looked plausible.

McDonald's first customer was prophetic: a nine-year-old girl who ordered a bag of hamburgers for her family's dinner. Too few followed. "Our new venture was a complete disaster," recalled Richard McDonald. "When word was out about our new system, our customers told us we must have gone insane." Those accustomed to the old system would pull into the parking lot, blow their horns for service, then drive off in frustration when no carhop appeared. What once was a bustling parking lot now resembled a bankrupt car dealer's. The old restaurant's carhops came by to snicker and gloat. Don't get rid of our old uniforms, they warned Richard and Maurice. They'd be needing them.

"We almost did call them back," said McDonald. "But our pride was at stake and we decided to hang on awhile." Although he and his brother nearly threw in the towel on three separate occasions, a new clientele gradually replaced the old one. Sales clerks, construction workers, and taxi drivers heard about McDonald's and liked what they heard. Young parents in need of a break began to come with their children for an affordable meal. Far from being put off by the brisk service of this new type of restaurant, they seemed intrigued by it. In his history of McDonald's, John Love called this new approach, "tailor-made for a postwar America that was faster paced, more mobile, and more oriented to convenience and instant gratification."

Within a year the McDonalds' new restaurant matched the volume of their old one, then exploded well beyond it. Word spread in the industry about their revolutionary new approach. Prospective imitators began to show up clutching notepads. They would order a burger and fries, then sit out in their cars taking notes, drawing sketches, trying to dope out the system. What they saw was a packed parking lot, two lines of customers stretching nearly to the curb, and a staff taking orders every ten seconds without breaking stride. The most impressive thing of all was that the Speedee Service System turned customers over twice as fast any drive-in could.

Trying to stay ahead of plagiarists, the McDonalds began to sell franchises. The first was bought by a Phoenix man in 1952. To simplify procedures for him, Richard and Maurice spent most of one night on the lighted tennis court of their colonial home walking a work crew through food-serving procedures. A draftsman used red chalk to record on the white surface exactly how these procedures and the new equipment itself would fit in the franchisee's kitchen. "We spent several hours changing the positions of the equipment to eliminate one step here and one in another location," said Richard McDonald. "This was essential to obtain the maximum speed for the new program."

In 1953 the McDonalds decided to spruce up their red-and-white building for the new franchisees. Richard spent an evening in his office sketching plans to give the building some height. First he tried columns like those on their home. These looked terrible. Then he drew a big arch parallel to the front of the building. This was an improvement. Adding a second arch and moving them to the sides looked even better. The only problem was that the McDonalds' architects refused to sully their building design with such cosmetic vulgarity. The brothers turned to a sign designer. He agreed that arches were just the thing. The sign maker suggested making them huge and yellow and bright so as to attract attention from drivers speeding by. The Phoenix McDonald's was the first one to be housed in a classic "golden arches" building. (It was a good thing the arches served no purpose, Richard later reflected. If they had, a car crashing into one could have done serious damage to the building.)

After Ray Kroc took over McDonald's franchising in 1954, he replicated this building and food delivery system throughout the country. Kroc had a clear vision of the world to come: one dominated by busy families whose members owned lots of cars and had extra money to spend—not just on food but on an "eating experience." Convenience and economy were not all that lured Americans to McDonald's. Watching the uniformed help assemble food with the speed and precision of a crack drill team seemed to mesmerize customers. "McDonald's," Kroc repeatedly told his franchisees and managers, "is not in the restaurant business; it's in show business."

In time the classic red-and-white buildings with their yellow arches seemed garish even to Ray Kroc. Beginning in the mid-1960s they were replaced by a more subdued mansard-roof version. One such building sits up the street from the former watchmaker's where my classic memory still resides. I don't care for it. It lacks character.

4

Fast Times

Who, a bare sixty years ago, seeing Queen Victoria in her pony-drawn bath-chair, could possibly have imagined that within a single lifetime, ladies of comparable age and dignity would be stepping on the gas along the Pennsylvania Turnpike . . . ?

—ALDOUS HUXLEY, 1961

The second generation of fast-food buildings were more sedate than the first, and even provided a few seats and tables. What didn't change was the emphasis on rapid turnover. Customers were to be greeted cordially, served quickly, then sent briskly on their way. Much ingenuity was devoted to getting them out of their seats as quickly as possible. The goal, admitted a Dunkin' Donuts architect, was to design an environment in which customers could feel "comfortable for five or ten minutes, and maybe a little crowded. You can't make it too comfortable . . ." Seats were crafted of hard plastic that caused the buttocks to grow uncomfortable in a few minutes' time. Interior walls were painted in stark primary colors—reds! oranges! pinks!—which consultants said would make eaters restless; anxious to gulp their food and get moving. Lively music was thought to have a similar effect.

If the increasing millions of Americans who ate out after the war felt that things seemed to be moving a little *faster,* they had more reasons than were apparent to feel this way. Not that restaurant patrons objected. If asked, most probably would have said they appreciated the briskness of service. Fast food met the needs of everyone involved. As restaurant historian Philip Langdon has observed, speed of service "enjoyed a widespread appeal even among people who weren't at the mercy of a tight schedule. Americans loved to 'save' time even when they had time to spare."

Hasty Homes

"Saving time" became an obsession after the war. Advice on how to do so was a staple of postwar magazines. Most such tips emphasized better scheduling and ways to move things along at a brisker clip. One 1956 compilation of "Nine Timesaving Secrets" included this corrective for morning bathroom dawdlers: "To speed your pace, try a small radio. You get news with tooth-brushing, plus step-on-it time signals. If you customarily bathe, switch to showers."

The reasoning here was that showering typically took half the time that bathing did. This is why built-in showers were such a popular feature in postwar homes. Tubs were usually included in such homes too, but measly, shrunken versions of the majestic old claw-footers. Showers were in far better tune with the postwar tempo. As my father once asked, how often do you hear someone say they're going to take a shower without adding that it will be "quick?" (i.e., "I'm going to take a quick shower.") The term "quick" is to "shower" as "splitting" is to "headache," "brand" to "new," "wide" to "awake" and "stark" to "naked." A country on the move found dashing in and out of rushing water more suited to its aspirations than soaking in still pools. Ogden Nash discussed this preference in verse:

> . . . it is obvious that the tubber is a sybaritic softie
> And will never accomplish anything lofty
> How different is the showerer . . .
> He has not time to waste on luxuriousness, but skims through
>   the spray with the speed of a Democratic politician
>   skimming through a Republican editorial

The bathroom was not the only part of the American home to reflect and accelerate the postwar pace of life. Another symbol of our changing attitudes toward time was the disappearing front porch. For a century before World War II, front porches were a staple of American homes. This was where family members went to enjoy cool breezes, pass time with neighbors, send toddlers out for their first ventures outside the house, and allow teenagers to court in a semi-private setting. Radio commentator Rod MacLeish once recalled the porches of his childhood as ideally suited to "spontaneous visiting, public courting, shared silences and random conversation to no end except its own pleasure."

But the more cars broke the silence with the roar of their engines and concealed the smell of jasmine beneath their exhaust, the less time people seemed to want to spend sitting on porches. (Certainly teenage couples didn't. There was nothing semi- about the privacy of courting in a car.) As streets grew dense with cars and living rooms with televisions, front porches were torn down, closed in, or simply used for storage. "It is a place to do messy projects or to break the Christmas *piñata,*" said one Oroville, California, woman of the front porch on her family's home. "It also held the pool table, which didn't fit anywhere else . . ."

Houses built after the war usually skipped porches altogether. A Levitt corporation official boasted that of 130,000 homes they'd built, nary a one featured a front porch. Meals that once were eaten on the porch moved to backyard patios of postwar homes, or into the kitchen itself. Eat-in kitchens were as popular as built-in showers in postwar homes, and for much the same reason. "Kitchen eating space will save you time, work and steps," *Better Homes and Gardens* advised readers in 1955.

More than any other room in the postwar home, the kitchen was a cathedral of time worship. In one typical ad, a radiant mother stood beside her ebullient young daughter in a spotless kitchen. "My AMERICAN KITCHEN Saves Me 2 Hours a Day to Spend as I Please!" read the copy. At the heart of postwar kitchens were the many appliances—some built-in—which were rolling off assembly lines no longer needed for tanks and guns. Americans reveled in their ability to buy the refrigerators, blenders, mixers, and freezers denied them during the conflict. Appliance makers vied to sell their wares as the fastest and most convenient ever. Push buttons were de rigueur. Blender makers engaged in a "battle of the buttons." Switches that once were limited to "on" and "off" now included "high" and "low." After Oster added "medium," the race was on. Before it ended some Sunbeam models featured twenty button settings. Blender makers were particularly creative in coming up with names for each function: whip, puree, chop, liquefy, crumb, mince, and grind were just a few. One Proctor-Silex engineer recalled staying up for two nights with seven colleagues and a thesaurus searching for short words that suggested accelerating speed and power.

Push buttons made no practical sense. If anything they were a step backward from the rheostat dials most replaced. Their significance was symbolic. As Thomas Hine noted in *Populuxe,* the postwar craze for push buttons carried a promise: "that one day all drudgery would disappear and that almost every task that was dirty or dangerous could be carried out by unseen machinery, activated by the tiniest flick of a finger . . . And you would be able to use the time you save[d] to have fun with your family."

For a time in the mid-1950s some cars even replaced manual gearshifts with automatic transmissions controlled by push buttons. Manufacturers weren't coy in explaining why. "You'll be a different woman with a Plymouth all your own," promised one 1957 ad. "A new Plymouth is as easy to drive as a baby buggy. You don't have to wrestle with the steering wheel. You never have to shift gears. Just push a button." This ad also pointed out that with her own car a housewife could participate in more civic activities, drive her kids to school, parties, and playmates' homes, and shop for bargains in distant locales.

Postwar buyers were quite receptive to this pitch. During the 1950s the number of American two-car families doubled (to 15%), then doubled again in the following decade. This trend was touted as an ideal solution to time-pressure problems. "The family with two cars gets twice as many chores completed," Chevrolet pointed out, "so there's more leisure to enjoy *together!*"

The Leisure Problem

With all the time- and labor-saving going on there was an understandable assumption that a tidal wave of free time was about to crash upon our shores. Were we up to the challenge? Commissions were appointed to study this question. Books discussed the "leisure problem," articles were written about it and speeches made. How would we spend all of our hard-earned free time? When pollsters put that question to Americans directly, the most common response was: *"What* free time?" John Robinson and other researchers found that contrary to their expectations, no increase in leisure was detectable in subjects' time use diaries. In fact, free time seemed to be declining for postwar Americans. If we were moving into a "leisure society," wrote Robinson of these findings, "it was not being detected by the time use studies."

Compared with similar studies done three decades earlier, the researchers found that subjects now averaged thirty to sixty-six fewer minutes of sleep per night. Eating time was down half an hour a day. Time spent reading, going to movies, listening to the radio, playing sports and games, engaging in conversations, driving for pleasure, dancing, and attending church services had also declined. By the mid-1960s American men worked nearly an hour longer every day, on the average, than they did before the war. Time devoted to commuting and other work-related travel was way up. The average mid-1960s American spent three and a half hours per week going to stores. Time spent on household chores had declined somewhat, but managing that job—including shopping and child care—actually took longer than it did in the 1930s. These were among the reasons for Robinson's observation that time-use analysis "provided little support for the scenario of the leisure-dominated society. Instead, decreased free time and increased shopping suggest a society increasingly faced with the time scarcity dilemma."

Such surveys found a substantial increase in the time women spent driving during the 50s and 60s. This was attributed to the increasing number of second cars. It was amazing how many time-consuming activities all those extra cars made possible. One homemaker of the time wondered if her car-bound life might not be harder than her ancestors'. True, her great-great-grandmother walked a lot, grew her own vegetables, and cooked without appliances, but "she also didn't drive her husband to the train in the morning, then drive the children to school, and then rush back home to put a load of clothes in the washer to wash while she prepared the day's garden harvest to be taken to the locker plant for fast freezing, stopping at the supermarket on the way back to load up the car with supplies, which left her just time enough to pick up the children at school, drop Janie off for her music lesson, and hurry home to unload the groceries and put dinner in the oven, when it was time to pick up Janie and meet father on the 6:05. Dinner over, children to bed, a meeting of the PTA . . ."

You Deserve a Break

Another woman gave this portrayal of family life in a mid-fifties suburb:

> . . . coming home from a board meeting of the Children's Home Society, I told the other women in the car how disturbed I was about all that "hurry" in our lives. Every one of them echoed the same sentiments. Doris said that she sometimes felt that her husband only came home to change his shirt between office conferences and civic meetings. As for herself, between Cub Scouts and the Safety Council, she found herself doing her housework along about midnight.
>
> Mary Jane confessed that, as parent-education chairman, she was so busy attending conferences on family life that she often rushed home too late to prepare a decent dinner. And if the children asked her a question, she'd snap at them . . .
>
> Lois added her dissatisfaction. When she gave up her job, she thought she'd be able to spend long hours trying out new recipes and taking up a hobby—but she found that she had less time at home now than when she had been working . . .
>
> There we all were—caught up in a dizzying tempo that left us too little time for the most important thing of all—peaceful family living.

This was a common lament. Though the terms may have differed, the *feeling* of being timelocked was little different in the 1950s than it is today. As a result, America's postwar mood was receptive to products of all kinds that promised to save time. The range of frozen foods expanded rapidly after the war, including pre-prepared meals. A watershed was reached with the 1951 introduction of beef and chicken pot pies by food magnate Carl Swanson. Two years later Swanson brought out turkey and gravy over corn bread with a side order of peas and sweet potatoes frozen in a three-compartment aluminum tray. As ever, convenience food merchants sold time over product. Chef Boy-Ar-Dee clocked preparation time for its packaged spaghetti dinner at twelve minutes flat. Sure-Jell came in at eleven for "homemade peach jam." Campbell's advertised four-minute sauces that could be made from its soups, and Junket sold a four-minute fudge mix. In 1972 French's broke the one-minute barrier when they introduced an instant product called "60 second gravy."

"For quite a while now, there has been a trend toward the quick," noted a Safeway executive that year. "It's evident throughout the store in everything from dinners to spray starch." Because they got large daily polls of consumer preferences, supermarkets became early-warning beacons of significant changes in postwar American life. One thing they noticed was a loss of business to fast-food outlets. Grocers also began to see an increase in nighttime trade. Both developments grew directly out of the fact that beginning in the mid-1960s a rivulet of housewives re-entering the job force was expanding into a river.

After veterans streamed home, women who had staffed the machines and desks in their absence beat a hasty retreat to the home front. Well over 2 million working women quit their jobs after V-J day. The idea of a married woman hanging on to a job which a vet might fill smacked of ingratitude. In case they didn't get the message, the gospel of sacred motherhood was revived (helping to fuel the baby boom). Not that working women went happily back to household chores. One postwar ad pictured a glowering young woman in an apron leaning over to clean a toilet bowl as she exclaimed, "I left an office for *THIS!*" But the solution to her frustration was not to go back to work. The solution was to buy Sani-Flush.

All of these new conveniences cost money. The American standard of living was shooting upward after the war, but not as fast as single salaries could take it. By 1960 nearly one-third of all married women in this country were working for income. Forty percent of mothers with school-age children held jobs then, up from 25% in 1948. By 1980 three out of five American mothers with school-age children worked outside the home.

No development contributed more to our sense of being timelocked than the rise of two-career families. Most were actually three-career families in which two members earned paychecks, and one (usually the woman) kept house besides. In time-use surveys, working women—especially those who had children—were more likely than any other group to report feeling "rushed." Their time-pressure scores were also highest, followed by those of employed men. Working mothers had less free time, slept less, and spent less time eating than did any other group. As John Robinson and his colleague Philip Converse noted, "Any sensitive contact with these materials rapidly creates an appreciation for the hectic lives imposed on women who desire to work while maintaining a family and household."

The Thirty-Second Minute

Another observation growing out of Robinson's research was this: "Television has had a far more profound impact on how we spend our time than any other technological innovation in this century, be it the automobile, or all of the various home appliances combined." According to subjects' time diaries, the average mid-sixties urban American spent two hours a day watching television, or one-third to one-half of available leisure time. This activity absorbed substantial amounts of time that used to be spent on other leisure activities, such as talking, reading the newspaper, or going to church.

In time TV-watching would also be blamed for reducing viewers' attention spans as it speeded up their thought processes. But this charge wasn't heard in television's early years. Hard as it is to fathom today, this medium is not intrinsically fast-paced. Early TV programs weren't up-tempo at all. Scripts for programs such as "The Hallmark Hall of Fame" or "Playhouse 90" were written to the rhythms of the theater. Series shows weren't much faster. "Your Show of Shows," originally a two-hour program, was still ninety minutes long in 1954. Most early productions were broadcast live. Even commercials were not commonly filmed until the mid-1950s.

Advertisers were quicker than programmers to appreciate videotape's potential to accelerate television's tempo. Throughout the 1960s they had used this medium to experiment with jump cuts, accelerated motion, and flashy graphics. The impact of such innovations went far beyond commerce. "Our culture is learning faster perception per second thanks to editing techniques that show us a hundred bottles of beer on a wall in twenty-seven seconds, or sixty-five pictures of McDonald's breakfasts in sixty seconds," noted ad critic Jonathan Price in the early 1970s, "we follow them, and when we return to the slower editing of regular programming—not to mention the scenes of real life—we may find the pace unaccountably dull."

As the 1970s began, admakers realized that they didn't even need sixty seconds to get their message across. Studies found that a thirty-second commercial could have nearly as much impact as one twice that length. In 1971 the average length of commercials was cut in half. That transition forced ad producers to squeeze virtually the same amount of content into half the time. They accomplished this by substituting imagery for story lines. Mr. Whipple was trampled underfoot by the Pepsi Generation. Viewers adjusted to the new tempo with surprising ease. After sponsoring a mid-1970s study in which the eyes of 250 Massachusetts housewives were observed while they watched television, one ad executive told his colleagues that they were wasting their time by letting a camera linger for four seconds on any one image. Before long they seldom did.

The shift from minute to half-minute commercials was a landmark event in the history of America's tempo. The pace of television (which is basically to say that of American life in general) became commercial-driven. In the 1980s many ads were halved again, to fifteen seconds, forcing programming to grow faster yet to keep up. The process was self-feeding. TV's accelerating tempo created viewer expectations which in turn put pressure on programmers to accelerate the pace of their product.

Even more than shorter ads, programmers blamed remote control devices for forcing them to speed up productions. In preremote days, it was taken for granted that viewers watching one show would probably watch the next one because they were too lazy to get up and change channels. Zenith found little demand for the wireless remote controllers first offered in 1955. With only five channels to watch at the most, and so little variety in network programming, the average viewer didn't see much point to changing stations. For nearly two decades after remotes were introduced they stayed in the gadget category and programming went its leisurely way.

The 1980s changed all that. During this decade a TV viewer's hand was as likely to hold a remote controller as a bottle of beer or can of soda. According to one mother of three, "Who's got it?" was a question which needed no further explanation in her home. The advent of cable programming gave viewers lots of reasons to change channels. This development forced drastic changes in program production. Once their audience was armed with remote controllers, producers could no longer take its attention for granted. They had to win and rewin viewers every minute. Producer Don Hewitt of "60 Minutes" attributed the ever more frantic pace of TV programming to "the clicker. That damn little thing millions of people hold in their hands and punch with sheer delight. If they don't like what they see, they can make a decision to hit that clicker in a matter of mini-seconds. And if you were on the screen, now you are gone. You better be constantly interesting." NBC Entertainment head Brandon Tartikoff concurred: "Once a guy didn't have to get up from his chair to change the channel, you could no longer take the same kind of time to set up characters and stories . . . a TV show which doesn't immediately grab the audience by the throat has an uphill battle today."

Many viewers treated the remote as an extension of their fingers. Studies found that some remote users changed stations as often as twenty-two times a minute, or once every 2.73 seconds. To the horror of advertisers, "A" market viewers—upscale urbanites—developed especially itchy trigger fingers. Such viewers were prone to turn on their televisions with no particular destination in mind, then take a couple of laps around the dial to see what caught their eye. They liked to move around. Dip in and out. Get some impressions. Catch part of one show while commercials were on during another. See how many programs they could follow at once. It took skill. According to one study nearly a quarter of all remote control users routinely watched more than one program at a time. Over half of the demographically prized 18- to 34-year-olds said they regularly watched two shows at once, and 20% claimed to be able to follow three or more. "It's an art to catch just enough of different story lines to follow all of them," explained one 18-year-old. "My parents can't take it. I usually end up alone in front of the television."

Grazing

"Grazers" is what media analysts called the new generation of TV scanners. This term caught on quickly. It seemed to epitomize not just an approach to TV watching but to life in general. With so much to do and so little time to do it, grazing described a style which involved nibbling at a growing smorgasbord of opportunities with less involvement per bite.

The term itself was originally coined by market researchers Leo Shapiro and Dwight Bombach. In a 1978 study of eating habits, Shapiro and Bombach pointed out that as recently as 1940 the average American family ate two meals a day at home. Preparing that food typically took four to six hours. Pre-war housewives were food producers as much as food consumers, devoting a large portion of their day to meal preparation. Within a generation, however, an explosion of time-saving appliances and pre-prepared foods revolutionized our eating patterns. Now up to twenty "food contacts" per day were the American norm. "In one generation," observed Shapiro and Bombach, "we have gone from a traditional food producing society to a food grazing society—one where we eat wherever we happen to be."

Since its members were going off in so many different directions, only one-quarter of all families now ate breakfast together. With income up and time down, one in five main meals was eaten "out." When families did eat dinner together at home, they often took less than twenty minutes to do so. In a follow-up study in 1984, Shapiro and Bombach found grazing more common than ever. Now, they said, this trend was so pronounced that one might consider the average American family to be more of a "herd" quickly nibbling small amounts of food in isolation throughout the day.

This new approach to eating was a fist to the chops of the traditional food and beverage industry. Coffee sales declined steadily after the early 1960s. Many explanations were offered for this trend. The most persuasive one of all was that a new generation of Americans didn't want to take time to brew coffee, even instant. What were they drinking instead? Soda from a can. "All hot drinks are going down," noted an industry analyst in 1982.

"People today are in a hurry. They want to slug something down and move on, particularly the younger ones."

According to market researcher Mona Doyle, 1982 was the year when the bottom fell out of the cake mix business. By then fewer and fewer customers felt that they had time to express their lovin' with something from the oven, even something that only required them to open a package, add liquid, stir and bake for half an hour. The market for canned foods was already in a tailspin because consumers no longer felt they could spare the time to open cans. Eventually even frozen foods began to seem pokey to consumers on the run.

Doyle made these discoveries during an ongoing poll of shoppers around the country that she began in the late 1970s. During that time no trend stood out more boldly than her subjects' growing lack of time. As baby boomers entered the workforce, married, and eventually had children, extraordinary time pressure was put on this huge segment of the population. Despite an occasional article heralding the arrival of "new husbands," most were decidedly old-fashioned when it came to sharing household chores, even when their wives held jobs. Something, or some things, had to give. Food preparation was an obvious choice. When Doyle began working in the food industry in the early 1970s, thirty minutes was considered a fast meal-preparation time. Eventually even that amount of time felt glacial. "Lifestyles were changing toward *minutes* of time for food preparation," said Doyle. By her calculation, seven minutes defined the upper limit of "fast" as the eighties waned.

Time scarcity became a pronounced trend in conjunction with the women's movement, Doyle noted during a conversation in her Philadelphia office overlooking the Schuylkill River. "We really could look and see when consumers started telling us that they were willing to trade off more money for time," she said. "The most telling example was hearing working mothers say 'I can pick up takeout' on their way home from work, and feel that they came out ahead. They felt that they could justify the expense, and the justification itself became a self-fulfilling prophecy. Then they took on more tasks and the process snowballed."

From Mona Doyle's perspective the microwave oven did more than any other single tool to allow postwar Americans to "compress time" and squeeze more activities into their day. "It's had as big an impact on eating habits as the airplane's had on travel," she said. There was nothing hypocritical about the microwave revolution. *Cosmopolitan*'s 1958 prediction that we'd spray the kitchen with artificial cooking smells while using microwave ovens seemed laughably quaint. In fact, microwave users made no bones about saving time in the purest sense. Using this appliance wasn't even regarded as cooking, necessarily (as was evident in the widespread use of terms such as "nuke it" or "zap it" to describe what happened to microwaved food). Microwaving was the first means of preparing food which hadn't existed since prehistory. This took getting used to. It was not until the late 1980s that microwave cookbooks became common. "Before that this would have been considered an oxymoron," noted Mona Doyle. Their recipes typically gave directions in numbers of seconds. Microwave ovens were as dependent on digital clocks as carpenters are on rulers. The analog clocks on conventional ovens gave more general reports of time which were often inaccurate. But it didn't matter. When food is cooked slowly for an extended period, a minute here or a minute there is unimportant. Not so with the microwave. Ten seconds one way or the other could make the difference between a triumph and a disaster.

Microwave ovens represented the ultimate victory of time over task. Microwaveable foods were not sold on the basis of quality, flavor, or even ease, but time alone. As the little girl called out to her mother while holding up a package at the supermarket, "This one's only six minutes, Mom." An accurate digital time readout was the throbbing heart of a microwave oven. This was true of many modern appliances. In the process of using them our time awareness grew more pervasive, and more precise than ever. As the 1980s came to a close, we seemed better equipped than ever to take charge of our time. The process that began with the invention of clocks more than six centuries before culminated in a world of devices controlled by history's highest quality of time. The World of Tomorrow—even the Day After Tomorrow—seemed to have arrived. We were exquisitely armed to do battle with time, and seek a little relief from its relentless grind. Why, then, as the nineties got under way, did so many of us feel more worn down than ever beneath time's merciless wheel?

How Life Got So Hectic

Why Time Is So Scarce

Who knows where the time goes?
—JUDY COLLINS
(SANDY DENNY, BMI)

One question commonly raised in focus groups was this: Why did my parents seem so much less pressed for time than I am? In most cases they only had one income. My mother didn't use microwaves or Dustbusters. Tater Tots and takeout pizza were not on their menu. They didn't always have two cars. With a higher standard of living and more time-saving conveniences, shouldn't my life be less hectic than my parents'?

In fact, the opposite feels true. The better off we've become, the scarcer time seems to have grown. In theory the wealthier one becomes, the more leisure one can afford. For most of history that was true. The wealthy class was also the leisure class. But those of us who earn rather than inherit money don't find this to be the case. The higher our income, the more strapped we usually feel for time. Roper's poll found that nearly half of those who make over $35,000 a year say they don't have enough time, compared with only one-third of all Americans who feel that way. A *USA Today* poll found that the most rushed Americans aged 25–44 were two-income couples, those making $35,000 a year or more, or both.

Many working couples feel that two paychecks are essential to support a minimal life-style. This is often the case. But compare what's considered "minimal" for a middle-class life today with one just a few decades ago. Start with homes. The average starter home in this country has more than doubled in size since 1950, from less than 900 square feet then to over 1800 square feet now. A vintage Levittown house measured 800 square feet. By 1990 the median size of a new American home was 1850 square feet. That's a lot more home to pay for, even if housing prices and mortgage rates hadn't gone up. It's also a lot more space to furnish, clean and maintain.

Inside our larger homes we consider far more items "standard" than our parents did. A second bathroom (or more) is a given. It used to be a luxury. So was air conditioning, wall-to-wall carpeting, and a remodeled kitchen. When it came to conveniences, our parents may have had one vacuum cleaner, a toaster, a blender, a washer-dryer, a refrigerator, and perhaps a freezer. The average house had one, or at most two phones (which were seldom used to make long distance calls). Most middle-class Americans owned a single black-and-white television set, a record player, and a radio or two. Wardrobes were far more limited. And if they included sneakers with a name on them, that name was usually Keds.

Now look about your own home. Most likely it includes more than one color television set, wired for cable. VCR. Stereo. CD player. Tape deck. Several radios. Walkman. A few telephones, at least one of them cordless. An answering machine. Probably more than one vacuum, including a Dustbuster. Coffeemaker. Microwave. Perhaps a Cuisinart. Maybe a computer. Garage door opener. Power tools. Disposable diapers. Substantial wardrobes (including many items that need dry cleaning). Designer clothing. Brand-name sneakers all around.

This is a short list of premium items that have become standard. (It doesn't even include such items as the surcharge we pay for convenience and takeout food, or long distance calls to keep up with scattered friends.) Add them up. A fairly typical, hardly luxurious middle-class life today is expensive. How do we afford it? We become two-paycheck families, we work overtime, we moonlight (women, increasingly). We clip coupons, send in for rebates, and drive long distances in search of "specials." Such time-consumers can feel essential to maintain a middle-class standard of living. But that standard is far higher than one previous generations even dreamed of. So when we say it takes more time than ever to keep up, this may be true. But we're "keeping up" at a much higher level than our parents did. To help us do so, America's consumer economy has become glutted with choices to make.

Over-Choice

Columnist Ellen Goodman was bemused by the reaction of a reporter friend who'd just returned from an extended stint in Moscow. For all of its aggravation, her friend said she missed the *absence* of choices to make in the Soviet Union's capital.

This reporter wasn't the only one to have such a reaction. After returning from almost four years in the Soviet Union in 1990, *Philadelphia Inquirer* correspondent Steve Goldstein found himself and his family struggling with input overload. "There are too many choices in the mall, the supermarket, in the endless stream of catalogs that flood into our home, or in trying to open a simple checking account," he wrote. "Too many comparisons to make to find the best buy on furniture, video recorders, children's clothing or small appliances." In less than four years' time the Goldsteins had missed out on the fax revolution, the proliferation of video rental stores, bank machines, untagged items in the supermarket, and car interiors that resembled airplane cockpits. Goldstein took nervous note of how many people seemed to be eating, talking on the phone, or even watching television while driving. On his own TV at home he found himself overwhelmed by the many programs to choose from on scores of cable channels. Help was available, of course, in a new kind of TV schedule. The only problem was that Goldstein grew dizzy as he tried to decipher television program grids.

"Is it possible," mused his wife, Margy, a philosophy major in college, "that more is less?"

Many have begun to ask that very question. The better able we are to buy goods and services, the more hectic our lives seem to have become. Why should this be?

The explanation has a lot to do with the increase in options our affluence has made possible. Making choices takes time. Choosing from among a dizzying range of possibilities—consumer products, CDs (both musical and financial), money market funds, TV programs, check colors, life-styles, convictions, people—can be exhausting. All the new options in life may increase our flexibility. They are also major time sponges.

For the first time in a decade my wife and I needed new phone service. We thought this meant simply calling for a hookup, then choosing between touch tone or pulse dialing. We were mistaken. First Muriel spent half an hour on the phone with a customer representative who tried to explain a range of options so complex she barely understood them herself. There were three plans for local service, two for extended area (including one with a local option), custom-calling options (four separate or two combined), various ways to pay our bill, three possible maintenance plans, and a decision to make about whether to wire the phone hookup ourselves or let their service person do it. We also had to choose a long distance carrier. Muriel took three pages of notes on this conversation. Then we reviewed these notes along with printed material the phone company sent, discussed our alternatives, and made some decisions. The whole process took a couple of hours and lots of mental energy. I don't think our life is any better for it.

This experience was symptomatic of changes taking place throughout society. We're deluged with choices to make. A Manhattan banking executive pointed out that when she started working at a bank branch in the late 1960s, there were few options to offer the customer: basically a savings account, checking account, or loan. Now her bank offers six different checking plans, twelve kinds of savings accounts, and eighteen types of loans. My own bank offers savings plans in a bewildering and constantly changing kaleidoscope. It can literally take hours to decipher and choose the right one. It wasn't so long ago that anyone who wanted to invest in a mutual fund had just a handful to choose from. By 1980 that figure had risen to 458. A decade later over 2200 stock and bond funds competed for our attention. What began as a way to simplify life for those who didn't want to buy individual stocks has become nearly as complicated as playing the stock market itself.

You could say we're in a state of over-choice. Alvin Toffler said just that two decades ago in *Future Shock* (the first paperback sold in a choice of jacket colors: six of them). "We are . . . racing toward 'overchoice,' " Toffler wrote in 1970,"—the point at which the advantage of diversity and individualization are canceled by the complexity of the buyer's decision-making process." At the time he said this there were several thousand fewer items on the typical supermarket's shelves, a handful of TV channels to watch, and only one telephone company to cope with. Coupons were in their infancy. So were rebates. In the twenty years since *Future Shock* appeared, the number of choices we must make in a given day has exploded. Few such decisions are earth-shaking. Together, however, they add up to scores of daily distractions, each one staking its claim on our time and attention.

The proliferation of choices is a trend that Roper has been studying for the past several years. They think it's a key source of the time pressure so many Americans feel. As compared with the more limited choices available a decade or two ago, explained Roper's Tom Miller, "people just don't have enough time to give to all of today's choices." Roper's poll routinely finds a common dissatisfaction with "brand clutter." Nearly 60% of those queried at the end of the 1980s said that the number of brands on supermarket shelves confused them. A decade earlier only 49% felt that way. Miller ticked off a wide range of other choice points cluttering our time: more television commercials pleading for attention; an average of 27.7 television stations to watch (up from 18.5 in 1985); more radio stations than ever to check out, more magazines to read (in the range of 12,000 in the United States alone at the end of the 1980s, double the number that existed two decades before), more brands of cars, more models of cars, and more options per car. "There's just isn't enough time to check out all of these automobiles," concluded Miller, "watch all those TV programs, read all these magazines."

One magazine that is doing better than ever is *Consumer Reports.* And no wonder. Today's range of choices makes us need its product ratings more than ever. Other media have pitched in with product comparisons of their own. But taking advantage of them takes time. Becoming a savvy consumer feels like being enrolled in an ongoing Consumption 101 course with lots of homework. Find and read product comparisons. Talk to friends. Study ads. Compare prices. Make some calls. Shop around. Make a choice. Buy a product. Take it home. Take it back. Start all over. Consumption is time-consuming. And the more alternatives we have to choose from, the more time choice-making takes.

In principle this has been true ever since Post Toasties began competing with Kellogg's Corn Flakes early this century. On the eve of the Depression an average American supermarket stocked 900 items. This figure rose to 3000 in 1946, and nearly 8000 by 1970. Today supermarkets typically carry 10,000 items or more. In 1989 an unprecedented 12,000 new products were introduced for Americans to consider, twelve times the number that were brought to market a decade earlier. Studies have found that shoppers give each brand they're interested in an average of four seconds' consideration. The more detailed labels grow, the more time this consideration takes. We now not only have more products to select from, but more to note about them. Not just the price but the unit price. The ingredients. (Are any toxic?) The expiration date of perishables (made hard to find by merchants who'd rather you didn't). And now, ecological information as well. Absorbing such information makes us more sophisticated consumers. But it makes shopping more complicated and time-consuming than ever. The result is mental clutter.

"Choices do not make life easier," noted Washington psychologist David A. Goslin. "As social scientists, we know that with an increase in choices, people tend to become more anxious."

This is not true just of product consumption. Over-choice also extends to the impressive array of activities, courses, and entertainments available to us today. In his Carlsbad, California, counseling practice, psychologist Larry Chamow has increasingly seen anxiety resulting from having too many options in all spheres of life. "What's most difficult for all of us," explained Chamow, "regardless of our age group, is dealing with all of these choices. Most of the people I see are frustrated by them. All of these things you *could* do. This causes an enormous amount of pressure. It's easy to get stalled."

One reason for the proliferation of social events is the opportunity they provide to "meet people." By one estimate, each one of us is likely to meet more people in a year than our grandparents did in a lifetime. It takes time to evaluate and choose those we might like to know better. Making and maintaining friendships takes even more time, especially if the people involved don't live near us. Unlike the geographically based community of her parents, observed a businesswoman in San Diego, "Our community is defined by other kinds of definitions, by interest, and so we go further, we commute for community. Whereas Mom's coffee klatch were the neighbors. Now we go across town to be with people."

Driving is the *sine qua non* of consumerism, for people and products alike. Most of our new options require time behind the wheel. In my own poll, 36% said they were spending more time running errands today than they did ten years ago, and 39% said errands took about the same amount of time. John Robinson has found a consistent upward trend in the amount of time Americans spend in cars running errands, going to restaurants, commuting, or shopping. Such shopping increasingly takes place on Sunday. By the mid-1980s Americans spent an average of more than forty minutes shopping every Sunday (up from twenty-five minutes in 1975). For many families Sunday has gone from a day when they go to church to a day when they go to the mall. This is part of a broader trend to fill time with productive activity which used to be considered time off.

Rocking Around the Clock

The borders between on and off time, work and play time, time to be up and time to let down have grown fuzzy. There are fewer and fewer periods of time when one can't do business. Not only diners and twenty-four-hour convenience stores but some copy centers, service stations, pharmacies, and even a few beauty parlors never close. In San Jose a special Yellow Pages lists nearly 200 area merchants who do business after 6 P.M. Pacific Bell planned to put out similar guides in other California cities. "We really looked at life-styles," explained the project's manager, "and this is the result."

Sociologist Murray Melbin calls our emerging round-the-clock society one of "incessance." Melbin has an interesting take on today's nonstop schedules. He sees America's newly populated night hours as analogous to its frontier in the last century. At that time sparsely populated western lands attracted those who felt crowded back East. In a similar migration, as time is used more intensively during the daytime, we invade the night in search of underexploited minutes. "Land fever is being replaced by time fever," Melbin suggested. "We can tell which dimension is society's main concern when its members consult clocks and calendars more often than they look at maps."

By now well over 30 million Americans are awake and active after midnight—nearly 10% of the population. As a result, hours that were once reserved for respite have grown increasingly businesslike. Up-to-date banks stay open into the late afternoon and early evening, at least part of Saturday, and in some cases Sunday too. Many automatic tellers never close (except to be repaired or refilled). "After hours" has become a good time to withdraw cash from an ATM, order a sweater, or make some investments. As Charles Schwab advertises, "We're there to take your order, any time of the day or night." Modern mail-order houses are open for business twenty-four hours a day, seven days a week. They're part of an emerging nonstop techno-commerce. Reduced phone rates motivate us to make calls late at night, join computer bulletin boards, or access data banks. Lower power costs can make nighttime a good time to do laundry or run the dishwasher. Many feel time has grown too valuable to "waste" on leisure. This is why the New York Stock Exchange has added nighttime trading hours. It can't afford not to. The global economy never shuts down, partly due to its range of time zones, partly because it's run by workaholics, but mostly because in an era when fortunes can literally be made or lost in *seconds,* time has taken on a value it never had before. Like land in Tokyo, modern time may have become *too* valuable. Our supply of time is even more finite than our supply of land. "If we have much to accomplish," noted Melbin, "we are reminded that time has limited room. In using time and needing more of it we try to fill it more thoroughly . . . Hours become dense to the point of crowding. Finally we can no more cram another activity in our day than cram another coat in the closet."

How do we manage? Timelocked individuals in focus groups, especially two-career parents, routinely said they cut back on sleep to squeeze more time out of their day. As his kids grew older, explained a New York lawyer, and went to bed later, his time for himself was getting pushed back. "In order to prolong that time I go to sleep later. But I still wake up at the same time. Some days I feel more drudged than others." Roper has found that more affluent Americans average half an hour less sleep per working day than others, which adds up to 125 hours a year, the equivalent of three full work weeks. A study done by two Michigan State University economists found that for every 25% wage increase a subject got, he or she would reduce sleep time by 1%. Were the wages of an average employee to double, that employee would spend twenty fewer minutes a day in bed. This seemed to be a tactic to maximize use of time as it grew more valuable. There are others.

Why Did God Only Give Us Two Hands?

John Robinson has found that the better educated his subjects, the more likely they are to engage in simultaneous activities. Here are some of the more interesting examples I've encountered of doing two or more things at once:

- floss teeth while driving (at stoplights only, praying no one you know pulls up alongside)
- change clothes while driving

- read with one hand while doing dishes with the other
- dictate memos while waiting in supermarket lines
- peddle an exercycle while paying bills at an attached desk and watching football on television

In a timelocked world, the ability to engage in simultaneous activities can feel like a test of one's ability to cope. When doing only one thing at a time it's easy to feel that we're not making full use of precious time. Why did God give us two hands if not to do two things at once?

Mona Doyle has found that this skill is particularly prized by younger consumers. That's how she and other market researchers explain their passion for "one-handed" food. America's key contribution to the world's cuisine has been food that can be held in one hand, freeing the other to do something else: hot dogs, hamburgers, ice cream cones, corn dogs. Through our genius we've even figured out a way to make hashed brown potatoes coagulate so they can be eaten with one hand. Other recent contributions to one-handed cuisine include french toast sticks, pocket pizza, Hot Bites, and, of course, the Egg McMuffin.

The secret to the success of such cuisine is that it allows busy commuters to save a few minutes they would otherwise waste by sitting down to eat. Eating while driving has become a national sport. Carmakers vie to include better-than-ever cupholders (the winner: Chrysler mini-vans, whose molded cupholders include a slot for mug handles). A lot of modern gadgetry is designed to help us engage in multiple activities: the Walkman, instructional tapes, cordless phones, cordless shavers, stationary bicycles with reading stands, and, of course, dashboard trays for food and drink. Nutritionist Sidney Mintz thinks contemporary eating habits simply reflect the fact that so many of us feel guilty if we're only doing one thing at a time. "Because of felt time pressure," Mintz observed, "we condense consumption pleasure by simultaneous consumption, consuming different things at the same time—such as popcorn and movies, or exercise and reading, or driving and drinking, or TV watching and eating . . . Maximum enjoyment in minimum time has come to mean both a higher frequency of occasions for consumption and more intense simultaneous consumption. Watching the Cowboys play the Steelers, while eating Fritos and drinking Coca Cola, while smoking a joint, while one's girl sits on one's lap, can seem like packing a great deal of enjoyment into a short time."

Focus group participants of all ages noted how routinely they did something else while "watching" television. "Even when I sit down to watch TV I have a magazine in my hand," said a businessman named George during a focus group outside Dallas. "I seldom do one thing at a time. In the office when I'm working on a program on the computer I may have something running on the computer and I'll have a magazine open in front of me or

I'll pull some work over from the side that I'll do for a minute or two while something's compiling."

Jed, a psychologist in the same group, said he had a tendency to leave the TV on while he was reading or doing other things. "I'm not really watching," explained Jed. "It's just there. It's background noise. I dictate with the TV on." A saleswoman named Denise said she kept her dictaphone on hand at all times to make use of spare moments: while waiting for appointments, say, or standing in lines. Denise used to dictate reports while driving, until she found herself too harried by the pressure of dictating, shifting gears, stopping for lights, and dealing with other drivers at the same time. "You wind up saying things on the tape that you don't want your secretary to hear," noted Denise.

Jed said he preferred to dictate while driving. In a car he wasn't interrupted by phone calls, his secretary asking questions, or his wife dropping by to visit. Jed actually looked forward to visiting a hospital an hour south of his office because he knew that would be time enough to knock out a report.

A 16-year-old named Laura, attending this group with her mother, marveled at all the things people seemed to be able to do at the same time. What was the point? "Like taking notes and listening and carrying on a conversation," said Laura. "It doesn't work. You can't do it. It doesn't all fit together."

"Why then," wondered Laura's mother, "is it comfortable for you to do your homework and have music going while you're talking on the phone?"

Her daughter blushed. Then Laura explained that she needed to talk to distant friends she didn't see that often, music was on "for comfort," and the homework was usually algebra which only took half a brain anyway.

Never Out of Touch

One reason video-phones have never caught on is that they make it virtually impossible to do something else while talking on the phone. Of those who filled out my questionnaire, 60% said that they were likely to do tasks ranging from paperwork to filing their nails while talking on the phone. (Only 36% said they usually did nothing else during phone conversations.) I have a friend with whom I rarely talk by phone without the clinking of dishes being washed in the background. Cordless phones have made it possible to conduct conversations while otherwise engaged in any part of the house—including the bathroom.

Most of us have a love-hate relationship with the telephone. Typically we love to be able to reach people, but hate being so reachable. We prize having a phone's buttons at our command but dread its jarring ring. (I've heard that there are people who can let ringing phones lie, but I've never actually met one.) Some arm themselves with defensive technology. A member of the Los Angeles focus group had two answering machines: one with a listed number for marginal calls; another with his unlisted number for important ones. Even deciding not to return a call consumes time and mental energy, however. Yet many of us can't stand the idea of being "out of touch." This is why so many fortunes have been made developing one innovation after another which makes it possible to never miss a call: answering machines, multiple lines, call waiting, call forwarding, cordless phones, cellular phones, and beepers.

My first son's birth was accompanied by the regular chirp of doctors' beepers. Users of this device tend to be ambivalent about being so reachable. On the one hand it allows them to go about their normal lives while on call. On the other hand a pager can feel like an electronic ball and chain. One study found that the vast majority of pager summons that doctors receive are not for true emergencies. Pointing out that the days when his was out of commission were among his most relaxed, a San Antonio physician thought that beepers were an ill-appreciated source of stress. "It's like having your mother with you everywhere," concurred a Philadelphia obstetrician of the pager on his belt. "You know: 'Get down here, at once!' "

Because they don't demand an immediate response, answering machines are less stressful than beepers, and therefore more widespread. By the end of the 1980s well over a third of all American homes owned this never-out-of-touch device. Some 38% of those who filled out my questionnaire termed the answering machine a "necessity" (behind washer-dryers, freezers, blow dryers, stereos, and a second car, but ahead of dishwashers, microwave ovens, garbage disposals, a VCR, or a second television). "It helps me stay in touch with people who work sane hours," said a night nurse in Cleveland. Others find that the power to screen calls and reduce telephone tag eases the stress in their lives. "Leaving messages" has become an art form. "Checking messages" has replaced reading the mail as the first thing many of us do after walking through the front door. The price we pay for this convenience is that such machines increase our volume of input. More calls go in and out of phones connected to answering machines. An actor in New York actually pulled the plug on his machine after he found that "the pressure of returning sixteen or seventeen calls a day became unbearable."

One of the sweetest rewards for taking a trip has always been getting away from the phone. Today, however, telephones beckon to us on trains and planes. ("Now how will I be able to pretend I'm not in?" moaned one traveling businessman confronting his first in-plane telephone.) Not everyone minds the idea of being this reachable. Cellular phone users typically feel that they improve their productivity and salvage lost hours by taking and making calls while driving. A Detroit lawyer and businessman estimated that over five years' time his car phone doubled the amount of work he got done. To him this was not just a productivity tool but a stress reducer because time spent in traffic jams could now be put to work. Many cellular phone users echo this sentiment. When stuck in traffic, lost, or late for an appointment, they call ahead and relax.

A few pioneers have begun to lug around transportable phones. At my son's nursery school's field day, one father put his minutes on the sideline to good use by making calls on a portable phone the size of a car battery. "It's saved me hours," a Washington lawyer said of the phone he totes everywhere to catch up on calls during idle moments. "But you have to be something of a Type A personality to fully enjoy it."

As cellular phones drop in size and price, we'll be able to carry them around like calculators. Futurists predict that in time phone numbers will be assigned to individuals rather than to phones. Anyone trying to reach us will simply dial our number and track us down. Many will resist becoming part of this process. But as never-out-of-touch technology reaches a critical mass, laggards everywhere will come under pressure to get on board. ("I've been trying to reach you. When are you going to stop being so pigheaded and get a universal phone number like everyone else?") It wasn't so long ago that many considered answering machines rude and unnecessary. I was among them. Then friends started asking why I didn't give them the opportunity to leave me a message so they could stop dialing my number. I now own an answering machine. Some day, perish the thought, I will probably carry a phone about in my shirt pocket.

Never-out-of-touchness is yet another illustration of how valuable time has grown in the modern mind; too valuable to waste by being unreachable. This returns us to the question with which this chapter began: With their lower standard of living, why did our forebears seem to enjoy a more relaxed pace of life?

Too Valuable to Waste on Leisure

Trying to determine why his parents' life seemed so much less harried than his, a Houston physician named Russell pointed to the modest salaries they made as an agricultural extension worker and school cafeteria employee. As a well-paid specialist he could command far more per hour than they ever dreamed of earning. Russell's time had grown precious, perhaps too precious, he thought. Being self-employed only added to his tendency to assign a monetary value to every waking hour. As a result, he explained:

When I "waste" time, whether it's fishing or taking my kids to the movies,
I feel guilt. Whereas I feel fairly certain my parents didn't have that
sensation. You went to church several times a week because that's what

you did to be a good member of society. You went out and visited those farms and ranches because that was part of the job. If things weren't real efficient, you didn't expect them to be real efficient. Maybe you got out to the farm and there wasn't anybody there to open the gate for you, but nobody got that worried about that sort of thing. Now, if I call my office at 8:30 in the morning; and my secretary doesn't answer the phone on the first ring, I start the day off angry. I think it has to do with the fact that we do look at time differently. I think they had the same absolute hourly demands that I do. They just didn't look at it the same way. I think it has to do with our assigning a monetary value to everything. Everything that happens is worth something. For example, if my fee for a certain procedure in medicine is $100 and it takes me an hour to do that, then for me to go to church for an hour means I can then sit there and say, "This is costing me $100." Obviously I don't consciously think of that, but I must have some concern that "Gosh, my time is worth more than this." I think it just wasn't that way in the fifties. If you didn't get your car out of the shop in time, well that's the way it was. Now, I expect them to furnish me a rental car. I have different demands than they did.

Is this crassly materialistic? I don't think so. I think it's just a candid description of an understandable reaction to finding that one's time has grown so valuable, perhaps *too* valuable. According to one school of economists there is a logical connection between affluence and time scarcity. In a nutshell, this is their explanation: The more money we can command, the more valuable our time grows. The more valuable our time grows, the harder it becomes to use it in "unproductive" ways (such as enjoying ourselves). If coconuts are worth only a penny apiece, you might as well sit under a palm tree as climb it to pick some. Should their value rise to 10 cents each, it might be worthwhile to spend part of your day picking coconuts. At $1 it would make sense to devote a considerable part of your waking hours hunting for coconuts. And should a coconut shortage drive their price up to $5 apiece, any time you spend lounging in the shade of palm fronds rather than harvesting its fruit could feel as though it's costing you a fortune.

This is the way many of us feel about leisure time. According to economist Gary Becker, the real cost of any leisure activity such as eating at a restaurant or going to the movies must be calculated as a combination of its actual price plus the amount of money that *could* have been made had that time been devoted to producing income. Added to our fabled workaholism, this formula helps explain why so many Americans can't enjoy leisure time. It's too expensive, in terms of foregone income. Becker thinks that the American time fetish fuels our consumer economy. It's symptomatic of a time-scarce culture that its members buy more and more goods, and use each one for briefer periods. This is especially true of newly disposable items such as ballpoint pens, calculators, or watches. By using products this way we are not just being wasteful. From Becker's perspective, being lavish about purchases but stingy with time makes perfect sense in an economy in which minutes have grown precious.

Many are feeling the effects of this equation in their work. Even those who work in industries once renowned for their leisurely pace are now held accountable for their minutes. Members of the banking industry make nostalgic jokes about "banker's hours." A San Antonio professor reported that for the first time in two decades of teaching college she was being asked to fill out time sheets. A hospice volunteer in that city reported the same thing (she quit). A Boston insurance broker said that his customer representatives were expected to handle four times as many policies as they did in the mid-1970s. This was possible in part because new technology had increased their efficiency. But his reps also didn't offer the same level of service that they used to. The broker didn't think this was a bad thing, necessarily, just a sign of the times. And he was grateful for the technology that made such productivity possible.

"If these things weren't there," agreed a DuPont product manager of the computers, phone systems, and fax machines that had become central to his work, "companies would not be making as much money. I wouldn't be paid as well." On the other hand, he added, "I get very frustrated now when I feel I have more tasks to do than I can get done in a particular amount of time."

The growing pressure to *produce* was a common theme in focus groups. Global competition was considered only one source of that stress. "There is serious pressure on our generation," said a San Diego journalist named Steve, referring to the huge volume of baby boomers jousting for a few top spots. "There are very real demographic reasons for those pressures. It's not just that we all need Cuisinarts."

"I work a lot of hard hours," concurred Charlie, also a journalist. "My parents had more choice. They had smaller houses and less vacation time. Most of us have roughly the same number of hours allowable for vacation. And then we don't take them. We dribble them out. We're afraid to leave our desks because the desks won't be there when we get back."

Steve thought that in trying to develop more innovative lives many baby boomers like himself had lost track of the time. By choosing to work more flexible hours from home he'd succeeded in filling his schedule fuller than it had ever been in an office. "It's in the search for time that we have these flexible jobs," Steve pointed out. "We get the fax, the copier, the computer." Rather than reducing his hours of work Steve found such conveniences had increased them. In the evening he took part in "bulletin board" conversations with other computer users. He also sent and received electronic messages, or E-mail. Steve could do this any time of the day or night.

One reason E-mail has grown so popular is that electronic mailboxes never close. Users can boot up their computers, read their mail, and send some out at any time of the day or night. There's no limit to how many messages can be transmitted, or the number of people to whom they can be sent.

That's the rub. Because it's so easy to convey information electronically, more messages than ever are being sent. With E-mail it's as easy to send the same memo to 1000 computers as to one. So what the heck; you might as well. Dealing in volume can make it feel like you're getting more done. At the receiving end, however, E-mail boxes bulge with messages with no tip-off about which ones should be given priority—no letterhead, no colors, no visual cues—nothing. To the computer a message letting you know that your mother has been taken to the hospital is equivalent to an announcement that Joe Jones has been made head of the Duluth office. The result is electronic junk mail. "It's a well-known phenomenon in large corporations," noted former Lotus Development Corporation Chairman Mitchell Kapor, "that when you come back from a long weekend you'll find fifty pieces of electronic mail in your mailbox, spend hours going through it, and end up with most of it being stuff you don't want to see."

Even if one responds to only a few such messages, it still takes time to consider them all. A University of California professor who participated in four professional bulletin boards as well as campus E-mail told me he was starting to feel overwhelmed by receiving fifty to a hundred messages a day. University of Pennsylvania communications professor George Gerbner said that it took him an hour a day to deal with his electronic mail.

What E-mail has become for many is a high-tech illustration of a much broader paradox in this society: Our time seems to grow crowded in direct proportion to the technology we develop to uncrowd it.

THE AFFLUENT SOCIETY

As they packed to spend a year with the Machiguenga Indians in Peru, Allen and Orna Johnson agonized over what to take. Both anthropologists had done fieldwork before, but never for this long or in such a remote location—the Amazon rain forest. Finally they decided to limit themselves to whatever would fit into two foot lockers. Neither had any idea how they'd get by with so little.

In fact, the Johnsons turned out to be "absurdly oversupplied," in Allen's words. At most he and Orna used 10% of what they took. A four-person tent was quickly discarded. So was a barbecue big enough for a tailgate party. A lantern which threw off enough light to read by proved useless. (Like their Machiguenga hosts, the Johnsons seldom stayed awake past sundown.)

After an extended rain Allen put his shoes out to dry in the sun: two pairs of boots, and two pairs of sneakers. Some barefoot Machiguenga men marveled at how many shoes he owned. One said that a fifth pair wasn't even in the sun. Johnson denied it. To prove his point the man went inside the anthropologist's palm-frond hut and returned with a pair of sneakers Johnson had thrown in a corner and forgotten about. "This was not the only occasion on which I could not keep track of my possessions," he later noted, "a deficiency unknown to the Machiguenga."

In time the Johnsons limited themselves to three sets of jeans and work shirts apiece, and one "good" shirt for Sundays. They also put away most of half a dozen table settings they'd brought, using only a single cup, plate, and spoon apiece. Did this make them feel deprived? Actually, said Orna Johnson, it was just the opposite: "When we had several utensils, there were always dirty dishes. So there was more work. When you only have one cup you just kind of rinse it out before you use it or after you use it and there's not as much work." As a bonus, their two cups were easier to keep track of. With six cups they'd always seemed to be looking for one.

The Machiguenga themselves had few possessions. A few machetes, some axes, and a shovel were their main concession to modernity. The Indians produced most of what they used: pots, baskets, cloth. Presumably this took a lot of time. This is what the Johnsons assumed. It wasn't so. A typical Machiguenga adult devoted only a few hours a day to making implements, farming, or foraging. Much of their time was given over to visiting each other, or simply taking it easy.

The Machiguenga never seemed harried. There was no word for "worried" in their vocabulary. Nor was there one for "time." (They indicated periods of the day by pointing to positions of the sun.) As a result, time didn't run short for the Machiguenga. They behaved as though this commodity was abundant. Allen Johnson—who now chairs UCLA's Anthropology Department—recalled watching two young boys pop corn. Their method was to pull one kernel at a time off a cob and place it by the glowing log of a campfire. After the kernel popped they put it into a container, pulled off another piece of corn, and repeated the process. With this method it took hours to come up with a decent snack. "It's a morning," recalled Allen. "There's kind of a relaxed quality to it. Not this popcorn popping up suddenly with an enormous eruption and then everybody sits down and starts chomping."

A leisurely tempo characterized most Machiguenga activity. After describing how their men spent hours meticulously carving a comb from bamboolike plants, Allen observed, "It's all done in a way that you have a feeling of complete relaxation. Not lazy or sluggish, but everything done at what feels like an utterly comfortable, unhurried, yet efficient speed. This is the feeling you have over and over again there. Right now, as the term's beginning here, that's an alien feeling. I'm constantly pushing, pushing to get the next thing on the list done."

During five visits to the Machiguenga totaling nearly two years, Allen Johnson found that after a few days he could literally *feel* time's pressure easing—in his body and in his mind. This was more true in the Amazon rain forest than during vacations back home. In the field there was no pressure to see sights, get his money's worth, or buy things. "In the States," explained Orna (who now lectures at UCLA in addition to raising their family), "you try to cram as much as you can in a day. There you didn't have the feeling of needing to get as much done. There wasn't the pressure of *accomplishing;* you didn't go to bed at the end of the day feeling 'Oh, I didn't do this and I didn't do that and I didn't do the other thing. Oh, my God, I better get up early. I better stay up late.' That never happened. Not having that pressure allows you to enjoy what you do a lot more.

"In our society we try to do so much. Most are things we set for ourselves that are not necessarily essential but that we perceive as expected of us. Organizing our papers, having the house clean in a certain way, all the things we set out for ourselves. And if we don't accomplish them we feel bad. No matter what you do, it's not enough; you accomplish something that's really important, then there's always the next thing that you have to do. And there's a sense of breathlessness because you were working under pressure. You almost feel like the pressure's necessary to get it done. In the field that wasn't the case. In the field you have a much smaller number of tasks. At the end of the day you've accomplished them. There's none of that harried sense of not having done what you had to do."

Does she ever think of going back?

"Many times," murmured Orna. "Many times."

So why don't the Johnsons take up permanent residence among the Machiguenga? They've often wondered. In addition to enjoying a refreshing pace of life both anthropologists found the Machiguenga to be good-humored, honest, and hospitable. But their life was not altogether idyllic. Among other things, a lack of modern medicines condemned them to suffer curable illnesses. This was high on the list of reasons not to move to Peru. In general, Allen Johnson felt, "We would have regarded a permanent life there as a great personal sacrifice. Orna and I came home partly because it is home, where our lives have meaning, and partly because we did not want to go without some creature comforts that we, for better or worse, regard as highly desirable."

At the same time, he added, "We've lived in a palm leaf house in the forest and we know it was very comfortable and we liked it. So we don't kid ourselves that some new luxury will somehow make our lives better."

With its microwave oven and multiple television sets the Johnsons know that their Los Angeles home offers no apparent evidence that its residents are nostalgic for a simple life in the forest. Yet both feel that experiencing such a life at least gave them some perspective. They live close to UCLA so Allen can bike to work. Like the Machiguenga, the Johnsons eat little meat. Orna tries to review their possessions on a regular basis, clothes especially, to see what can be given away. Seeing Machiguenga children enjoy life with virtually no toys helped them resist the temptation to shower Pound Puppies and Cabbage Patch Kids on their three girls. In general they've tried to retain an awareness of how much time buying and maintaining consumer items can cost. "The main thing it taught me," said Orna Johnson of her year in the field, "is that you can get by on very little. You don't need possessions in order to feel well off."

There are many ways to define affluence. One way, our way, is by the money we make and possessions we own. Another way, the Machiguenga way, is by the amount and quality of time one has at one's disposal. They are poor in possessions, rich in time. The cost of this type of affluence is material. By our standards these Indians live a meager life. They don't starve. In fact, says Allen Johnson, the Machiguenga's diet is balanced and appetizing. Nor were their homes lacking. In Beverly Hills one might look like a shack. But in the rain forest, the Machiguenga's wood and palm-frond shelters were appropriate: sturdy, well-ventilated and comfortable. In fact, other than modern medicine, all the Machiguenga lacked was modern conveniences.

One day a local man was about to punch some holes in a piece of leather to make a child's drum. Allen took out his Swiss Army knife to offer him the use of its leather punch. By the time he had the punch out, however, this man had already made a perfectly good hole with a piece of broken knife he kept at hand for that purpose. In the meantime Johnson's knife drew the attention of some other Machiguenga men. They'd never seen anything like it, and asked Johnson to explain the purpose of each of its many tools. They wanted to know where they could buy one.

"I interpreted this experience in two ways," Johnson later reflected. "First, the knife was overelaborate. The Machiguenga met all their own needs for clothing, shelter, and containers with much simpler tools. Second, the elaborateness of the knife was itself an attraction, and its remarkable design and quality of materials could not help but draw the men's attention."

Before leaving, he gave them his Swiss Army knife, but not without misgivings. Based on his experience among the Machiguenga—and his appreciation of their low-key life—Johnson was ambivalent about helping them acquire modern implements. Even the few metal tools they had already obtained from Peruvian traders enabled them to till the soil rather than forage for food at the expense of working longer hours. Were the Machiguenga to be inspired by a dream of making their lives easier through the use of conveniences, could they ever again enjoy the luxury of time?

6

The Convenience Catch

Americans have more timesaving devices and less time than any other group of people in the world.

—DUNCAN CALDWELL

Rummage sales are a graveyard of shattered dreams. Here is a Presto hamburger maker, still in its box. There is a Veg-O-Matic that doesn't look as if it sliced too many cucumbers. Several hot lather dispensers sit forlornly by a speed dialer with unsmudged buttons. One whole table groans beneath the weight of hot-air popcorn makers, automatic can openers, electric carving knives, and a single Cuisinart struggling to maintain its dignity. Most such conveniences look barely used. They usually are. And no wonder. Devices that promise to simplify our lives and save us time rarely succeed. At best they have no net impact. At worst they actually complicate our lives and cost us time.

Saving time seems to be an impossible dream. On balance there may be no such thing as "time-saving." Any time saved in one place is squandered in another, usually with interest.

Consider lawns. Until the rotary lawn mower was invented late last century, there were few lawns to be mowed. Only those homeowners who could afford to hire gardeners with scythes and sickles—or who kept a few sheep—enjoyed trimmed lawns. Early this century an improved push mower made it possible for the burgeoning population of suburban Americans to grow and mow their own grass. This convenience made the job easier, but one that had to be done more often because push mowers couldn't cut tall grass. They also needed a specialist for sharpening.

Lawns still weren't cut that meticulously. Mowing technology just didn't permit it. The internal combustion engine is what made today's pristine lawns possible. In cars this engine allowed more and more people to live on suburban land suited to growing grass. Applied to mowers, gasoline engines made it possible to mow lawns neatly and often—once a week or

more. Today this is the norm for American homeowners. The easier it
became to cut grass, the higher our standards rose and the more often we
felt a need to do so. By now many homeowners consider any lawn a failure
that doesn't look as if it could sustain a few holes of golf. On balance an
ostensible convenience—the lawn mower—ended up costing far more time
than it saved.

This is the convenience catch. The more convenient our lives become,
the more pressed we feel for time. Time grows scarce in direct proportion
to the number of conveniences purchased to save time. Any minutes saved
in one realm of our lives are usually spent in another, with interest.

It seems paradoxical that in any age of microchips and fiber optics we
should have less time than ever. It's not. Modern conveniences not only
speed and simplify chores but allow us to do more of them. Cuisinarts
reduce drudgery and accelerate certain tasks but also raise expectations
about the quality of our meals. Dustbusters make it possible to suck dirt
from spaces that used to be inaccessible. Rolodexes and speed dialers make
it easier to contact people, so we end up contacting more of them. It's the
convenience catch.

This catch applies to the office as surely it as does to the home. Take
the Xerox machine. No piece of office machinery ever filled in the blank so
quickly on the question: "How did we ever get along without _____?" Two
decades after Xerography was introduced in 1959, an estimated 177 billion
copies were being made annually here, or about 750 for every man, woman
and child in the United States. By conservative estimates at least 25% of
all this photocopying was absolutely unnecessary. Not that it mattered.
Once any document within reach of a Xerox machine could be copied, it was
amazing how many things turned out to need copying. Letters, poems,
rumors, jokes, manifestoes, party invitations, recipes, body parts, and
Johnny's latest drawing for Grandma Kate in Albuquerque all were subjected to the moving green light. Seventeen copies of Bob Underhill's
memo on why the ratchet assembly division shouldn't be moved to Cleveland may not have been absolutely necessary, but with that many on file,
one might outlive Bob himself.

A retiree once said that what he missed more than anything else about
his old office—more than the people, the phone, or the prestige—was the
photocopier. That same feeling is what motivated me to buy a copier for
my own home office over a decade ago. One thought I had was that this
would save lots of time that used to be spent in trips to the library or copy
shop. Its effect was exactly the opposite. With a copier just steps away, lots
of extra copying became possible. Duplicates, triplicates and quadruplicates
of documents for cross-filing. Letters. Birth announcements. My father's
poems. Our children's artwork. After the first copier died I returned to copy
shops and libraries for a few years. My Xerox habit dwindled. Then I bought

another copier. As before, in the short run this device saved me time and effort, possibly even money. But once again I'm far more willing to make copies. A copier close at hand robs you of discipline. I accidentally copy material I've already copied. I reproduce material from the library to read "later" (and seldom do). At best the time-saving is a wash, at worst a loss. In a way photocopying is too *great* a convenience; too *easy* to use. As a Sacramento doctor observed, "If I spent all the time during my entire medical career reading out of one standard textbook the time I spent Xeroxing articles, I'd be a lot smarter."

Time-Consuming Time Savers

It's no coincidence that Xerography is an American invention. Although the convenience catch applies to all people everywhere, Americans have always had a particular genius for spending time trying to save time. From early on our love of gadgetry was as noted as our hectic pace of life. Historian Marshall Davidson thought the two might be connected. Davidson wrote of our "ingenuity in . . . finding the quickest and easiest, if often not the best, way of getting things done. That penchant for saving time became such a fixed and fundamental habit that the typical Yankee came to use the leisure he derived from a labor- or time-saving device to think up a new such device so that he would have more time to think up still other labor-saving devices in a non-stop spiral of time-consuming effort."

Ever since the first apple parer graced a colonial pine shelf, we've puzzled over the fact that so many devices artfully designed to save time and labor on balance did neither. The mistake we made was to assume that "labor-saving" technology existed in the same setting it entered. This just isn't the case. Each such device—no matter how modest—creates a new reality, one which can make added demands on our time. Moving food preparation from the hearth to the stove killed off one-pot meals, permitting the use of more pots (and dishes) which then needed cleaning. Once basic kitchen tasks such as chopping, beating, or whipping were made easier, we found many more reasons to do such tasks. Even the eggbeater—America's first big appliance success—proved more time consumer than saver. When eggbeaters eased the burden of whisking eggs for mid-nineteenth century cooks, angel food cakes grew popular. This meant that more than a dozen whites now had to be separated from yolks, then beat with a vengeance. As a result, any initial time saved by the eggbeater was squandered and turned into a net deficit.

When it comes to saving time, one must always consider the *net*. At the outset many conveniences save a few minutes here and there, but in the end they usually consume more. On the time front we typically win battles and lose wars. The very tools we buy to simplify our lives end up complicating them. Hoping to ease my burden, I once bought an automatic phone dialer. After several frustrating hours spent trying to install it I called a neighbor for help. Once he did the wiring I spent more hours studying the dialer's manual to learn how to enter numbers for automatic dialing (it could do a lot of other things, too, but those I ignored). Power outages made it necessary to reenter these numbers. Eventually my automatic dialer saved me a bit of effort in dialing frequently called numbers. But this device never recouped the hours it took to get it up and running. I'm not even convinced that my fingers didn't dial faster than my "speed dialer." One effect of using this device was that I promptly forgot nearly every number programmed into the dialer. Therefore whenever I was away from this convenience I had to look them up. After one last power outage I didn't bother to reprogram my dialer. It's still wired into my system, but I haven't touched it in years. This high-tech time saver just cost me too much time.

So has our VCR. For some reason this wondrous device can reduce otherwise competent grown-ups to whimpering states of ineptitude. When she went to college, one student asked her mother to tape some programs for her at odd hours, such as three in the morning. Her mother did: by staying up to turn the recorder on and off. She couldn't figure out any other way to do it.

In theory videotape recorders give us powerful control over our time. By being able to record programs for later viewing, zap commercials, and fast forward through slow parts, we've supposedly grown more frugal in the time we devote to television watching. Ha! No matter how much we enjoy the convenience of VCRs, they make enormous demands on our time. After we waste several hours trying to install the device and hire someone else to do it, we are equipped to tape shows that are on when we're out. In order to choose them, we must read expanded television schedules in greater detail than we used to, including the wee morning hours our eyes used to skip over. (One woman I know has designed an elaborate weekly grid with which to plan her weekly taping.) Then a blank tape must be found and the recorder set (after making sure its clock is still accurate and resetting it if necessary). Success at this process allows us to watch shows that we might otherwise have missed. But it also imposes the burden of actually doing so. Recording a tape doesn't necessarily mean we'll watch it. There aren't enough hours in the day. I record and watch in about a 3:1 ratio. But you can't tape over a program once you've gone to the trouble of recording, labeling, and shelving it, can you? So there they sit, recorded tapes by the dozen, glaring at me and hoping beyond reason that someday I'll find time to watch them. One whole tape is occupied by a three-hour ABC special on postwar America that I was too tired to see when it aired in 1985 and am still too tired to see. Several unwatched John Wayne movies are left over from an aborted project on the actor. Three tapes incorporate all nine and a half hours of *Shoah,* which I definitely plan to watch, as soon as I finish reading *War and Peace.*

The Time-Saving Fallacy

Home videotaping is just one among many techno-saviors which end up costing great gobs of time in the guise of saving some. Low technology had a positive self-limiting effect that kept the volume of tasks manageable. The easier any task becomes to do, the more often we tend to do it. The reason that conveniences are such dismal failures at saving time and effort can be summed up in four basic points. Conveniences:

- convert a few big, time-consuming tasks into many smaller ones that can consume more time overall;
- create new tasks altogether;
- raise standards;
- require added time to master, maintain, and repair.

This process can be seen at work throughout the typical modern home. By making it easier to dry wet hair, blow dryers encouraged us to wash it more often. Unlike yesterday's heavy vacuum cleaners, today's "electric brooms" and hand-held vacuums are meant to be used continually. ("Brush after every meal," says Panasonic of their electric broom. "For the other six days of the week," advertises Dustbuster.) The net effect of many such advances in household technology can be to increase our volume of tasks, and the amount of time those tasks consume.

One survey of several studies done on housework since the 1920s concluded that "The proliferation of some small appliances has extended rather than eliminated tasks. Thus, the net effect of technological change is not time saving." Almost without exception, all such studies reached the same conclusion: Labor-savers may relieve housework of its drudgery and speed up particular tasks, but they don't save time. The University of Michigan's Survey Research Center found virtually no difference in time spent on housework between those who owned many appliances and those who didn't. When center sociologist Joann Vanek compared time spent on household chores between the mid-1920s and mid-1960s, she found very little difference in overall time expenditure over four decades' time. However, Vanek did find revealing differences in the *way* time was spent. Appliances had indeed reduced or eliminated the amount of time devoted to specific tasks: ironing, for example, beating rugs, or canning food. But laundry took the average mid-sixties woman one hour *more* a week, and general home care was up two and a half hours weekly.

Compared with previous laundering methods, automatic washing machines have saved lots of time and effort. What no one foresaw, however, was how much more laundry it became possible to do once that task was simplified. This was especially true after the introduction of wash-and-wear clothing. Now sheets, underwear, and socks could be changed more often. Laundry hampers grew larger. What was once a weekly task became an endless one. "Over the long run," noted housework historian Susan Strasser, "the automatic washer probably restructured rather than reduced laundry time . . . Eventually, by allowing women to wash 'whenever you get a load,' the automatic washer, the dryer, and the synthetic fabrics that ended ironing probably increased the weekly household laundry load."

In Sacramento, Arlene, a 47-year-old mother of two who grew up on a North Dakota farm, observed that she probably spent about as much time on laundry as her mother did. Arlene thought that this was because "we don't wear our clothes to the limit. We do more laundry. I might spend a little less time because it is more efficient, but I do significantly more laundry than my mother did."

No one else in this focus group disagreed. But Nancy, a secretary and mother of three, did put in a word for her favorite appliance: the dishwasher. "You rinse the stuff off and put it in there," Nancy said. "When you have a full load, you put it on."

"Let me tell you what happens," interjected her husband, Hal. "She tells you in theory what happens, but what really happens is that after we rinse the dishes, a surgeon could use these things. They are hermetically sealed—they're so sterile. Then, after that, they're put in the dishwasher. Basically it's a big holding bin where you're storing dishes before you put them away."

"I think they don't save that much time," agreed Arlene's husband, Michael. "You don't have to dry them, but then you could let them drain too. I think you use more dishes."

Arlene concurred. "As children," she recalled, "if we were having a snack, we didn't get out a plate and use it, we'd get out a piece of wax paper and throw it out. Now I just grab a dish. Then that dish needs to be washed."

It's a misnomer to call contemporary life "easier" than it used to be. True, the drudgery level is way down. But the nuisance level is way up. We may no longer haul water, split wood, trim wicks, clean lamps, boil clothes, feed horses, or bake bread, but we do stand in supermarket lines, chauffeur kids, endure traffic jams, fend off telemarketers, and repeatedly try to figure out how to reset digital clocks (to say nothing of working extra hours to pay for all of our conveniences). In effect we've swapped hard labor for a longer sentence.

Anyone who's ever taken a day off from work hoping the refrigerator repairman will show up may question the time-saving qualities of modern conveniences. Or got stuck in an endless electronic switchboard. Or bought anything with "some assembly required." Or had to run out for fresh batteries to placate a wailing child whose radio-controlled car just stopped moving. Today's tasks may be simpler, but there are more of them. Having reduced the amount of time we spend per task, we've increased the number of tasks overall. Physical exhaustion has been replaced by the psychic kind. It's all part of the convenience catch.

The Automatic Blues

An understandable mistake is to assume that "automatic" conveniences save time and simplify chores. More often it's the other way around. Consider the rubber sink stopper. There is nothing complicated about it. The worst fate that could befall such a stopper was that it would wear out or get lost, making it necessary to buy a new one for a dollar or so. Today most tub and sink drains employ lever-operated metal stoppers. Metal lever stoppers are a bit easier to use. Unplugging them doesn't require getting your hands wet. But they don't really save time. If anything, metal lever stoppers can cost time. When something goes wrong with one, you can gather up your wrenches to repair or replace it. Or else you can call a $60-an-hour plumber whom you hope will come when promised.

One paradoxical reason that life has grown so complicated is the very emphasis we put on conveniences being "automatic." The more sophisticated technology becomes, the more likely it is to need expert counsel. Automatic devices typically have more complex mechanisms than manual ones. Such mechanisms divorce them from users' ability to understand, trouble-shoot, and service their own gear. The inner workings of manual devices tend to be self-evident. Even when broken, low- to medium-tech tools can be encouraged to limp along. Gay Talese kept a battered old Olivetti typewriter going for years by using dental floss to hold loose keys in place. Andy Rooney got a service manual from his dealer so he could maintain his own Underwood. By contrast, an electronic typewriter, like an electronic anything, either works or doesn't work. There is not much in between. Automatic devices require specialists to tell us how to get them going, and to repair them when they don't.

Compared with a previous generation of medium-tech gadgets whose operations were basically self-explanatory, the operation of electronic ones is anything but. Most require scriptural analysis of manuals to reveal their secrets. What's worse, manuals are not only necessary to get modern conveniences up and running but to do even the simplest maintenance. As a result countless home computers, memory phones, food processors, and electronic notepads are sitting in boxes in closets, rarely used if used at all because their owners are too intimidated to figure out how to use them and too embarrassed to ask for help.

A friend of ours named Elise once treated herself to an automatic breadmaker. Having technology bake her bread seemed like it might be an improvement over letting Safeway do it. But every time we visited Elise, the breadmaker sat in a corner of her kitchen, still inside its carton. She kept "meaning" to use it, Elise told us, but just hadn't found the time. After this went on for several weeks, Elise finally broke down and admitted the truth: She couldn't face the breadmaker's manual. If she could find time to read— and decipher—the manual, Elise assured us, she might use the appliance yet. She was hopeful that this would happen. Soon. (Update: Elise gave it to her father-in-law.)

We live in an age of manual proliferation. At one time I kept all of our manuals in one folder. Now we need over half a dozen folders: for big appliances, small appliances, stereo, electronic goods, kids' items, digital timepieces and "misc." When we moved and accidentally left half of our manual folders behind, we were lost. What does that flashing symbol on the camera readout mean? How do we change the time on the camcorder? What's involved in resetting station buttons on the car radio?

To help answer such questions, many manufacturers now have 800 numbers. Like a suicide hotline these services offer help, reassurance, and anonymity. The GE Technical Assistance Center fields 8000 calls a day. More questions are asked about VCRs than any other convenience, especially how to reset the clock once its numbers start blinking. More than one owner has finally solved this problem by covering the blinking numbers with tape.

Digital clocks are particularly intimidating to consumers of a certain age. Even George Bush took the occasion of a presidential speech to stump for a nation where every citizen would be able to set their own VCR's clock. A common topic of conversation around the twice-yearly time switch is how demanding a chore it's become to reset the many timepieces in our homes. This task has gone from a simple, easily executed twist of the wrist to a complicated pushing of buttons in mysterious sequences. And this button-pushing must now be done on a proliferating number of products. Look around your home. Note how many conveniences now include a built-in digital clock. We have a total of twenty-two digital clocks in our three-bedroom house. One woman in New York counted 18 in her apartment: one on the microwave, two on VCRs, six on time-display telephones, two on answering machines (which not only displayed the time but announced it after every message), one on her fax machine, another on the automatic coffeemaker ("I never use the automatic turn-on," she explained, "but I can't let it display the wrong time, can I?"), a digital watch ("Where is the instruction booklet?"), and clocks in the kitchen, bedroom, bathroom, and car. "Changing all these clocks takes a lot of time," she moaned, "and before you know it, you've used up the better part of that hour you thought you gained—or was it lost?"

Let Them Read Manuals

I recently bought a vintage digital clock at a garage sale. This clock is electric but not electronic. Its painted-on numbers don't glow with authority. Nonetheless, several things impress me about this clock. A power outage only stops its time for as long as the power's out. Resetting the clock then calls for adding on just that amount of time. To do this you stick your finger inside a hole in the back and turn the number wheels manually. This takes a few seconds. Best of all, the whole process is self-evident. No manual is needed. Including the time it takes to scout up a manual to tell me what to do, I can seldom reset any modern digital timepieces in less than a few minutes.

A University of California/San Diego professor named Donald Norman has a long-term interest in the challenge posed by the design of modern conveniences. A friend once told Norman that he thought it would take an engineering degree from MIT to get his new digital watch to work. Norman has such a degree. But, as he pointed out to his friend, he is no better at setting a digital timepiece than anyone else. "Give me a few hours and I can figure out the watch," Norman wrote in a book on the maddening design of today's conveniences. "But why should it take hours? I have talked with many people who can't use all the features of their washing machines or cameras, who can't figure out how to work a sewing machine or a videocassette recorder, who habitually turn on the wrong stove burner."

For the past several years Norman (now a psychologist who chairs his university's Cognitive Science Department) has crusaded for a more intelligent approach to product design. Among his least favorite are single-handle shower faucets and sleek but confusing controls on high-tech stoves. Such products are designed to be more beautiful than functional, Norman has concluded. He's found that the pricier the product, the harder it can be to use. This is because such products usually offer added functions with more complicated controls and longer manuals to explain them all. Such manuals are usually written at the tail end of a design process by team members so immersed in their product's details that they have trouble communicating with first-time users. An added complication is that so many manuals are translated from another language into English, not always coherently. As a result many of us—Norman included—are repeatedly frustrated by our inability to master modern implements. This clumsiness feels like a reflection on our ability to cope with contemporary life. Because we feel so guilty about appearing to be techno-dolts, most of us keep mum. This only perpetuates the problem. In Norman's words: "People blame themselves, when the real culprit is bad design."

A design engineer who was trained at MIT once recalled how little concern for product users was included in his education. In fact the opposite was true. "At MIT a lot of people laughed at the idea of making things easier to use," said engineer Richard Koffler. "The mentality for many was, 'If they can't use my design, they don't deserve it.' " This attitude helps explain why many supposed conveniences are maddeningly difficult and time consuming to use for anyone who wasn't in on their development. Intelligence or education has nothing to do with it. The founder of Digital Equipment Corporation—who has *two* engineering degrees from MIT— once confessed that he couldn't figure out how to heat a cup of coffee in the office microwave. For a long time he had lots of company. In the mid-1970s, John Robinson found that microwave owners commonly used this appliance as a breadbox. By now, of course, many have deciphered microwave controls, or some of them anyway (especially "defrost" and "reheat"). If any modern convenience was endorsed as a time- and labor-saver by focus group members, it was the microwave oven. "Invaluable," "a lifesaver," and "the biggest invention since the automobile," were among the phrases used by working mothers to describe their microwaves. A bank executive in New York said that her microwave had made it unnecessary to spend all of Sunday cooking meals for the week to come. "Instead," she said during a chat in her office, "I come in here."

Exactly. Like any appliance, microwave ovens are subject to the convenience catch. Even this miraculous tool doesn't save time on balance; it merely shifts it. "They've allowed us to schedule a whole lot more things in our day," said a Dallas nurse-practitioner about microwave ovens. "Because you don't have to get up early enough in the morning to get something out of the freezer to put it in the crock pot to have it ready for dinner when you come home. Now you have that time to go to an earlier meeting, schedule an earlier patient. You still get all that done plus you're doing meal preparation. I don't think it's been labor-saving. It's just allowed you to channel your labor into other things."

Like most appliances, microwave ovens save more drudgery than time. One reason for this was noted by a secretary in Los Angeles: Because it was so quick and easy to use, her microwave made it possible to eat more often. It is a grazer's dream. Those who actually cook in their microwaves find that directions for doing so are both complicated and stern. Microwave recipes include more finger-wagging warnings than a 1950s sex educator. They brim with words such as "never," "don't," and "always." Nor does microwave cooking necessarily save time. A friend of mine once compared several recipes that accompanied her new microwave oven with similar ones in *The Joy of Cooking*. For some dishes the former actually took more time than the latter. Even a simple roast took as much time or more (in addition to needing an extra "browning sauce"). Microwave cookbook author Barbara Kafka has conceded that this convenience isn't always faster than a conventional oven, though it is usually cooler and cleaner, and in some cases can provide better results. More important to its users, microwaves virtually eliminate any need to plan ahead. Their appeal is based more on convenience than time-saving as such. This is particularly true when it comes to "microwaveable" foods. Once you factor in the time it takes to drive to the supermarket, make selections, and stand in line at the checkout, convenience foods save precious little time. Add the extra time one must work to afford their premium prices and they could even be a net time-loser. Yet the apparent time- and trouble-saving appeal of such a product can defy logic. Mona Doyle recalled a young intern in her office who added cold water to a cup of dried soup, put it in the microwave, punched a few buttons, then stood waiting for results. Doyle noticed that a recently used kettle of water was still steaming on the adjacent stove. She pointed this out to the young woman. Why didn't she just pour hot water into her cup and have the soup ready right away? "Too much trouble," responded the intern.

Compu-Confusion

Just as some Americans tend to techno-phobia, others are techno-philes—younger ones especially. Having learned to tell time digitally, do sums on calculators, and write on computers, they could hardly be anything else. A senior at Brown University said that recalling the primitive days when he still had to type papers made him shudder. Many expressed similar sentiments. During focus group discussions, the one task for which computers received nearly unanimous praise was word processing. "I'm not a terribly good typist," explained an aspiring writer in Ohio, "and you can just correct as you go. Before I always had White-Out all over." A Los Angeles screenwriter said that in four hours he could print out a script that used to take him two weeks to type. Variations on this theme were routine. But one teacher in Providence, Rhode Island, had a partial dissent. Much as she loved her word processor, said the teacher, she didn't think it was actually saving her time. Now that it was so easy, explained the teacher, she spent more time than ever revising her copy.

This certainly has been my experience. Like so many writers, I'm a word processing convert. It's hard to describe how much more relaxed and flexible the act of writing on a screen can be than it ever was on paper. Also how much more productive one can feel with a computer partner. At a keyboard I feel as if I'm generating twice the prose in half the time that typewriting used to take me. This conviction would probably not stand up to objective scrutiny. Any time I've saved has almost certainly been squandered on extra revisions and added printouts. The evidence is on my office floor, which is cluttered with more piles of printout paper than it ever was of typewriter paper. I doubt that my computer has actually saved me time. Certainly not when you factor in the number of hours it took to research which computer to buy, and which modem, printer, and word processing program (which in turn took many more hours to master). When one computer I bought didn't work out I had to return it and buy another. Add several time-consuming calls to hardware and software companies for technical support, and I'm probably a net loser on the time front when it comes to computers.

Computers are no less subject to the convenience catch than any egg-beater. The more potent they grow, the more susceptible computers make us to the "can do it/will do it" syndrome. Research on the social impact of home computers has found that far from saving time, such conveniences were actually extending the workday of users. "Because they allow you to do so much more," observed an economist of the spreadsheet programs he brought home from work, "that's what you end up doing."

The real time-consuming danger takes place when it occurs to a computer user that the techno-tool which has been such a wonderful writing or number-crunching partner ought to be a big help with other chores as well. Writer James Fallows, an early convert to word processing, found that he quickly grew so enamored of computing that he began staying up late at night electronically indexing the names and addresses of everyone he ever knew and writing a program to help him pay his taxes. This cost him far more time than it saved, he admitted, but was a temptation he couldn't resist. A writer I know computerized his daily schedule. I once called him to arrange a meeting. Before confirming the date and time he had to boot up his computer so he could access his datebook. This took a minute or two. Looking at a paper calendar would have taken a second or two.

If we stuck to simplifying existing tasks with the computer's help, we'd save time and effort by the kilobyte. But it doesn't work that way. New capacities generate new work. A University of Illinois professor was impressed that the size of his department's staff and its workload didn't seem to decline even after they acquired state-of-the-art computers. When he asked why, the department secretaries explained that their workload had remained constant because their standards had risen. The evidence was before his eyes. "When the departmental newsletter comes out every week," explained the professor, "it now has pictures on it. Also an ornamental heading."

In Crystal River, Florida, a filmmaker named Joel said that although computers had helped him simplify a couple of his business's tasks, timewise "The vast majority of the things that we have tried to do on those computers have been a net loss." Whenever you buy a new computer, Joel pointed out during a focus group, "You get a stack of manuals two feet thick and you've got to read the damned things. Plus you've got to do the prep, you've got to do the set-up, you've got to do the maintenance."

Joel's wife, Marie, a writer, did feel that she had saved time processing words on her computer. But Marie confessed to wasting countless hours trying to master its more obscure functions. She recently logged on to most Florida libraries to do research. When compared with doing so by mail or phone, this had saved her enormous amounts of time, Marie said. But like other database users, Marie found that once she could retrieve so much information so easily, she did—in an ever-expanding volume. As a result her research now took longer than ever.

Prentice, a computer consultant, said he'd made a lot of money rescuing users who bought elaborate systems to simplify their work, then couldn't figure out what to do with them. In desperation such users sought him out to write a program that would clean up their mess. "I experience a lot of technology as being too cheap," Prentice observed. "I see a lot of people who say 'I'll have that,' before they figure out what it is they're trying to do. Then they become driven by technology. The technology is just so cheap that they buy these things that drive them. I've never seen a labor-saving device. It seems to me labor is constant. Then you have all these things to help you do more of it. Then you need a computer to organize them all. That's how I make a living."

On balance, the very notion of "saving time" may be a fantasy. Any time we save in one part of our life gets spent in another, compounded with interest. The more we can do, the more we will do. Any means we devise to save time and effort typically ends up increasing our volume of work, and the tempo of our lives as well. Far from easing the pace of life, techniques designed to save time and labor usually accelerate it.

THINK FAST

I had just finished giving a talk on time pressure and was catching my breath in an empty room next to the auditorium. Someone knocked on the door. It was a woman, tall, slim, with curly hair the color of a golden oak gunstock. She asked if she could join me. Sure, I said. What's on your mind? "Want to hear one more story about the mind-boggling pace of life?" the woman asked. Her green eyes flashed like a Rolling Rock sign outside a cheap bar as she said this, and her long fingers stroked the air.

The blonde's name was Nicole. She was 35. Her husband was with the FBI. At one time Nicole had sold radio ads. Then she raised funds for a college. In 1985 Nicole was offered a job with a big database in Kansas City. She'd be working with a team of eight, aged 26–40. Nicole wasn't sure. She went there to check the operation out. They showed her a bank of computers. Name an author, one guy said. She did. The guy tapped a few letters on the keyboard: L-E-O-N-A-R-D, E-L-M-O-R-E. In ten seconds he handed her a complete list of Leonard's books, from *The Bounty Hunters* to *Glitz*. Also some articles he'd written and quite a few about him. Nicole was impressed. "It was like, wow!" she said, covering her wide eyes with those long fingers. "This is magic!"

Nicole took the job: market planner, medical division. She'd been there five years. Sounded as though she enjoyed it, I said. Enjoy wasn't the word. Craved was more like it. Nicole said she couldn't wait to turn on her computer in the morning. She needed to hear its fan humming, sense its hard disk warming up, feel the machine's instant response as her fingers caressed its keyboard. But the magic was wearing off. Access times that once made Nicole's cheeks flush now left her cold. The bank of computers that once seemed so magical now felt like an old flame who'd lost a step and gained a few pounds. In a word, these computers felt: slow.

Nicole's teammates felt the same way. They were losing patience with their hardware. First these technological dreamboats had introduced them to a fast life; now they couldn't keep up. Their users wondered what could. Having grown so used to nanosecond responses, nothing less could satisfy them. Their spouses seemed pokey. So did their kids. Nicole didn't have kids. But she did have a husband, and he'd begun to notice how quickly she lost patience with him. Her husband was no slouch. Years of sting operations had taught him split-second timing. But nanoseconds were beyond him. They were beyond any human being.

Nicole felt as if she'd entered a warp speed zone where few humans could survive. She noticed it on the highway. Before Nicole began working in the fast lane, she hadn't minded if the guy in front of her didn't move when the light turned green. Now she minded. She honked her horn. She made strange gestures. She used language she didn't use to use.

Nicole felt as though she was being wired with faster and faster chips. If a customer wanted a market plan in a month, she promised to have it in two weeks. If the customer wanted it in two weeks, she'd try for one. And deliver. Her only problems were the nightly headaches, and the near-collapse she endured at the end of every week. Nicole wondered if she'd ever be the woman she used to be.

The parents among her co-workers were finding the same thing, but on different terms. Their families couldn't keep up with them. "Come on, come on," they found themselves murmuring to their slowpoke kids. One woman heard about a test for people like them. Start a stopwatch. Close your eyes and start counting. Stop when you think a minute has passed. Open your eyes. See how much time has actually passed. Most did about forty seconds. One woman stopped at eighteen. Nicole made it to forty-seven. She was the calmest one in her group. She didn't look calm to me.

Nicole didn't feel calm to herself. She was worried. Had she lost her capacity to slow down? Something had happened recently that gave her hope. Nicole took a vacation with her husband in the Minnesota wilderness. The first thing she did there was take off her watch. She put it on the cabin's dresser and didn't look at it the whole week. They told time by the sun. If it was high, it must be noon; low, it must be dinnertime. No more sun, no more activity. Then it was time for bed. By the end of the week Nicole could hear leaves falling and smell distant campfires. She felt at ease with her husband in a way she thought was no longer possible.

Then it was time to go home, back to the database and the world of nanosecond responses. Nicole could feel her muscles tighten. She felt a flutter in her breastbone. The last thing Nicole did before closing the door of their cabin was to put her watch back on.

You make it sound like a wrist cuff, I said. That's exactly how it feels, said Nicole.

7

The Speed Trap

Folks used to be willing to wait patiently for a slow-moving stage coach, but now they kick like the dickens if they miss one revolution of a revolving door.

—ED WYNN

Nicole's story may have been unique, but her feelings weren't. A sense that the pace of life is getting out of hand is widespread, particularly among those who work with state-of-the-art communications technology. During a focus group outside Philadelphia, a banker named Jacqueline said that no piece of technology had had a greater impact on the tempo of her day than the fax machine. "When people are talking to me about services they want to buy, I can no longer say, 'Well, I'll mail that to you,'" Jacqueline explained. "You can't even say, 'I'll put it in the overnight mail.' It's 'Fax it to me. I want it in half an hour. Give it to me now.' That's stepped up the pace tremendously."

"It leads to bouncing the ball back and forth much faster," agreed Walter, a computer engineer. "You feel like you've got to move faster. When mail comes through on the fax, you shouldn't have to feel like you have to turn it around faster, but you do."

"I think it's terrific," said a builder named Hank. "I use fax all the time. Even though we've only had it for two or three years, I can't fathom business life without it. You do something, you do a piece of it, you fax it over to them, they fax back their piece. Something that used to take two weeks you can do in a matter of hours."

"Personally, I hate them," said Hank's wife, Eileen, an interior designer. "What fax machines have done is make people think they should think as fast as their machines. In our business, it's become like, 'I want the solution immediately. I'm not going to wait a couple of days for a solution. Give it to me *now*. I don't care what it is. Just give it to me.' Fax machines don't give you time to look at the problem. I think you get second-rate solutions that way."

"That's not a problem of the fax machine," argued Jeffrey, a research scientist. "That's a problem of the way it's being used. When I get a review to write and they say they want it in the mail in a week, then they give me a fax number, that's a chance to get two extra days. I get two extra days to think about it and it'll be in their office at the same time."

"With the fax machine when somebody's asking for something, they aren't usually saying it has to be perfect," added Jacqueline. "It's more like, 'Show me what you've got. As if I was in the office with you.' You can fax sketches of things back and forth and save yourself a lot of hassle compared to sending a formal letter waiting a week for a reply. With fax you can get more quickly down to what you both agree on. But there's no excuses, either. I miss the lag time, but I like the informality, so it's a bit of a tradeoff."

Fran didn't see any tradeoff at all. "The devil's tool," was what she called fax machines. A hospital administrator, Fran had just returned from a conference in Hawaii where she spent too many hours sitting beside a fax machine responding to urgent messages from her boss back in Philadelphia. To her it felt like a high-tech ball and chain. Although she was thousands of miles away, Fran's boss *knew* in an instant whether she was by the fax as she was supposed to be or out enjoying Honolulu's surf. "There's no more 'float,'" moaned Fran. "With the fax there are just no excuses."

Few pieces of technology have accelerated the pace at which we do business as quickly as the fax machine has. Virtually overnight, facsimile transmission made possible a quantum leap in the speed of transactions. One day we were wondering if the mail would arrive in the next hour or two; the next day we were murmuring, "come on, come on," as we waited the few seconds it took for a letter to roll off the fax. Once the ability to transmit printed material this fast became common in the late 1980s, users routinely began to fax material not only around the world but across campus, down the street, and between floors of the same building. In one bold stroke, faxing leapfrogged regular mail, overnight mail, and Federal Express alike to establish a new standard of document transmission speed—virtual instantaneity. Fax has more in common with Nescafé than it does with conventional mail. Facsimile transmission doesn't just accelerate time; it virtually repeals it.

Many users consider faxing a godsend. On my questionnaire, 16% called fax a "necessity," an extraordinary figure for a technology in common use for less than three years at the time. Yet in focus group discussions, even the most fervent faxers admitted that they didn't always appreciate the rate of exchange involved. Being able to transmit time-sensitive material in an instant is wonderful. So is getting needed material quickly. But receiving material that demands a quick response before you're ready to give one is less than wonderful. Faxed communications imply that the receiver should respond in kind; no excuses. "You can't say you don't have it because they know you do," said a Cincinnati lawyer. "Because of the fax machine you sometimes have to drop everything you're doing to address a particular thing."

According to one study, faxing has doubled the average rate of interruption for executives: from every eight minutes to every four. Yet not all of the faxed communications causing these interruptions really merit such urgency. "Someone downtown called and asked me to fax something to him," reported a college president in Fort Myers. "I said, 'You don't need it for a week.' He said, 'Well, faxing is much faster.' "

Such reports were common. "Every day this week somebody said to me, 'I'll fax it to you,' " Joel, the filmmaker, told focus group members in Crystal River. In only one case did he think such urgency was actually necessary. "But I'm going out and getting a fax machine. It's gotten to the point where I don't want to discuss it anymore. 'Yes, please, fax all day long if you like.' " Joel wasn't excited by the prospect. "Once we have it," he said, "we'll really have to boogie because everybody else is boogieing."

The upside of faxing's speed is purchased with a downside of stress. "Can't catch your breath," was the phrase used by many to describe their reaction to communicating by fax. This means of communication typifies our accelerating pace of life. Such a technological advance speeds up life's tempo far more than we anticipate. Today it's the fax, computer, and microwave oven that are leading the faster charge. Yesterday it was the telephone, jet plane, and pressure cookers. Before that came telegrams, railroads, and cookstoves. Each response to our call for more speed ends up accelerating life's pace beyond our expectations. Over time it's hard to tell what's cause and what's effect. Which came first: grazing or fast food? Did the twenty-four-second shot clock reflect the faster pace of pro basketball or produce it? Has the fax machine promoted a breathless work pace or did the breathless pace of work make fax machines essential? Can we ever know?

A process of syncopation is at work here: call and response. In an attempt to save time we develop ways to do tasks faster. These innovations establish a new standard of speed. The new standard eventually becomes the norm, then begins to feel slow. Once again a need is felt for more speed. Then the cycle begins all over again. In the process three things happen that are at the heart of our accelerating tempo:

- pauses—catch-your-breath moments—are eliminated
- new norms lead to speed inflation
- innovations such as the fax machine set a torrid pace, become "pacers" whose tempo we try desperately to match

The Vanishing Pause

Until recently technological limits put natural brakes on our tendency to overaccelerate. There was little need to think about limiting the pace of our activities. Technology—rather, lack of technology—did it for us. This is no longer true. One restraint after another has fallen. There are few remaining barriers to how fast we can go: in travel, communication, or the means to do our work.

Consider the following progress chart:

Speed Limits On	Limits Lifting	Limits Off
buttons	zippers	Velcro
stove	pressure cooker	microwave
washboard	wringer washer	washer-dryer
pen	typewriter	word processor
index cards	flip-up file	Rolodex
U.S. mail	Federal Express	fax
carbon paper	photostat	Xerox
snapshots	home movies	home video
tellers	drive-up banking	bank machines
DC 3	jet liner	Concorde
roads	parkways	superhighways
abacus	adding machine	calculator
diner	drive-in	drive-through
operator	rotary dial	touch tone
skittles	pinball	video games

What this chart illustrates is how many *pauses* we've eliminated from everyday life. Microwaves make it unnecessary to boil water. Solid-state electronics have virtually eliminated "warm up" time in entertainment hardware. My CD player starts the music a split second after I push the "play" button, well before my record-trained ear is ready to listen. (It then displays the seconds elapsed for each selection, but that's another story.) Word processors make it unnecessary to remove paper from a typewriter and feed in new sheets. Calculators don't waste a second in doing our math. Then there are long-lost pauses such as stropping a straight razor and mixing lather; filling and lighting a pipe; pulling out a pocket watch and snapping open its case; adding ink to a fountain pen. On a conscious level we may not miss any of these interruptions. Many were little more than nuisances. But they did fill the day with brief respites. During each such pause our body took a break. The cumulative effect of eliminating one opportunity after another to catch our breath is to create a breathless society.

Faster, more sophisticated tools were developed to relieve us of drudgery. But drudgery at least gave us moments of pause (especially for those doing brain work all day long). Physical tasks—sharpening a pencil, cooking a meal—provided an opportunity to mull over what we were doing, and where we were headed. As we eliminate one such moment after another, they rarely get replaced with other opportunities to take five. "The man or woman in the technological society has suppressed the natural respites in their rhythm," wrote historian Jacques Ellul. "The time for choosing, adapting and collecting oneself no longer exists."

One of those whom I consulted for this project was Robert Inman, a veteran journalist and Charlotte, North Carolina's top-rated news anchor. When Inman started broadcasting in 1965, television news was filmed, then driven to the studio for processing and editing. This created an unavoidable delay of several hours between covering and reporting most stories. The delay gave reporters an opportunity to reflect on the events they'd covered before reporting them. Inman still recalls the day he realized that this party was over. It was in late 1975. He'd gone with a cameraman carrying a new hand-held video camera to interview a congressional candidate in the next county. They returned to the station just before that evening's newscast and broadcast their hour-old tape raw. Inman was stunned by the rapidity of it all. Now this approach is standard. So is live coverage of more or less newsworthy events in a breathless "Action News" manner. During the Falkland Islands crisis in 1982, Inman reported live from London and Buenos Aires via satellite—"as instantaneous as you can get"—a process he's repeated many times since. (Live reporting during the Gulf War, with its many gaffes, illustrated both the drama and drawbacks of satellite journalism.) While he thought that all of these developments have made for better, more up-to-date newscasts, Inman has found that for news*casters* they've meant that "you no longer have an incubation period. You can't make that extra call. You don't have time to even think about it."

The great virtue of low-tech hardware was that it built in interludes: waiting for a call to go through, for the radio to warm up, or for our bank balances to be tallied by a teller. To our brains such pauses may feel frustrating. But our nervous systems don't necessarily agree. It takes a breather. Because enforced pauses can feel so frustrating (especially when we're in a hurry), much time and effort have gone into eliminating as many of them as possible. But we've lost something in the process. When we expect our day to be filled with regular interludes, we pace ourselves accordingly.

By current standards my first computer was dinosaur-slow. As a result, I fell into step. While the computer took what felt like minutes to search for items, save files on disks, or print out my day's work, I would go to the bathroom, get a snack, stand up and stretch, look over my notes, mull over what I was working on, or simply daydream. Now I have a far faster, more up-to-date computer (and printer) that barely hesitates at all. I love it. And I miss the little off moments that used to be imposed on me.

Whenever a computer, microwave, fax or other convenience "saves time" in a welcome way, it also eliminates occasions to pause. Add up all the lost pauses. Their loss has a lot to do with today's sense that the pace of life is getting out of hand. The overall effect of eliminating pauses is to speed up the whole in a process of time compression. This is comparable to eliminating all rests from a symphony, or every descriptive passage from a book. Doing so makes for more efficient use of time. You can "get through" pieces of music and works of literature faster that way. But why would you want to?

I once took a course in speed reading. This course promised to make me able to "read" books in an hour or two with good comprehension. In a sense it succeeded. After completing the course (which basically taught you to read straight down the page rather than from side to side) I could race through novels in a fraction of the time it used to take me, while picking up the key points. But this style of reading was so tense that it made time spent with a book excruciating rather than relaxing. Pausing to consider a point or to appreciate a well-honed sentence felt against the rules. I quickly stopped speed reading any but the most cursory material. Reading books in the old way once again became a pleasure.

Others have similar feelings about cooking. Once they're equipped with microwave ovens, convenience foods, and canned ice tea, many find they miss the slowing down which conventional food preparation requires. Their children are another story. Kids who grow up with microwaves, calculators, and video games develop a different sense of the normal pace of things than that of their parents. They figure food preparation time in seconds, just as I calculate it in minutes and my grandmother did in hours. To me the amount of time it takes to heat a can of soup on the stove is just about the right interlude between work and lunch. It may have something to do with the fact that I grew up eating Chicken Noodle soup and Scotch Broth. Their preparation time suits the tempo I was raised on. To my 10-year-old, waiting for a pot of soup to boil is agonizing. Perhaps cans of soup felt too hurried for my mother. She used an old Royal typewriter. At times my mother sat me on her lap as she pushed its keys down in a rhythmic series of thunks. Today my 3-year-old sometimes sits on my lap as I click away at a computer's keyboard. His brother used to enjoy pushing the keys of my IBM typewriter. Did my mother sit on *her* mother's lap as she wrote with a fountain pen? How can each generation not grow up with a different sense of life's proper pace?

As children we're imprinted with a certain tempo that feels like the "right" one. For most of the time there was no difference between that tempo and the one our parents grew up with. In modern times, however, each generation has lived at a faster pace than their forebears did. My contemporaries have adapted to a world of nanoseconds. Our children know nothing else. Those who grow up surrounded by fast forward buttons, Velcro fasteners and zero wait-states are bound to have a different sense of life's "natural" tempo than those who didn't. My 10-year-old was amazed to discover that basketball was once played without a shot clock. So many of life's tasks have been easier and quicker for him than they were for his parents: learning to tell time digitally, doing sums by calculator, writing by computer, pushing buttons to make a call. Even the time required to tie shoes has given way to the convenience and speed of Velcro straps. Like so many parents I'm grateful for Velcro fasteners of all kinds. Yet I wonder what price will come due as one such element of speed builds on another.

Speed Inflation

More than two decades ago Andy Warhol said that we'd all be world famous for fifteen minutes. In recent years I've seen this prediction reduced to 15 seconds. Not long before his death in 1987, Warhol himself said that considering the way things had speeded up, "I now give 'em eight and a half seconds."

Like a runaway vehicle hurtling downhill, life's acceleration seems to have developed its own momentum. Each response to the faster tempo speeds it up even more. No one is more painfully aware of this fact than restaurateurs. Fast food began as a way to shave a few minutes off their meal for time-pressed customers. In time what was once a brisk eating experience began to feel normal, then slow. Today fast-food operators are hustling to keep pace with new demands for speed. They talk of customers who have moved beyond "grazing" into "gulping." In an attempt to accelerate the food delivery process they've tried self-ordering by computerized touch pad (to eliminate eight to ten seconds of "talk time"), taking orders from those standing in line, and guaranteeing food delivery speed.

What is hard to foresee is the way in which accelerators such as fast food enter into a syncopation with life's tempo, first reflecting our hunger for a brisker pace, then accelerating it even more. In the process new standards are set that need to be broken. Today's fastest means make yesterday's seem agonizingly slow. Having to turn a radio dial can feel maddening after one's fingers have grown accustomed to preset buttons and the search and scan functions of modern car radios. VCRs can make watching broadcast television frustrating because there's no fast forward button to hit. Laserdiscs are about to make videotape seem primitive because one must wait for spooling tape to get to where one wants to go, rather than gain instant access through the magic of laser beams.

This is speed inflation at work. Nowhere is this process more evident than in the world of computers. When buying a new computer, it takes superhuman will not to be seduced by talk of faster-than-ever operating speeds. Twenty megahertz sounds better than 12.5, doesn't it? Would you rather have the regular model or a turbo version? Sixty milliseconds of access time or twenty-eight? Can I sell you one with a zero wait-state or a wait-state of one second? Well, zero, I guess. And while you're at it, make my access time twenty-eight milliseconds and the operating speed twenty megahertz. And by all means give me the turbo model.

The differences we're talking about are the wink of an eyelid. A few seconds at most. But once you try a faster computer—even one just a second or two faster—going back to a slower model can feel excruciating. This is something I hear repeatedly. "I got this new computer," a writing colleague told me. "Now I just can't tolerate the old one. We're talking about *seconds*. But your brain gets trained. It's Pavlovian. My accountant says the same thing. He has a new computer like mine. 'Now whenever I go to a client's office with a slow computer,' he told me, 'I'm tearing my hair.'"

Feelings are mixed on this score. Those who work with computers tend to welcome any added millisecond of speed they can afford. "The PC [personal computer] that's going to help me the most," said such a user, "is the one that . . . creates fewer wait-states in me." Eliminating unnecessary delays increases their productivity, such users feel, and brings the computer's speed more in line with their own thought processes. Some go further. Should their computer's speed exceed their brain's, more's the better. Just as pokey computers used to slow us down, faster ones can speed us up. "If your system is fast and responsive," suggested computer consultant Jonathan Seybold, "then you are fast and responsive."

But a tax must be paid on such an asset. Once we speed up to match the computer's new tempo, can we then slow down? Even before today's blazing speed levels had been achieved, one computer user found that his ability to read and comprehend text scrolling down the screen had accelerated to keep pace with the computer's tempo. The only problem came when he wanted to gear down, to return to a more leisurely pace. "Now," he pointed out, "when I read a book, I must consciously slow down my reading so my thoughts can catch up. Otherwise, I unconsciously want to skip anything that isn't instantly graspable. As I bounce between pausing and rushing, my sense of time changes. Already contemplation takes more concentration than it used to. My mind wants either to be stimulated or to be numb. I can still think with deliberation, but when I've been computing steadily, I don't feel any reason to."

It's well established that many of those who work with computers try to mimic its tempo in their own thought processes. There's a lot of computer envy among up-tempo types who try to emulate the split-second responses of microchips. Psychologists have noted a common syndrome among those who work all day with high-speed computers, then find themselves frustrated by trying to relate to slower, nonelectronic entities: their spouses, say, or their children. This can be as hard on users as on those around them. A common complaint in focus groups had to do with the implicit pressure computer users felt to work at the speed of a microchip. As one New York lawyer put it, "You just think that you should be able to think things through at the pace that you can transmit the answer."

Chasing the Metal Rabbit

Electronic data processing can make it possible to do a given task faster. In doing so it establishes new standards of working speed. From an employer's standpoint this is generally to the good. For computer-driven employees, however, this daily electronic dash can be exhausting. It's estimated that as many as 10 million Americans—claims adjusters, data entry clerks, telephone operators—now have their output monitored electronically. Word processing supervisors can tell in an instant how many keystrokes each member of an office staff is generating. Operators have an average number of seconds to field each call, as monitored by a computer. One Georgia clothing factory found seconds too crude and began to determine every worker's output by Time Measurement Units (TMUs) of one-twenty-eighth of a second. Front-pocket stitchers were allowed 95 TMUs or 3.42 seconds per pocket. A computer terminal at each worker's station kept track of output, TMUs, and subsequent salary.

Computers head the list of what I call "pacers," technological advances that set a fast, uniform pace human beings are expected to match. Like the metal rabbits that make greyhounds pant their way around a racetrack, today's technology establishes a pace no flesh and blood organism could hope to sustain. Not that we don't try. The fast-talking, short attention span, doing-two-or-three-things-at-a-time person has become a culture hero. Breathless television personalities set the tempo for our national conversation. While promoting books on television in 1973, 1976, 1980, and 1985, I was struck each time by how much faster that medium's discourse had become. TV-speak is a language with its own cadence, vocabulary, and grammar. There is little need for modifiers, or even for complete sentences in this language. Such talk wastes time. Before a rolling camera one quickly learns that any idea that can't be expressed in ten words or less might as well not be expressed at all. After a few words the average interviewer first loses interest, then begins to look panicky—usually in response to frantic gestures from an off-camera producer. Guests learn fast. In the late 1970s an average political "sound bite" lasted for 45 seconds. By the 1984 election this had dropped to 14.7 seconds. Four years later the average sound bite was down to 9 seconds.

Television is second only to computers in setting today's pace. The key reason is not artistic but commercial. Ever since thirty-second commercials became the norm in the early 1970s, we've been subjected to more ads per hour featuring a greater number of images flashing by at an increasingly faster rate. The "ad clutter" resulting from twice as many commercials in the same amount of time has forced advertisers to tap dance at an ever more frantic pace trying to get our attention. Some advertisers have found that they can pack more content into less time by editing out dead spots and speeding up the whole in a process known as "time compression." The same process is sometimes used to shave up to 10% of a film's running time so that it can fit a given time slot on television. (Director Nicholas Meyer protested to no avail when twenty-three minutes were compressed out of *The Day After,* his post–nuclear holocaust movie: "Never mind what such speeding up does to the intended pace or rhythm of the film.") Actually, viewers have adjusted to television's accelerating tempo with surprising ease. One reason that modern experiments in live television routinely fail is that their pacing is just too slow compared to highly edited videotaped productions. "Because we've become accustomed to video editing," noted media consultant Roger Ailes, "our minds skip ahead . . . Videotape and its editing process have tightened up not only television but the way we communicate. This has contributed significantly to making us a more impatient society."

Television's pacing is rarely at a conscious level. Our synapses have grown so accustomed to quick-take broadcasting that we're seldom conscious of how fast-paced it really is. But try an experiment. Simply turn off the sound during an average commercial program and pay attention to how brief each visual image really is. Or try watching television from a distance, paying attention to flicker more than pictures as such. When we're unable to actually see what's on the screen, we become aware simply of how often the light changes. Outside of soap operas, few images on commercial television last longer than a second or two. This has become such a commonplace that we seldom notice, at least not consciously. Former adman Jerry Mander is convinced that it's not our minds so much as our nervous systems that have adapted to television's pace. As Mander has noted, "When watching TV, you live in a much more rapid perceptual universe. Rapidly changing images, 15 edits per minute, incredible condensation of time, movement backward in time and forward, cartoons on and off, outdoor images and then suddenly indoors, music, whirling, rising images, a potpourri of hyperactive stimuli most of which is impossible in ordinary life."

One seldom-considered way in which technology has accelerated life's tempo is by generating a by-product of noise. It's a rare piece of hardware that doesn't charge a sound tax. Today's lawn mower–leaf blower–air conditioner–dishwasher–hair dryer–vacuum cleaner cacophony has created a terrible din in exchange for help with our chores. A clear connection between noise and tension is well established. What's less well appreciated is the way in which ambient sounds can accelerate the pace of our lives. Some years ago a German physiologist found that by speeding up or slowing down the rate of a clock's ticking he could accelerate or decelerate the heartbeats of those listening. In another experiment, subjects placed in a noisy room were found to estimate that ten minutes had passed when only seven really had. In a quiet room their average estimates—nine minutes— were more nearly accurate. Such results lend indirect confirmation to the restaurant folklore that up-tempo music encourages customers to eat quickly and be on their way. To study this hypothesis, University of Kentucky marketing professor Ronald Milliman tested patron turnover in the same restaurant with different tempos of music playing in the background. While listening to slow-paced music, customers took an average of fifty-six minutes to complete their meal and depart. Those served while faster music played took only forty-five minutes. "The best part," Milliman advised restaurateurs, "is that virtually none of your patrons know they are being influenced by atmospherics. In fact, our studies reveal that if they are asked, for instance, 'Was there music playing in the restaurant while you were eating?' nearly everyone will say 'no' . . ."

Probably this is true on a broader scale: We may not be aware of the rising crescendo of noise in our daily lives, but our nervous systems are. They register the louder sounds as a call to action. Ascending levels of noise are one among many conscious and unconscious pacers that make our lives feel set on fast forward. Like so many pacers, this is a by-product of advances we prize. Technological progress responded to our wish for faster service by eliminating pauses. This contributed to a process of speed inflation and set a torrid pace beyond any we'd imagined possible. A critical mass has been achieved. The ability to move faster has created its own momentum. The dream of saving time has gone from hours to minutes to seconds to milliseconds. Our original goal of "saving time" by speeding up the whole has faded from memory. Speed has become its own reward. Ultimately, however, speed inflation debases the currency. We lose our ability to keep track of what's really urgent and what isn't. Do we really need to get our photos developed in an hour? Is a five-minute pizza essential for the good life? What's the hurry? We hustle to get places sooner. Once there we can't remember what the rush was.

A Love-Hate Relationship

For all our complaints about the brutal pace of life, would we have it any other way? Just look at our aphorisms. "On the double," "get a move on," and "hit the ground running" have a positive ring. "Saunter along," "take your time," and "a leisurely pace" do not. Asked to choose between the statements "I find today's pace of life stimulating," and "I find today's pace of life nerve-wracking," 55% of those who filled out my questionnaire chose the former, 38% the latter.* Only 17% felt, "I miss the days when travel was more leisurely;" 81% said "We're lucky to live in an age when jet planes, Metroliners and interstate highways make travel so much faster and easier." As for the statement "I like the lively pace of today's television programs," 60% agreed, while 23% concurred with, "I have trouble keeping up with the pace of today's television programs."

It's not just technology that we're dealing with here; it's values. Technology does our bidding. If life seems to be moving awfully fast these days, it's because basically that's what we want. At the same time there's an obvious concern about the price we're paying for today's accelerating tempo. And there ought to be. Living in a fast forward society takes its toll.

The next section will consider what price we pay for our hectic way of life. In some obvious and not so obvious ways we put our physical health at risk by fast and furious living. Our spirit, too, can be eroded by what I call "rushaholism." Finally, the health of family life is awfully hard to sustain when its members are constantly on the go. This is timelock's toll.

*Since some of those who filled out the questionnaire did not respond to every question, the totals here and elsewhere do not add up to 100%.

III

Timelock's Toll

8

The Hurried Body

Those who rush arrive first at the grave.
—SPANISH PROVERB

On his way to the focus group, Harry missed a turn. He nearly panicked at the thought of being late. By his own admission, the Boston sales manager was time obsessed. Harry had used an appointment calendar since he was in high school and organized his life around it. He'd spent years searching for the perfect calendar. "I live by an appointment book and a watch," Harry explained. At work he scheduled appointments every fifteen minutes: "like a doctor." Breakfast meetings at 7 A.M. were sometimes on his calendar. Harry told his wife, Sandy, and their two daughters that if they needed time with him, they should write themselves down on his calendar.

Harry—who was the first one to arrive—gave the group this report without embarrassment. In fact he took pride in being so well organized and conscientious about time. Harry pointed out that scheduling his life so carefully made it possible to participate in a lot of civic activities. "If you want to get a job done, give it to a busy man," he reminded the group. To help get the most out of his time, Harry embraced new technology with a passion: electronic typewriters, computers, fax, multibutton office phones, and a cellular phone in his car. The car phone not only allowed him to complete deals faster, said Harry, but also made it possible to "call my mother and listen to her talk for ten miles or whatever."

Harry's attitude toward the pace of his life overall was this: "The faster the better as far as I'm concerned."

Although congenial, and successful in his work, the sales manager was clearly tense. Another member of the group asked Harry if rushing around so much and feeling constantly pressured by time had any impact on his health. "Yes, it does," he replied. "I have a very bad stomach. I take a lot of medication. I have an ulcer. I've had an ulcer since I was 14 years old. So these time pressures are there. I've learned to live with them more now,

109

say in the last five or six years, than I ever did before. There was a time when I was absolutely a wreck. If I had an appointment for seven, I'd be there quarter to seven. I'd drive around the block. I'm not so much like that now.

"But I noticed coming here tonight and knowing what the topic was, I took a wrong turn, and the first thing I did was look at the clock on the dashboard and I said, 'Oh no, I only have three minutes.' I'm maniacal about time."

Within reason we can survive a fast and furious pace unscathed. There may even be some benefit in terms of increased vigor, intensity, and concentration. But many of us have gone well beyond any benefit in accelerating the pace of our lives. We've lost control of that pace, often without realizing it. Even when our minds don't register the faster tempo to which they've had to adapt, our bodies do.

One reason we love vacations (assuming our need for speed isn't chronic) and find post-vacation reentry so difficult is that once we "lose track of time," our bodies revert to a more normal rhythm. Then our nervous systems tell us in no uncertain terms how much they prefer this tempo. Peace Corps volunteers assigned to slower-paced societies have found resuming a faster pace the hardest part of coming home. Their bodies resist getting back in step. Any time away from the rush can have such an effect. After a former Republican official in Pennsylvania was sent to prison for extortion, he found that the severe headaches from which he had suffered for thirty years disappeared. His doctor attributed this cure to the fact that the man's time behind bars was "the most relaxed period in his life."

Although human beings can adapt to a rapidly accelerating pace of life, they pay a price. Our nervous systems evolved to function at a much slower tempo. Until quite recently in human history, bodies seldom moved faster than 5 miles an hour; the speed of a brisk walk. Our daily routines were comparably slow. Whether we can "adapt" to more rapid speeds isn't the issue. Of course we can. We can function at very fast tempos indeed. But the ability to get used to a steadily accelerating pace and the ability to *flourish* are two different things. The question is, What price do we pay for our hectic way of life?

Time Sickness

The physical toll exacted by time's pressure is an issue that has concerned Larry Dossey for years. Dossey, a Dallas physician, thinks our society is in the grips of a "time sickness" epidemic. He defines this disorder as one in which we feel so overwhelmed by overloaded schedules that our bodies rebel. This is the physical response to timelock. Like a Pavlovian dog, we begin to respond inappropriately to all manner of ringing bells—alarm clocks, beeping watches, the ring of phones—by alerting our nervous system to get ready for action. If subjected to constant time pressure, the human nervous system begins to regard clocks as a threat little different than snarling tigers, or swirling hurricanes. Time literally becomes its enemy. When we're in a state of chronic timelock, our bodies respond with continual "fight or flight" arousal. They go on perpetual combat alert. They pump stress hormones, which in turn suppress immune responses, advise the liver to produce more cholesterol, and increase the stomach's acidity. Our sweat glands work overtime, our muscles grow tense, and electrical signals in our hearts grow unstable. These are just some of the effects Dossey and others see in bodies responding to the pressure of time. "The end result," he noted, "is frequently some form of 'hurry sickness'—expressed as heart disease, high blood pressure, or depression of our immune function leading to an increased susceptibility to infection and cancer."

A connection between time pressure and physical disease is not one its victims usually make consciously. "But the body, being smarter than the mind, at some point begins to rebel," Dossey said during a conversation at his home in a Dallas suburb. "That's where time sickness comes in. Enter headaches, insomnia, irritable bowel syndrome. These are amber lights before red ones, such as a [heart attack]. They're telling us to slow down, pay attention."

Dossey described two composite patients based on hundreds he'd seen in his Dallas office: first, a young engineer from Texas Instruments who can't ignore his physical symptoms anymore. He may have had a heart attack, an ulcer, and high blood pressure. He is mildly overweight, can't sleep, and has tension headaches. The engineer just can't figure out what's going on. His response to time pressure is to try to ignore it. As long as he does this, his prognosis is poor. Another example is a young mother who spends three or four hours a day running errands, car pooling, and ferrying her kids to ballet and soccer. She spends Sunday morning in church, then gets ready to face Monday. This woman suffers from insomnia. She has irritable bowel syndrome and frequent headaches. She feels generally awful and wonders if low blood sugar might be her problem.

"If you think these cases are unusual," said Dossey, "hang out in any internist's office for half a day. This type of patient comes in continually. They want tests for hypoglycemia, chronic yeast infections, environmental allergies, or chronic fatigue syndrome attributable to Epstein-Barr virus (EB virus is big now) when a simple case history about how they live in time is what they really need. Occasionally you'll find a needle in a haystack.

But when you're in Texas and hear hoofbeats, think of horses, not zebras. This is easier to say than do. People will go to enormous lengths—diets, exercise programs, magical cures, reading books—they'll do *anything* before they'll revise their schedules."

Dossey included himself in this category. Tall, broad-shouldered, with a large jaw, Dossey played high school football in the Texas town where he grew up. Compared to his more relaxed twin brother (now a dentist), he was always obsessed with time: measuring it, racing with it, trying to beat it into submission. This gave him the drive to get through medical school and establish a successful practice, including a stint as chief of staff at Medical City Dallas Hospital. Even after he concluded that time pressure was the real cause of so many symptoms he was treating, Dossey didn't reduce his own schedule. To the contrary, he developed an additional career, writing and lecturing on the dangers of time sickness. After several years of sixty- to eighty-hour weeks, Dossey suffered a ruptured disk. He has no doubt that the schedule he was trying to maintain contributed to his own condition. To use one of his favorite phrases, "My body got smart before I did." In the three months Dossey spent recuperating, he decided to take his own advice and drastically reduce his commitments. His choice was to give up the active practice of medicine and continue his career as the Paul Revere of time sickness, lecturing frequently and writing three books on different aspects of the need for more relaxed and humane styles of life.

Dossey's medical colleagues have been less than receptive to the suggestion that they prescribe reduced schedules for time-pressed patients. The traditional approach has been to treat their symptoms with tranquilizers ("for people who don't have time to slow down"). Dossey thinks one reason for this is that doctors are as timelocked as anyone, and no better able to create a humane schedule for themselves. He sees signs that this may be changing, however. Throughout the 1980s Dossey noted a growing awareness among doctors of time-related anxiety as a contributing factor to a wide range of health problems. Some areas of concern and types of treatment identified by him and others include:

• *Clogged Arteries.* Several studies have confirmed that stress can stimulate the release of compensating hormones that raise levels of cholesterol, fats, and other artery-clogging substances. This is as true of time-related stress as any other. In one study, the cholesterol level of a group of accountants was found to skyrocket in the weeks preceding January 1 and April 15 tax deadlines. Dr. Dean Ornish, director of the Preventive Medicine Research Institute in Sausalito, California, has found that artery blockage can be significantly reduced by a combination of dietary changes, regular exercise, and stress management. Ornish emphasized that relaxation techniques are central to this regimen. He felt that such techniques are too often overlooked when treating arterial obstruction.

• ***Poor Nutrition.*** In general, the more pre-prepared our food is, the less our body benefits from it. Fast food's high fat and salt content is common knowledge by now. Health counselor Ralph La Forge, former manager of the Preventive Medicine and Cardiac Rehabilitation Division of San Diego's Sharp Memorial Hospital, called such meals "nutritive substance abuse." When rushed, said La Forge, we understandably want food that can be delivered quickly, eaten easily, and that promises a fast taste return. This translates into fried, salty entrees, crunchy snacks, and sweet, fizzy drinks. Under the pressure of time, said La Forge, "we invariably go for the Pepsi and fried foods at mealtime. We basically go for such food when we're circulating stress hormones." During an energy sag in the midafternoon we tend to eat high-sugar foods originally meant to be desserts. At the end of a harried day "We want to drink Corona [beer] and eat chips while watching Dan Rather." La Forge called this diet one of "quick-fix calories." Eventually these preferences become habitual, even when we have time to eat better. The cure is not so much to force different food choices on ourselves as to revise our schedules, said La Forge. Only after decelerating the overall pace of our lives do we grow more receptive to salads over sandwiches, juice instead of Pepsi, and feel able to eat a baked potato instead of gulping french fries.

Another risk in fast eating is this: Food that gets caught in the throat and blocks wind passages invariably hasn't been chewed enough. Insufficient chewing usually results from trying to rush through a meal.

• ***Repetitive Motion Disorders.*** Among the fastest spreading modern maladies are repetitive motion disorders such as carpal tunnel syndrome, or CTS. This refers to the recurring, debilitating hand and wrist pain that usually results from using these limbs for small, repetitive motions over an extended period of time. In response, joint tissues swell and irritate nerves. According to a study done by the U.S. Department of Labor, repetitive motion disorders were the source of 18% of reported workplace injuries in 1981, and 48% in 1988. The reason this syndrome is spreading so quickly is that modern technology has reduced so many tasks from large, varied activities of different tempos to continually repeated, fast-moving ones. Productivity pressures are pushing workers in factories and offices alike to work at tempos to which their bodies aren't suited. A variety of tasks and breaks in routine give tissues a chance to heal. Increasingly they don't have that opportunity. Assembly line meat cutters are one afflicted group. Supermarket checkout clerks—who repeatedly twist their wrists sweeping products over scanners—are another. Computer users are among the most afflicted. In New Jersey's tax collection office, where data entry clerks are expected to make at least 8000 keystrokes an hour, over 80% experienced pain in their shoulders, arms, wrists, or hands, 47% felt numbness or tingling in their fingers, and 7% suffered full-scale carpal tunnel syndrome. Similar problems have been found among newspaper reporters and others who use computer keyboards all day long. CTS specialist Dr. Abner Bevin of the University of North Carolina's Hand Rehabilitation Center pointed out that today's keyboards make it possible to type 40% faster than was possible with typewriters. "The technological revolution has outpaced human evolution, it seems," said Bevin. "We are not biologically equipped to perform thousands of repetitive motions an hour." To prevent CTS he and others recommend creating as much variety as possible in one's physical work routines: changing movements, using different equipment, taking breaks. Resisting the urge to work faster to get more done in less time can help prevent serious injury.

• *Sleep Deprivation.* By one estimate the average American gets ninety minutes less sleep per night than is healthy. Most of us can get by on less sleep than necessary, but we pay a price in reduced alertness and resistance to disease. Some sleep researchers suggest that the widespread attempt to work more by sleeping less is costing us billions of dollars in lost productivity on the part of exhausted, inefficient workers. "Walking zombies" are what Cornell University psychologist James Maas has called the growing army of sleep-deprived employees. The U.S. Congress has commissioned a major study of the economic and health consequences of sleep deprivation. Among them are thought to be short-term memory loss, inability to concentrate, and chronic fatigue. Sleep-deprived individuals are also more prone to abuse caffeine, Dexedrine, amphetamines, and other stimulants.

One study found a clear connection between those who regularly slept less than others and "Type A" behavior. The so-called short sleepers not only got about 20% less sleep than others but 25% less REM (rapid eye movement) sleep, the most restful kind. In experiments with both animals and humans, REM-deprived individuals have been found less able to deal with problems through reflection and flexibility rather than instant, often aggressive activity. This is characteristic of Type A behavior and could be a precursor of cardiac disease.

• *Coronary Heart Disease.* Research done at the Meyer Friedman Institute in San Francisco has found that Type A personalities—driven, time-obsessed, chronically angry individuals—were up to twice as likely to suffer heart attacks as more phlegmatic Type Bs. Staff members determine whether a client is A or B through an intake interview. In this videotaped session a series of questions are posed that are designed to assess key Type A traits such as hostility and "time urgency." Topics covered include irritability at being made to wait in stores or restaurants, the compulsion to do two things at once, difficulty relaxing, and a fetish about being on time. Careful attention is paid to such tipoffs as tense posture, rapid eye blinking, fast speech patterns, and frequent interruption of the interviewer.

In a group discussion with new clients and their spouses, intake nurse Nancy Fleischmann once had them all close their eyes and point to where they thought the clock was on the room's wall. The spouses pointed in many directions. Nearly all the clients pointed right to it. Such behavior is considered symptomatic of what institute staffers call "hurry sickness." An obsession with numbers, schedules, and not wasting a moment is at the heart of this malady. To illustrate this point, Dr. Meyer Friedman will sometimes show new clients jam-packed pages from the calendars of Type A heart attack victims—especially for the day or two preceding their attack. Such a frantic sense of time urgency, Friedman wrote in a book with institute director Diane Ulmer, "arises from an insatiable desire to accomplish too much or to take part in too many events in the amount of time available."

"Probably the most common feeling is the feeling that you always need to rush, get on to something more important," Diane Ulmer said during an interview in her San Francisco office. "The inability to focus on one thing without your mind flitting. Waking up in the middle of the night because you have so many things on your mind. Becoming absolutely frantic about being delayed even a minute. Getting enraged when somebody cuts you off in traffic or keeps you from going where you're going for even a few seconds. Not being able to relax. Feeling restless when sitting still, or not having anything to do."

In order to make maximum use of time, Type As usually rely on two basic strategies. First they try to speed up any and all activities. (One patient put his food through a blender so he wouldn't have to waste time chewing.) Then they engage in constant attempts to accomplish more than one thing at a time. One institute client bragged that he could watch programs on four television sets at once—while riding his exercise bike—and paying bills during the commercials. Another installed a hinged board beside his toilet to get some paperwork done while sitting there. Completing bodily functions provides excellent opportunities for Type As to maximize their use of time. After calculating that he wasted a week a year walking to the office men's room, one institute client had a bathroom built right next to his office. Another kept a bottle by his desk that he used to relieve himself without having to leave his chair. The most impressive patient of all saved time by disciplining himself to only defecate every third day, after taking a laxative.

What's the point? Where is the payoff for such obsessiveness about time? "An intricate feedback system comes into play that we don't understand too well," said Ulmer of the patients she's worked with for over a decade. "Something happens that makes people feel wed to speed. The feedback the body gets from all that rapid moving about is that there must be real time urgency."

The Harried Heart

Robert Levine, the psychologist who's studied the pace of life around the world, has generally found a clear correlation between the tempo of a given setting and mortality rates from coronary heart disease. Although the reason for this connection is unclear, Levine speculated that its underlying cause was the fact that fast-paced locales tend to attract more than their share of Type A residents who in turn keep the throttle pushed to its limits. Even though time pressure *per se* is not toxic, Levine concluded, in conjunction with Type A tendencies it can be highly toxic. "My position is that time urgency *is* related to coronary heart disease," explained Levine, "in and of itself, or tied in to other factors."

Some exceptions were revealing, however. In Levine's studies, the Japanese were the only people whose pace of life exceeded our own. Yet their rate of death due to heart disease—although rising slowly—is far lower. No one knows why this should be. Levine thinks that the answer may be found in their emphasis on cooperation. A researcher studying job performance in that country found that the question "Do you like competition on your job?" could not be translated directly into Japanese. The closest possible translation was, "Do you like impoliteness on your job?" Levine thinks that this spirit of conciliation may buffer the frantic schedules they keep. By contrast, "in our own culture . . . there is often a fine line between speed/time urgency on the one hand and competition/hostility on the other—and the combination can be life-threatening."

Studies by other researchers have suggested that free-floating hostility is the Type A trait most likely to trigger a heart attack. Redford Williams, a Duke University physician, has concluded that Type A traits such as time urgency and competitiveness "appear to be harmful only to the extent that they activate one's hostility and anger." If Williams is right, then rushing to your next appointment may not be toxic by itself. Getting furious at the driver ahead of you who is only going 50 miles an hour when you want to go 60 could be lethal.

Separating time urgency from hostility is no simple task, however. Even if hurrying *per se* is not necessarily risky, the problem is that few people hurry *per se*. Redford Williams has given a good illustration of this connection: himself. Despite his awareness of the danger, wrote Williams, "I still find myself harboring nasty thoughts about the motives of slow people ahead of me in supermarket lines, of drivers who are still sitting there after the traffic light has changed to green, even of unseen folks on some other floor of the building when the elevator doesn't arrive fast enough to suit me."

As Williams's self-portrait suggests, time stress and rage are two sides of the same coin. When under constant pressure from time, it's virtually impossible not to feel hostile toward anyone who might slow you down. This incorporates a lot of people. When you're in a hurry, anyone who gets in your way is going to get you ticked off. Getting ticked off is easier because you're already on edge. It's hard *not* to be touchy when you're feeling rushed.

Logan Wright, past president of the American Psychological Association, has an interesting perspective on this syndrome. Himself an admitted Type A, Wright has compared ultra-time urgency to religious fervor. Type As resemble idol worshipers, suggested Wright. Time is their idol. This idolatry sets them up to get angry, especially during "situations in which others' infidel-like insensitivity to time impacts us . . . directly," he noted. "They are late and thus delay us. They drive too slowly and will not let us pass. They are the ones responsible for slow-moving lines (e.g., the proverbial person at a supermarket who has both coupons to cash in and a check to write) . . . because we are time worshipers, we become angry at anything or anyone who wastes our 'precious time.' "

Meyer Friedman has said he's seldom seen an impatient person who wasn't hostile as well. Friedman Institute staff members find that Type A personalities first exhibit symptoms of unrelenting time pressure, then develop irrational rage at those who they imagine to be adding to that pressure. "I'm not sure that you can always tell the difference between time urgency and hostility," observed Nancy Fleischmann. "Time urgency can be a form of hostility."

Institute clients are treated with a range of treatment designed to modify if not eliminate Type A tendencies. According to Friedman's research, those who stay with the program can reduce their risk of coronary heart disease by half or more. Part of the program consists of doing regular drills such as deliberately driving in the slowest lane, standing in the longest lines, not wearing a watch for one day a week, spending a specified amount of time at meals (chewing slowly), and doing absolutely nothing but recalling pleasant memories or listening to soothing music for fifteen minutes twice a day. They are also expected to take part in a weekly meeting with other Type As to discuss and try to modify the stressful lives they're leading.

Late one fall afternoon such a group met at the institute offices. This group consisted of executives from several local corporations, an advertising man, and a member of the San Francisco Symphony. Some had already suffered heart attacks. Others were hoping to avoid them.

Diane Ulmer, slim, blonde, and low-keyed, kicked off the discussion by reading this quote from Lord Chesterfield: "Whoever is in a hurry shows that the thing he is about is too big for him." The source of hurry sickness, Ulmer suggested, is what Meyer Friedman called "greed"—trying to squeeze too many activities into too little time. By attempting to be *too* productive we usually just wind up exhausted, physically and emotionally. No one debated the point. Members of this group felt like living illustrations. An accountant said that in the three months since his heart attack he'd found himself slipping back into his hurried ways: driving too fast, rushing about at work, not paying attention when his wife spoke to him. The adman sympathized. "There are times I move so fast I get frightened," he told the group. "At times my life is moving so fast all I can do is steer it, not change the pace. But as it picks up speed, it's harder to steer." The adman hadn't had a heart attack, didn't want to have a heart attack, and was looking for ways to get off the race track before that happened.

A corporate executive in his mid-40s talked about trying to balance pressures at work and at home where he was kept up around the clock helping his wife feed their new twins. "I go from feeling, 'Aren't they cute?'" he said of the twins, "to thinking 'Twenty years from now, when I'm 66, I'll be spending $80,000 on their college.'"

Late in the discussion, after an older executive spoke at length about the tremendous pressure he felt at work, from infighting colleagues to an insensitive boss, a man named Richard Collins* discussed the need to sort out real from imagined stress. "Sometimes the person we work for is a bad person, a truly rotten Type A," he told the others. "Other times we imagine threats. Separating real threats from imaginary ones is a problem I'm struggling with. When I'm subjected to outside pressures, do I do relaxation techniques? Do I take time? Do I order, prioritize? At the same time, how do I build up my own sense of self-worth so I'll be resilient when those pressures present themselves?"

On that note the group ended. Before leaving they held hands and said a brief secular prayer. Richard Collins told the others he'd be missing the next two meetings because he was about to go to New York for meetings at the home office of his investment firm. He wasn't looking forward to the trip. "New York's a struggle," Collins explained, "yelling, screaming, pounding, frantic pushing. I don't react well to that. It brings out my Type A tendencies."

The rest nodded sympathetically. They wished him well.

*Pseudonym

TYPE A+

Richard Collins's time in New York went about as he expected it would. The pressure of that city's pace made it hard not to respond in kind. "They're in a constant state of agitation," he noted of his colleagues in Manhattan. "It's very difficult to get people to sit down and relax and *think* about things."

Collins told me this early one morning midway through his eastern sojourn. During a meeting the day before he'd found others constantly interrupting him, finishing his sentences, answering their own questions, or rephrasing them whenever he paused to consider his response. Finally Collins had to ask his colleagues to let him think about what he wanted to say, and complete his own sentences. "They slowed down a little after that," he chuckled. "But it's very difficult for them."

One woman at the meeting was about to go on vacation. This was her getaway day. Collins set the scene: "At the same time we're having our meeting, she's preparing a sales analysis for the boss's boss that had to get done that day. She had a staff meeting at four o'clock and here it is three o'clock and she's got people running in and out of the meeting. So not only is she trying to do this sales analysis and trying to get ready for her four o'clock meeting but she's also rushing to get out because she's got a presentation to get off to a potential customer. It was crazy, just chaotic. So I sat back, took a couple of breaths, got in my relaxation mode and just watched this go on."

It hadn't been so long ago that Collins himself was dashing in and out of meetings like that. Impeccably dressed, trim, and dark-haired, the corporate vice-president described himself as impatient and short-tempered by nature. It wasn't hard to picture his ruddy cheeks flaring red. For years Collins had a standing rule that he would wait no longer than fifteen minutes for a seat at a restaurant. He stormed angrily out of more than one restaurant when they violated his rule. Slowpoke drivers also drove Collins into a rage. On one occasion he and the driver ahead of him were both waiting to turn. Collins felt that she was taking too long, grew impatient, sped up to go around, and rear-ended the other driver's car. At work he took on too many assignments, then tried to complete them all by working late and on weekends. The twice-divorced bachelor in his late 40s was also dating several women, working with local charities, attending concerts, taking a college course, traveling, and quietly unraveling. The morning a colleague innocently asked him a question and got chewed out by a furious Collins for presuming to impose on his time, he knew he had a problem.

At the suggestion of his boss, Collins went to the Meyer Friedman

Institute. As he sat in the waiting room reading their literature about Type A behavior, Collins got the impression that they'd been eavesdropping on his life. Then he was ushered into a back room for a videotaped intake interview. Anyone who scores over twenty-seven on this structured interview is considered Type A. Collins came in at seventy-seven. This was the highest score ever recorded. No previous client had come within ten points of this figure. When Friedman announced this distinction at the therapy group to which Collins was assigned, he felt embarrassed and upset, but more motivated than ever to do something about his Type A behavior.

By the time I met Richard Collins he'd been enrolled in the institute's program for nearly two years. During that time he had learned how to modify his frenzied behavior. Not completely; that was impossible. Collins unselfconsciously referred to himself as "a recovering Type A." But he now drove his car at a reasonable speed, no longer minded waiting for a seat in a restaurant, and took actual vacations—ones in which he didn't keep calling back to the office. Although he's well over six feet tall, Collins now found that when he walked with business colleagues they had to constantly stop and wait for him to catch up. Before he had always done the waiting. "I'm not nearly as rushed," said Collins. "Time isn't that big a deal to me anymore. I've reordered my priorities, tried to focus on fundamental issues in the world. Not on whether the waitress gave me the right cup of coffee or something."

Getting to this point took effort. Participating in weekly group sessions at the institute helped him ratchet down. He was also faithful about completing "assignments" such as taking time off every day, talking more slowly, asking others about themselves, and actually *listening* to what they said. Growing out of another drill—picking the longest line to stand in—Collins had even come to find line-waiting rather pleasant. "It's an incredible time to be able to do creative thinking," he said. "It's just great time. I find when I'm in that situation—at restaurants, movies, wherever—there's a lot of time to think. I cherish that time. I use it for think time. I reorder what I'm doing. That helps me to be more productive.

"One of the problems of us Type As is that we never stop to contemplate things. We're constantly moving from one thing to another at a very superficial level. Now, I've tried to learn to appreciate my job, appreciate the people more, stop and look at things, smell the roses. I'm sorry that's trite, but that's really what you're doing. You stop and you think about what you're doing and you enjoy and appreciate what you're involved in—whether it be walking, jogging, seeing a play, talking with someone—you enjoy it and relax a little bit instead of doing so many things at a very superficial level."

Far from reducing his effectiveness at work Collins felt that gearing down had made him more productive. By pruning his schedule and taking time to reflect he'd learned to focus better on the task at hand, work on one thing at a time, and take a genuine interest in co-workers. This made it easier to delegate tasks. Before, his distrust of others and need to control every detail of assignments made it nearly impossible for him to give work away.

When he was given responsibility for installing a companywide software program, rather than simply adding this task to his already overcrowded calendar and trying to do it all himself, Collins first relinquished some existing responsibilities and postponed others. Then he took time to think carefully about the new program and to identify its major components. After that Collins delegated as many of its other elements as possible. Only then did he start to implement the program. As a result it went on line smoothly and he was not sent into a frenzy in the process.

Collins said co-workers noticed the difference in his working style and commented on how calm he seemed. " 'It's more pleasant to deal with you,' they say. I'm really pleased to have that happen." He attributed the change to having grown more comfortable with himself. Looking back on where he'd come from, Collins put particular emphasis on the low self-esteem underlying so much Type A behavior. He felt sure it underlay his. Why else would he have needed to be so compulsively busy if not to *prove* his worth by doing more and more in less and less time? "One of the big fears Type As have is that we're going to get fired tomorrow," Collins explained. "We live in constant fear of losing our jobs, or losing our careers, or losing our spouses, whatever it may be. We're going to be failures. That's why we do more and more things because the more things we do, the more valuable we are, the more we're needed. There is a need for us to *prove* that we have value as human beings, that we can accomplish a *lot.*" This, he thought, was the real reason for the time pressure that Type As like himself welcome, and actually court.

In retrospect Collins felt that his marriages broke up largely because of his chronic impatience and subsequent hostility. "You lose patience with people who aren't Type A, who aren't as Type A as you are," he explained. "The time urgency and the hostility are so intertwined." He also realized that trying to get so much done in so little time—at the office, in civic activities, by traveling—was a way of escaping the pressures of marriage.

Collins was in Los Angeles on business when he heard there had been an earthquake in San Francisco. The Marina district, where he lived, was particularly hard hit. Collins flew right back. He spent the next week unloading food from trucks, setting up cots, and helping comfort those in despair. In conjunction with his Type A modification, that experience completely changed his attitude toward people, Collins felt. "I can't tell you how much it has affected my own particular concerns about family and friends and reordering my priorities," he said. "It's made me think very hard about what's important. Frivolous things just don't seem to matter anymore when you've seen people—personal friends and relatives—get impacted by something that devastating. Partying and socializing with multiple dates, those kinds of thing just aren't as important to me as having an intimate relationship, a relationship with somebody I really care about. A phenomenal number of people told me that immediately after the earthquake they either ate, or made love. Both of those things are life affirming. One of the things I missed, and I think a lot of people miss if they're not in that kind of relationship, is (1) having support from that person and that concern, and (2) being able to hug that person and care for them and know you're there for them and they're there for you.

"After the earthquake I had a lot of people call to find out how I was doing. That was very, very heartwarming. People I hadn't heard from in a while, too." The day he said this Collins was about to visit two siblings with whom he'd been out of touch. "I feel a need to get closer to them," he explained, "and I'm hoping this weekend that we will. It's just become more important to me. I care about them so much. I like them and I *think* they like me, and we just don't talk that much. And we should. We should be more concerned about each other."

9

Rushaholics Anonymous

Still—in a way—nobody sees a flower—really—it is so small—we haven't time—and to see takes time, like to have a friend takes time.

—GEORGIA O'KEEFE

Health reporter Jane Brody once wrote a vivid account of her former life on the go. Before learning how to slow down, Brody reported in the *New York Times,* she was "worried about every wasted moment, anxious about every missed train or bus, hostile in every traffic jam, unable to wait in any line. I must have said 'hurry up' to my young sons at least a dozen times a day. I pushed ahead of people without even seeing them. I would start sprinting when I came within a block of the subway station, which earned me the nickname 'road runner' from my husband. I regarded busy signals, overly protective secretaries, and slow-moving salespeople as deliberate obstacles to my attempts to get more and more done in less and less time.

"Though as a 35-year-old woman I wasn't worried about heart disease, I didn't like what I saw. My easily provoked tension and anxiety could not have made me fun to be around. Nor did they make life pleasant for me."

Does this sound familiar? It's a candid portrayal of rushaholism, the compulsive need to make haste and fill every spare second with activity. This compulsion is an American passion. If you doubt that we hurry needlessly, watch passengers in a just-landed airplane unfasten their seat belts, then huddle in the aisle, angling their heads so as not to hit the overhead compartments. This makes it possible to deplane a minute or two sooner so they can get to the baggage claim area faster and wait longer for their luggage. It's classic rushaholism, a need to make haste whether this makes sense or not. Illustrations are all about: drivers switching lanes on busy roads only to have to stop at the next light and let steadier drivers catch up; passengers running to catch a subway that runs every three minutes; pedestrians dashing across streets against the light, risking their lives to save a few seconds. In such cases hurrying has become a way of life rather

123

than a means to an end. It satisfies an inner craving for speed more than it gets us where we're going faster.

Why do we do this to ourselves? The answer may be similar to the one so many of us give for consuming caffeine. We know that this stimulant isn't good for us, but we don't know how to stay in gear without it. Many of us need time pressure to produce. We are deadline workers. We can't focus on the task at hand until our backs are against the wall. We need time's pressure to tell us what has to get done.

Marian, a Providence high school teacher, found that whenever she bought a datebook, she'd only use it for a few days, then go back to using little slips of paper stuffed in her purse or taped to the wall above her desk. "Because I'm disorganized, I've always felt rushed," she said during a focus group. "I always do things at the last minute. But I've decided I like to be rushed. Because when I try to do things ahead of time, that's when I leave things out and don't do the whole thing. I'm much better if I just start at the very last minute. That's the way I operate best. I tend to correct my papers right up to bedtime even if I've had time earlier to do it. So I do go around in a perpetual rush. 'Running around with ripped socks' my husband calls it. But I like rushing around." Marian said she'd thought about getting out of the rat race, but knew she'd have trouble living without it. Toward the end of vacations Marian couldn't wait to get back on track. "I just like the rush, rush, rush," she reiterated.

Marian was just one of many focus group members who felt they couldn't function without being in a hurry. What's the point? Why are so many of us constantly on the go? There are many reasons (other than actual necessity). Among them are:

- Our temperament makes some of us feel we have no choice.
- In this society there is more status in being too busy than in not being busy enough.
- Staying in constant motion makes it unnecessary to reflect on where we're headed.
- Moving fast can literally be a "rush" that is as addictive as any other.
- Being in a perpetual hurry is a good way to avoid entangling personal alliances.

Do We Do It to Ourselves?

In Fort Myers, a teacher named Barbara described a schedule so jammed with work, household chores, and raising two children that she had little time for herself. "For me to find time to shave my legs is difficult," is the way Barbara put it. "I try to take time for myself. We'll have family meetings and discuss it. 'Your mother needs time for herself,' I'll say. It works out for a couple of days, then everybody forgets and we're back to the same routine."

But as the discussion wore on, this picture grew more blurred. "The kids and I have told her," said Barbara's husband Greg, "that you need to take whatever it is, a half hour, an hour, for yourself, and no one's going to keep telling you that. You've got to do it for yourself. If you don't, no one else is going to watch out for you."

"So I'm trying to drop a few things and just do them when I have the time to do them," conceded Barbara. "It's very hard to change when you have that type personality."

Greg, also a teacher, described himself as more casual about time than his wife was. He didn't like the impersonality of dealing with drive-in tellers and would go inside the bank just to have a face to talk to. Barbara wouldn't dream of doing such a thing. "Greg is a slower-paced person than I am," she agreed. "I probably bring a lot of it on myself. I create the pressure and the stress and I know I need to take life a little easier. But he has the time to go inside [the bank] and chat a little bit. I don't have that time, at least I don't think I do."

A need to be constantly on the go has at least as much to do with inner as outer pressure. The loudest complaints about today's brutal schedules come from those who have chosen to do hectic work in fast-paced environments. Anyone with a strong interest in this topic (including your author) is usually feeling serious time pressure. We'd like to assume that this pressure is imposed on us by our work, our families, and the pace of modern life. Some of it is. But much is self-inflicted.

On the way to interview a Los Angeles counselor who treats "hurry sickness" and lectures on its perils, I got quite lost and arrived fifteen minutes late. In the early part of our conversation the counselor noted pointedly that one Type A characteristic was an inability to leave enough extra time should one be delayed *en route*. We then discussed the Type A compulsion to do two things at once. Throughout our visit the counselor arranged flowers for a party she was hosting that night. She admitted to having only partially tamed her own hurry sickness. Her husband had a secret signal—one upraised finger—that he used to let her know she was spinning her conversational wheels too fast in social situations. "That's something I need to work on in my own life," confessed the counselor, popping another flower in a vase, "time urgency, free-floating hostility."

Her own feeling was that a chronic sense of time urgency originated in one's personality, that if so inclined one could be just as hassled in Des Moines as in Los Angeles. Many others agreed. A commonly recurring observation on questionnaires and in discussion groups was: "We do it to ourselves." Nancy, a U.S. Air Force employee near Dayton, thought that "people have an anxiety level to get comfortable with that has to do with time and pressure; things they impose on themselves. I look around and see that people have more leisure time, but they fill it up. Renovating your house becomes something you have to do, or your volunteer activities, or other commitments. It's self-imposed and we may not recognize it unless we step away from it."

Mitzie, a Dayton stenographer, agreed with Nancy. She'd raised three children on her own, which left her with little time for anything but work and family. The pace was frantic. "Once they left home I found I had to create a pace for myself," she told a focus group. "In fact I created that hurried pace more and more ... I've structured my life with so many things I like to do that I've created so much time pressure on myself. But without it I'd go batty. When I don't keep myself busy I begin to feel down."

A 1987 study confirmed the old saw, "If you want to get something done, ask a busy person." This study found that those who described themselves as having the least amount of time at their disposal were also the ones most likely to engage in volunteer activities. Any number of focus group members were living illustrations. "I was a professional volunteer," said Betty, a middle-aged housewife in Crystal River, "so I guess you don't have to work for money to stay busy. Buck [her husband] always said that if anybody ever said, 'Will you do something?' my hand automatically came up. But I learned several years ago that I could just sit there and sit on my hands. I didn't have to do all those things and it's much better."

What changed her attitude?

"I guess Buck did. He thought I was too active, that I volunteered too much."

"She was cooking instant grits," interjected Buck, a retired contractor, "and when you start cooking instant grits you don't have enough time."

Heidi—who raised six children in addition to directing a church choir and doing volunteer work on the side—told the group in Fort Myers that she'd cut back her schedule after beginning to suffer migraine headaches. "Now I'm feeling guilty about not being the busy busy person I once was," she said, "and I'm feeling that I'm not doing enough. That's why when I come down here to Fort Myers in the winter I get myself into volunteer work and do whatever I can. But that's my kind of internal pressure."

Heidi is a German-American from Milwaukee. Recently she'd returned to her parents' homeland in search of her origins. What struck Heidi more than anything else was how hard the average German worked; how clean they kept their homes; how filled they kept their time. After returning home she saw herself more clearly, and her mother too. "My mother came to visit recently," said Heidi, "and she gets up early and I have to have something prepared for her to do, some sewing or mending so that if she gets up before me she isn't idle."

Calendar Display

It's simplistic to call timelock a consequence of external or internal pressures alone. It is probably safe to say that if one is predisposed to a frantic pace, today's tempo will make that easier than ever to achieve. Appearing to be overoccupied has higher status than ever, far more, certainly, than seeming to have time on one's hands. A visibly full schedule suggests that your time—and by implication, you—is exceedingly valuable. This lends cachet to what's been called "conspicuous busyness." Among the conspicuously busy, nothing is so shameful as to appear underoccupied. Pride is taken in a look of harassment and preoccupation as part of a general can't-spare-a-second attitude. Proof is offered in the form of crowded datebooks that are whipped out at the merest provocation.

In the world of conspicuous busyness, datebooks have near-icon status. Calendar display is an important ritual in this world. There's an art to it. One pulls out a crowded datebook, holding it at a certain angle so that the scrawls filling its every time slot are plainly visible (writing some in red is a good touch). Then as much time as is decently possible is devoted to flipping through the book's pages, while murmuring sighs and expressions of despair. "After several minutes spent studiously going through page after page," advised writer Marlys Harris, a student of calendar display, "you come up with some impossibly far-off date . . ."

One reason retirement involves such a loss of status is that retirees rarely have datebooks to press upon each other. During a focus group in Fort Lauderdale, one retired couple showed us their wall calendar. Virtually every date on that calendar was filled with activities. This couple did not want us to get the idea that they were idle. They understood this society's values. One reason that fast-paced busyness has always been so prestigious in America is that we're youth-obsessed and age phobic. Oldtimers add to their loss of status by walking slowly, thinking things over, and always seeming to have time to talk. As a *Vogue* writer told that magazine's readers, "It's become a status symbol to be too busy to talk."

Being able to avoid time-consuming conversations is a major payoff for being on the go. Another reward is that the faster we go, and the more crowded our schedules, the less likely it is that we'll have to stop and think about where we're headed. Busyness can be an effective filter. Having too many things to do provides a built-in excuse for not dealing with things we'd rather not deal with: people, thoughts, ourselves.

No Time to Think

An admitted workaholic named Lawrence Wright once gave this report of how he felt about taking a weekend off at his wife's insistence: It scared him to death. Not working for a couple of days forced Wright to consider the possibility that he might have been kidding himself about his time problems. He'd always imagined that his biggest problem about time was not having enough of it. Struggling with free time forced him to realize that his actual problem was just the opposite: "My real fear of time is having too much of it . . . My worst nightmare is to be caught for a few hours with nothing to do."

Even when there was no need to get somewhere fast, Wright rushed out of habit. The many hours he spent stuck in traffic drove him into a rage. Because statistics showed he'd probably spend a full half year of his life this way, why couldn't he just sit back, relax, meditate, or listen to the radio rather than constantly glance at his watch? "It's because when I'm idle, I feel in danger," Wright concluded. "When I'm forced to be disengaged, the cold breeze of mortality catches up to me, and I become confounded by the Big Questions. I wonder why I'm doing this, who I am after all. I suddenly become aware of myself as just another life form, no more consequential in the eyes of the indifferent universe than a drifting protozoan in the sea of time. Then the light changes, and I rush ahead, trying to keep abreast of the mob."

Protecting our psyche against unwelcome intrusions is one reward for living at a fast and furious pace. During an earlier project on risk taking, I was struck repeatedly by how unreflective those I interviewed—skydivers, rock climbers, standup comedians, entrepreneurs—were as a group. It was almost as if stopping to think about the risks they were taking might mean they'd stop taking them. Another way to interpret their attitude might be to speculate that staying in constant motion (most were quite hyper) made it impossible for them to take a moment to reflect. I think this was how they wanted it.

One reason they regularly gave for taking the chances they took was that feeling in danger forced them to focus on the task at hand and eliminated distractions. Those who made speed their vocation, or their avocation—race drivers, motorcyclists, downhill skiers—routinely cited this reward for going fast. In a state of ultrahigh speed, concentration was absolute. And (though they seldom said so explicitly), their sense of ecstasy in the midst of speed could be orgasmic. "I feel the earth molding herself under me," reported T. E. Lawrence (Lawrence of Arabia) about how it felt to roar across the Salisbury Plain on a motorcycle doing 80 miles an hour. "It is me piling up this hill, hollowing this valley, stretching out this level space. That's a thing the slow coach will never feel. It is the reward of speed. I could write you pages on the lustfulness of moving swiftly." Extreme rushaholics such as Lawrence completely and unabashedly crave the sensation of going fast. "The speed is electrifying," is the way race driver Linda Snyder put it. "Once you've tasted it, you're hooked."

Mainlining Speed

It's not just daredevils who find rushing addictive. Being in a constant hurry adds zip to many an ordinary day. A fear of boredom underlies much rushaholism. "I 'run' so fast," wrote one woman on her questionnaire, "that I'm bored during relaxation time." Many of us keep the throttle wide open to make sure this can't happen. Hurrying can be exciting. Cramming too many activities into too little time, then having to rush to complete them gets the pulse rate up. So does dashing to make planes or trains, and speeding in cars. Studies of chronic speeders have found that although most say that they drive fast to "make time," few actually do. The bigger payoff for driving fast is that it's more arousing than driving slow. Psychologists say that speeding is the most common form of sensation seeking. In such cases, speed has become an end rather than a means, a craving rather than a choice. As a result of this craving many of us have lost our ability to live without filling every spare second with frenzied activity. We cannot relax without literally suffering withdrawal symptoms. We are rushaholics.

Anyone who has spent the first few fidgety days of a vacation thinking he or she ought to be back at work knows this feeling. Only when forced to slow down for an extended period of time do we realize how accustomed we've become to being constantly pressed for time. In his inaugural address as president of the American Psychological Association, Logan Wright wondered if time urgency might not be addictive. Wright pointed out that discomfort when idle is a basic characteristic of Type A personalities such as himself. This even occurs when they're dropping off to sleep and after they wake up. Might such discomfort be a form of withdrawal suffered in the absence of time pressure? Type As tend to get going as soon as their feet hit the floor in the morning, Wright pointed out. Perhaps to them hectic activity from the day's very beginning is like a morning cup of coffee for a caffeine addict, or a first cigarette for one dependent on nicotine: "a way of starting the adrenaline flowing and thus ridding themselves of withdrawal-based discomfort."

This analysis may not be as farfetched as it sounds. There is a well-known syndrome of stress addiction that may incorporate rushaholism. To the nervous system, being constantly pressed for time is simply one more source of stress. To cope with such arousal our glands secrete "stress hormones": stimulating neurochemicals such as adrenaline and natural opiates such as endorphins. It's well established that stress does release such mood-elevating natural opiates. Always being in a hurry is one way to stay stressed. Therefore making sure you never slow down can be an effective way to elevate mood. In other words, rushaholism could be a self-prescribed antidepressant, one that is highly addictive. Eventually we become hooked—not on speed itself, but on the addictive opiates released by fast and furious living. In their absence we crash. We have become rushaholics; compelled to make haste even when there's no need to do so.

Pieces of Mind

As with any addiction, a dependency on making haste is seldom the result of conscious choice. Hurrying builds its own momentum. Busyness sneaks up on us. One task builds on another. Before we know it there aren't enough hours in the day. Yet the addictiveness of rushaholism can make it feel easier to keep our schedule crowded than to cut it back.

Eventually, however, a psychic as well as a physical bill comes due for our rushaholism. It is possible to stay constantly on the go, trying to do two or three things at once, and squeezing every bit of productivity possible from the seconds of our lives. But the emotional price is steep. When we try to make the most of our time by filling it too full, the effect is to make any time hard to enjoy. We lose the ability to savor what we're doing without thinking about what we might be doing. "If I'm reading, I think I should be writing," writer Letty Cottin Pogrebin once lamented. "If I'm writing, I wonder if I should have gone to that meeting instead. If I go to the meeting, I think maybe I should have spent the evening on the phone fundraising for a woman's conference or doing my filing."

Although he professed to like the fullness of his schedule and pace of his life, Harry, the Boston sales manager, did have reservations. "Because, quite frankly, my mind is always running," he said. "I find it scary sometimes. I have a hard time winding down. My mind is always going ahead and I'm always thinking about what I have to do." According to Diane Ulmer, this attitude typifies Friedman Institute clients. "Probably the most common feeling is the feeling that you always need to rush, get on to something more important," said Ulmer. "The inability to focus on one thing without your mind flitting. Mind always racing. Waking up in the middle of the night because you have so many things on your mind."

By living at too-frantic a pace we develop a habit of never giving anything, or anyone, our full attention. Take the too-common experience of dialing a phone and forgetting who you'd called when they answer. This is rarely a symptom of premature Alzheimer's disease. Rather it most often results from: (1) calling too long a list of people; (2) having a lot of things on one's mind when making a call; (3) trying to do other tasks while on the phone; or (4) all of these. Such phone conversations are seldom satisfying. Nor are ones conducted with someone wearing a Walkman (your teenager, say). Or those murmured during commercials of a television program, or in the middle of a movie. But a declining quality of human interaction is part and parcel of our fast-paced, hectic lives.

Consider the doing-two-or-three-things-at-a-time syndrome. Once this skill is mastered, it's easy to feel guilty when not doing more than one thing. But the psychic toll is high. Psychologist Bruce Baldwin has warned that once we're so habituated, "Doing just one thing at a time makes individuals feel uncomfortable. The result is an individual who is no longer able to psychologically 'let go' to enjoy just one activity. Instead, they are plagued by distractions that stem from the learned habit of constantly splitting their focus. As a result, genuine relaxation becomes difficult."

Among the most common forms of multiple activity is thinking about one thing while discussing another. On my questionnaire I asked this question: "How would you rate your ability to conduct a conversation and appear to be paying attention while thinking about something else at the same time?" Of those who filled out this form, 20% said "excellent," 38% "good," 27% "fair" and 12% "poor." In other words, 85% were able to carry on a conversation without really listening, at least on occasion. To the related question "How good are you at glancing at your watch or a clock without anyone else noticing?" over half rated themselves as "good" (27%) or "very good" (24%). Another third said they were "fair," and 11% "not good at all."

Needless to say such an approach does not make for a high quality of human interaction. This is characteristic of rushaholism. Relationships with others are the first thing to suffer. By now it's estimated that we size up new acquaintances in less than a minute. In a rushed society of people giving each other quick once-overs, one doesn't want to leave too much of what psychologists call "impression management" to chance. In more leisurely times we could allow our identities to unfold gradually. Today that's risky. For those on the fly, an esthetic shorthand is necessary. Wearing advertisements can be seen as a courtesy to others who are trying to decide whether they like you or not. Hence the popularity of visible brand labels on our clothing, and sound bites borrowed from television that pepper our conversation. ("Where's the beef?" "Make my day." "Don't have a cow, man.") Our concept must be high. According to Roger Ailes we're all broadcasters now. Not just our clothing but our conversational techniques must be "punchy and graphic . . . We transmit our own programs. We receive ratings from our audiences."

Sound bites lead to listen bites. Who's got the time for an extended conversation, let alone the attention? By some estimates, the average American's attention span is now eight seconds and falling. The inability to pay sustained attention is one reason so many relationships are in such disrepair. Miss Manners (Judith Martin) has observed that the civilized art of engaging in opening gambits to find common ground for a conversation is giving way to "a new reluctance to engage in banal preliminaries for fear of losing a stranger's attention before real conversation can begin. The idea seems to be that one is allowed only a few seconds for an audition, and that if an opening line is dull or offensive, one will be dismissed."

Timelock has forced us to develop new ways of connecting. Among them are "touching base," "checking in," and "grazing" (in the social sense). Such techniques involve brief, hurried contact with a large number of people who don't know us too well. In today's singles services such techniques have become an art form. "Our system allows you to get to know a large quantity of quality singles in a short amount of time," advertised one. Another is based on a system they call "Quick Connections." In this system an energetic evening is promised with loads of guided activities leading up to a trademarked activity called "Short Talks." According to this service's publicity: "Short Talks are brief, time-limited conversations that enable you to get information that interests you from a variety of people, one at a time . . . Short Talks last for 8–10 minutes and then the emcee tells everyone to move on to a new person. This way, parting is not awkward and you have different Short Talks with all of the people you would like to meet. If a Short Talk doesn't lead to greater interest, only a few minutes have been lost . . ."

The Rolodex Syndrome

In the movie *Modern Romance,* Albert Brooks played a lonely, jilted lover who spins his packed address wheel exclaiming, "Look how many friends I've got!" This is the Rolodex Syndrome. A Rolodex is one of many devices that allow us to expand the number of "contacts" in our lives at the expense of actual intimacy. Modern phones make it possible to reach out and touch more people than ever, while reducing the depth of such relationships. Call waiting swaps sustained conversation for never-out-of-touchness. It permits the most mundane sales call to interrupt the most intimate chat. This convenience is one of many that increases the quantity of our relationships while reducing their quality. Too many contacts, too little time. Yet time is an absolute prerequisite for genuine human connection. Building intimacy takes patience. Lasting relationships can't be brought to a rapid boil. They must simmer. Most of us don't have that kind of time. Therefore we have little intimacy in our lives. Things are moving too fast. Our calendars are too crowded.

Novelist Maureen Howard once described a visit with a friend that she'd arranged six weeks earlier, "the best we could do flipping through our calendars . . . Dazed by the laundry list of our commitments, we spoke in hasty fragments, like a tape on fast-forward, of what we planned to do on our day. Drive out of town, lunch, rummage antique shops—irresponsible pleasures, our fantasy as schedule-laden as our working lives. Now the idyll is upon us, cut to a half holiday and confined to the neighborhood. Something has gone wrong, terribly wrong. It is absurd to pencil in friendship, to be grateful for our few hours as though favored by the gods."

Difficulty connecting with others—even those with whom we would like to connect—is an inevitable consequence of timelock. Any decent human relationship is based on paying attention to another person and actually *hearing* what they're trying to say. But actually hearing what other people are saying is hard when we're rushed and have so many things on our mind. The French have a word to describe what they consider a necessary precondition for friendship: *disponibilité.* There is no exact translation of this word, but it suggests a certain openness, receptivity, having time for, being able to listen to, and being at the disposal of another person. "Availability" might be the closest English word, though it lacks the resonance of the French term. French or English, this state of receptivity to others is nearly impossible when we're pressed for time.

Friendships are put to the test by timelock. Too often they are reduced to the Christmas card category. Not having time for friends was a common concern among those who filled out questionnaires and took part in focus groups. "My friends are as busy as I am," wrote one woman on her questionnaire, "so we have to schedule time together like appointments." In response to the question "How often do you find yourself wishing you had more time to spend with family members or friends?" 65% responded either "constantly" or "often." Half said that with so many other demands on their time they found it hard to keep up friendships. The will was there; 48% indicated that they tried to make time to see their friends on a regular basis. To an open question about what they would do with six months to live, many said they'd look up old friends. But in the following question, about how that wish compared with their lives today, few indicated they were actually doing so.

A 42-year-old Los Angeles filmmaker pointed out that most of his friends were as busy as he was. Therefore they seldom saw or heard from each other. "We're all comfortable going long periods of time as friends without needing to be in touch," he explained, "without feeling we need to nurture the friendship on a daily or weekly basis." A 27-year-old pool maintenance man contrasted his Los Angeles neighborhood with the Pittsburgh community where he grew up: "Most of the people were tradesmen, plumbers, carpenters, that sort of thing. They came home from work every day and talked about their day, and sat around on weekends and drank and talked about their week. It was an ongoing kind of thing. They used to have big block parties and pig roasts, stuff like that. But neighborhoods like this, unless the kids know each other, there's not too much in common."

During a focus group held in Katonah, a town north of New York City, a 46-year-old management consultant named Schuyler pointed out that even twenty years ago our circle of friends or that of our parents was not likely to be very widely dispersed. There was more opportunity then for the daily contact that fertilizes ongoing friendships. Like so many, however, Schuyler found his friends scattered and hard to keep up with. "I make excuses," he said of his inability even to respond to letters. "I think times have changed grossly as far as how much time people spend writing to each other."

Schuyler's observation struck a responsive chord. All the others in this group were baby boomer–aged parents. Like him, most found their friends were scattered throughout the country. Few had been successful at staying in touch with them. "It's because I haven't written letters," admitted Becky, a mother of two. "I've had friendships end."

"It's hard even to write postcards," agreed Cheryl, a free-lance screenwriter with one child and another on the way. "It's a time thing. You have to get yourself into a mindset and clear all the other shit off your desk and say 'OK, the kid's in bed, I have a little bit of energy left. Should I spend it speaking to my husband or should I engross myself in a letter?' Christmas cards were the last time I wrote."

Jack, Becky's husband, was the only one present who made a special effort to keep up with old friends through letters, calls, and visits. "Friendship overrides time as a value to me," said Jack. "And also as a value judgment. If it doesn't for you, you're living a minimal life. If time is more important to you than friendship, then it has to be inspected."

Needless to say, this observation didn't sit too well with the others. Cheryl pointed out that Jack had Becky to take care of their two kids while he took time to keep up with friends. Marilyn, a mother of two, said that she'd rather spend her one day off a week with her family than with friends. "I guess I miss the friendship," Marilyn concluded. "But I like being with the kids. So I make friends who have children."

Although they never got sitters just to spend time with each other, Marilyn continued, she and her mother-friends did visit with kids in tow, even though this made actual conversation difficult. Her husband, Paul, thought that women were far more likely than men to seek each other out even on that limited a basis. Men seemed prone just to forgo friendship as a tax on growing older. Schuyler didn't agree. "I don't think it's gender based," he said. "I talk to a lot of women at work who complain to me that they don't have enough time to keep up with their friends because of work. I really think it's time based."

ALICIA (CONT.)

This book began with the story of Alicia, the Chicago executive who was trying to combine a demanding career with serious time pressure at home. There's more to the story.

Alicia and Bill were childhood sweethearts in a Chicago suburb near the one where they now live. After graduating from college with liberal arts degrees, both took corporate "line" jobs; ones bestowing a lot of responsibility in exchange for a major time commitment. Alicia later got an MBA and became head of a product development group. In essence she was managing a business: marketing new products, solving problems in the field, hiring and firing. Although it meant being constantly on call, Alicia loved that job and still misses it. But within a two-year period in the mid-1980s, several things altered her perspective. Most important, her son, Matthew, was born. The next day Bill's sister died of cancer. A few months after that the stock market crashed. Within weeks Alicia began to notice productive employees with twenty years' experience cleaning out their desks.

The last straw was her sister's wedding. In order to attend, Alicia had to miss an important strategic planning session at work. This was not considered a smart career move by her colleagues. Alicia realized that from their perspective, family obligations were "kind of a wimpy excuse" for missing an important meeting. But from her new perspective, Alicia had begun to ask herself questions like this one: In ten years' time, what would matter more—missing her sister's wedding, or pleasing a boss who would probably be gone by then? Alicia went to the wedding, and paid the price. Just as she assumed would happen, "I probably was not regarded the same after that."

But Alicia was regarding herself differently. The strain of trying to maintain a grueling work schedule and be there for her family as well was taking its toll. One night when Matt was still nursing she woke up, got out of bed, put a coat over her nightgown, and headed for the door.

"Where are you going?" asked Bill.

"To the train," Alicia replied.

"Hadn't you better get dressed first?" said her husband.

Soon after that Alicia did something she never thought she'd do: She transferred from a line to a staff job. As a staff person Alicia became one more middle manager. This felt like swapping a field general's assignment for one as a master sergeant. Staff people didn't call shots. Superiors gave them things to do and they did them. But if they left their desks and headed for the door at 5 P.M., no one seemed to mind (most other staff members had families too). They weren't expected to be on call during evenings or weekends. Nor did staffers take many business trips. So if Alicia's current life looked hectic, it could have been worse. She could still have been on the line.

Bill still was. As a commodities trader, his hours continued to be long and unpredictable. Like Alicia in her product development job, he loved his work and paid the price. At the same time, if anything, Bill was more disturbed by the effect of their schedules on their family life than Alicia was. Bill loved fathering. Alicia's husband said he wouldn't even mind taking care of Matt full-time. He helped raise their son as much as his schedule permitted. Whenever possible Bill picked him up at his aunt's in the evening. This meant staying in constant phone contact with Alicia, seeing who would be where when. So far neither felt that their demanding schedule was hurting them or Matt. But after Alicia gave birth to a second child in the fall, neither knew how they'd manage. How would Matt react? Could Alicia's sister take care of two children? If not, how would they feel about leaving their children with a sitter? Would she and Bill have any time left for each other once another kid was in the house? Could they pay enough attention to Matt as he grew older?

"Once we can't control his environment to the degree that we do now, I'm not so sure," worried Alicia, "once he's in school. Who will his friends be? How will he handle that environment? I can't tell you what next year will be like."

Alicia was reluctant to cut her work back any further. She was willing to be less career-oriented than before, but there were limits. "I wouldn't want to reduce my standard of living," Alicia explained. "I'm not sure if more flexibility at work would be worth a financial loss." Her father had held two jobs to make ends meet. Alicia had vivid memories of watching her mother hunched over the kitchen table trying to balance their checkbook. She had sworn never to do that herself, and never to have her children watch their parents worry about money. So far that hadn't been necessary. Alicia hoped it never would be. But she was growing ambivalent on this point. Late in our conversation Alicia said that for the first time she'd actually begun to consider the possibility of trading money for time at home with her family. Not quitting, or even going part-time necessarily, but trying to find work that could be done partly from home, or perhaps starting a business. Something that would leave her more time to spend with her family, to take part in community activities, and to go to church on occasion. This seemed like a distant dream.

Alicia didn't feel alone with her dilemma. Most of the parents she knew were struggling with time conflicts. In a working mothers' support group that Alicia attended, the two dozen other women all felt caught in a time vise. Many came to their monthly lunch meetings in a frenzy, if they came at all. Common topics of conversation included husbands who were seldom home for dinner; sitters who didn't show up; and kids displaying symptoms of time-stress. Some of the other mothers even envied Alicia for having a sister to take care of her son, and a husband who helped out at home.

What if Alicia thought that her demanding schedule and that of her husband were actually putting their children at risk? "I would stop working in a second," she replied without hesitating, "even if it meant having to sell our house and scale back."

What's most striking about Alicia's case is that it's really not striking at all. A little exaggerated, perhaps. But untold millions of parents are struggling with their own versions of the timelocked American family: trying to give proper time to their careers, their children, their spouses, and themselves, while fearing that they're cheating all four.

10

The Timelocked Family

If I had my life to live over again I would have waxed less and listened more.

—ERMA BOMBECK

The day after his second year of school ended, we were startled to find our son writing himself a schedule. We've kept it as a reminder that perhaps we all needed to loosen up a bit. This was what David wrote:

9:00–9:30	[play] computer
9:30–10:00	get dressed
9:45–10:00	play with Scott [his brother] /or work on my [computer] file
10:00–10:20	read a book
10:20–10:30	computer
10:30–10:45	Daddy check my work
10:45–11:00	play outside
11:00–11:30	Square One [TV program]
11:30–12:00	Reading Rainbow [TV program]
12:00–12:30	anything but TV [at his parents' behest]
4:30–4:45	read a book
4:45–5:00	play outside
5:00–5:30	Reading Rainbow
5:30–6:00	Double Dare [TV program]
6:00–7:00	help dinner
7:00–7:30	eat dinner
7:30–7:45	play Hacky Sack [a ball-type game]
7:45–8:00	play with Scott

8:00–6:00   sleep
6:00–7:15   go back to sleep

(Don't ask me what he did from 12:30 to 4:30 that day.)

I don't know what was more striking, the fact that David composed this schedule or the fact that he stuck to it, religiously checking each entry against the clock before moving on to the next activity.

Most of us did not learn how to schedule our lives until we grew up. Our kids virtually learn that style with their earliest feedings (themselves often on a schedule). What does this signify in the long run? We don't know what effect today's time pressures will have on children raised in that context. We do know that children acquire attitudes toward time from the society in which they are raised.

At the playground recently with Scott, our 3-year-old, Muriel realized she needed to know the time but wasn't wearing a watch. She looked around. A boy and girl nearby had pastel-colored digital watches on their wrists. Both looked about 6 years old. Muriel asked them what time it was. In unison they told her, "Five-two-three."

Because they're so easy to read and so ubiquitous, digital timekeepers make kids aware of time at an early age, and in a very precise fashion. When I told him it was time for his nap, Scott once asked me what time it actually was. In the modern way I said, "one-three-oh." Scott then brought to my attention that, according to the clock on the VCR, it actually was "one-three-one." Such stories are a commonplace in today's world. A kindergartner in one family tells anyone who wants to hear that he goes to school "at eight-two-two." Time to him is a very specific, precise commodity. None of this "around 8:20" business, or "about half-past." Eight twenty-two it is. And this child gets antsy if the clock reads 8:23 and they haven't left yet.

In Plano, an affluent community north of Dallas, stress counselor Leslie Kolkmeier sees an increasing number of time-pressed children. One 10-year-old was constantly absent from school due to migraine headaches. Her main source of anxiety seemed to be the clock. "If I'm not ready to go with the keys in my hand by three minutes after eight," explained her mother, "my little girl gets sick." Kolkmeier asked if her daughter was ever actually penalized for being late to school. "No," replied the mother. "She just seemed to know that if we didn't get there on time we'd be 'running late.' "

This is an extreme example of an increasingly common phenomenon. Kids are feeling the pressure of time at younger and younger ages. It could hardly be otherwise. Today's children wear watches and carry calendars at a far earlier age than their predecessors, in fact and in spirit. They can hardly develop anything other than a fast-paced, hyper-scheduled approach to time. It's what they smell in the air around them. This attitude toward time will have a lot to do with the flavor of their lives to come. It's the flavor of the contemporary family.

Fast Families

Families bear the brunt of timelock. At one time the home was considered a refuge from work pressures. Now its inhabitants march to a businesslike beat. The pace at home has become little different from that at work. It calls for huge calendars on the kitchen wall, constant cross-checking of everyone's schedules, and sophisticated use of complex telephone systems so everyone can stay coordinated. "Today's 'combination women' are remarkable," marveled market researcher Mona Doyle. "My daughter-in-law has an awesome calendar on her refrigerator. It covers thirty to thirty-one days, broken in thirds, and shows who's responsible for their child at any given time. The scheduling it takes to run a two-income family leaves little time left over."

The tempo of the office and much of its paraphernalia—datebooks, Rolodexes, phone systems, computers, even faxes—have invaded the home. In the process our family lives have become ultra-scheduled. They must. How else could we cope with the multiple time demands tugging at every family member? "I have a calendar and I'm totally lost without it," said Kathy, a substitute teacher and mother of two in Crystal River. "If I didn't keep appointments, children's activities, school sports, days the kids have dental appointments, the days I'm going to work, etc., etc., written on my calendar, I'd be lost. I'd go crazy. When I'm without my calendar I'm like a lost person."

Because its members are so busy, family life today must be *organized* to an unprecedented degree: schedules compared, calendars coordinated, watches synchronized. This isn't necessarily wrong, or bad. In the current context it's necessary for families to schedule their activities carefully. The risk, however, is of raising busy little clones of our timelocked selves.

"If my daughter is slow on the street," admitted one mother, "I tend to pull her. I used to think it was so inconsiderate when I saw parents hauling little children around. Now I realize it's because the post office closes at five or the bank closes at three. Sometimes rushing a child just can't be helped." Another mother wrote on her questionnaire, "I hate it when I find myself yelling at my kids to hurry up—we'll be late—we'll miss the bus, etc.—and knowing I'm passing along the stress as a learned thing."

Among my own least favorite, and too frequent, occasions as a parent have been those mornings when we're urging our kids to step it up or we'll be late. "Come on Scott, let's go. Get a move on. We haven't got all day. Pick out a toy and let's get to the car." This makes us all tense and unhappy.

When we don't have to rush, mornings are a different experience altogether. Then Scott watches some "Sesame Street" before dawdling
through breakfast. He "reads" the cereal boxes, asks questions, looks for
birds out the window. Then he may play with a truck, or work on a puzzle.
After getting dressed Scott stands by his toy shelf trying to decide which
one to take to day care. Sometimes this involves two or three false decisions before he settles on one. Then he struggles into his jacket and heads
for the door, pushing the coffeemaker button as we leave. Between the door
and the car Scott may pause two or three times, to pick up a rock or because
he's seen a worm. He stops, stoops, picks up something, and excitedly
rushes it over to me: a piece of broken acorn. "Daddy, look, a squirrel ate
them!"

When there's time to dawdle that way, we're all happier. ("Dawdling,"
after all, is not a problem for kids, only for parents.) Leaving Scott at day
care is much easier when I don't have to rush out the door, when I can sit
and start a puzzle with him for a few minutes or sing a song with his friends.
Day care workers note with a combination of sadness and sympathy how
few parents have that option. Every morning they have to peel at least some
pupils off their parents' legs so their mom or dad can dash out the door and
get to work on time. This is not necessarily a knock on such parents. When
you have to get to work, you have to get to work.

Well-Scheduled Children

At Tot Town*, a day care center north of Washington, D.C., staff
members have a ringside seat every morning to observe hurried parents
and their anxious children struggling to break away from each other. "They
both have tears in their eyes," reported one veteran teacher during a staff
meeting, "particularly in the early part of the year."

"Some of these kids are here when I arrive at eight," added another
teacher, "and they're still here when I leave at five. That's a *long* day."

Tot Town's staff members didn't find that these children's parents were
uncaring, or unreceptive to suggestions for easing their kids' schedules.
With the staff's encouragement, a few made a point of taking time off for
"home days" with their children. Others tried to spend extra time with them
in the summer. But in some cases this was problematic. More than one Tot
Town parent had asked teachers to help them prepare a list of activities to
engage in during extended time off with their children. "It seems like they
always have to be busy," observed one staff member. "They always have
to be *doing* things. They can't just relax."

*Pseudonym

Tot Town itself made a big point of being low-key. Nonetheless, its teachers had to schedule their children's activities far more than they liked: free play till nine, organized activities after that, straighten up the room, lunch at noon, clean up afterward, then everyone onto cots for a nap at one. The easiest day to get the kids to nap was Monday, because the kids' weekends were even more hectic than their weekdays. Many had already begun to take music lessons and dance lessons and to play on soccer teams with uniforms.

In an after-school program run by Tot Town, the pupils' lives were even more activity-driven. It wasn't uncommon for these 6- to 12-year-olds to be in a near-panic toward the end of the day, saying things like, "if my mom doesn't get here any minute I'm not gonna have time to eat and get to soccer" (or play rehearsal, or roller skating, or any one of a number of organized activities). One year the director of this program felt compelled to send parents a reminder that it was *not* part of their job to have kids dressed, ready, and waiting for their next activity. Older teachers were struck by how much busier students' lives seemed to grow each year. "That's why you see so many kids in something like soccer who are burned out by 12," one teacher said. "They begin to drop out. 'Hey I've been doing this since I was little,' they seem to say. 'I'm burned out.' "

Do they use that word?

"They sure do. That's just what they say. 'I'm burned out.' "

Early in a focus group involving eight fourth graders (many of them Tot Town graduates), a boy named Jason said, "It would be nice not to fall asleep in class." Why was that happening? asked his friend Chip. "I don't always get enough sleep," Jason explained. "I usually go to bed around ten, then I have to get up at six to walk the dog." Chip asked why he didn't go to bed earlier. "Because I have to practice my instruments," Jason replied. As he told the group, Jason played both violin and trombone in addition to being on baseball and soccer teams, taking part in intramural sports, going to church, practicing for choir, and throwing pots in a pottery class.

This type of schedule was little different from those reported by others in the group. Most listed their activities on a day-by-day basis: "Hebrew school on Tuesdays," said Beth, ticking off on her fingers. "Then piano on Thursday, gymnastics on Saturday, oh, and Sunday school." (Her family was interfaith.) Beth also took acting classes on some evenings. "Dance, piano, flute, Girl Scouts," were the activities Kristen reported. "I used to play baseball but I didn't like flies in my mouth. I'm also in plays." After detailing his weekly schedule Chip added, "Friday is completely free. That's the best." Ashley said she took part in some activity every day of the week. Yet after listing them all—piano lessons, gymnastics, drama, softball— Ashley said that she wanted to add ballet.

The only child present without a full complement of activities was

Molly. Molly explained that this was because she had such a "long day."
She left for private school every morning at seven and didn't return until
five. Her evenings were taken up with homework. "It's just all school," said
Molly. "There's no free time."

Did these children enjoy having such full schedules? Feelings were
mixed. "I like to be busy," said Ashley. "I don't like to be . . ." "Bored,"
chimed in Beth. "Right," agreed Ashley. "I don't like to be bored." But later
Ashley said, "I'm too busy. I always feel rushed." Others murmured assent.
"When you have a lot of activities to do," explained Beth, "sometimes you
don't have enough time to just stay home and read, like I love to do, or dress
my dolls or something. I always feel rushed." Most of the others also felt
hurried at times. "Like when I have baseball," said Jason, "and somebody
else is picking me up and I eat half a hot dog and then have to go."

Did the children think their parents were this busy when they were
kids? None did. "Relaxed, totally," was what Chip imagined his parents'
childhood was like. "I don't think my mom, when she was my age, was as
busy as I am," Beth felt. "Sometimes when I come home with my knees
bruised, she'll say, 'Oh, I used to get bruised all the time. I used to roller
skate up and down the street.' So I think like she'd go out with friends, not
go to classes as much as I do." How did she feel about that? Beth pondered
the question, then replied, "I think I'm better off because I have more
activities. I don't really enjoy roller skating or anything. Well, at a rink I do.
But not up and down the street with all those bumps."

Although busy, this group was probably less stressed than many. All
came from stable, two-parent families, albeit ones where both parents
worked (Beth's mother excepted). The full schedules they reported are
probably typical of their demographic peers, and not as hectic as some. The
unanswered question for such kids and their parents alike is why so many
children today lead such organized lives. This question came up repeatedly
during adult focus groups. Unlike the clock and calendar-driven lives of their
children, most participants remembered a more relaxed childhood in which
they and their friends seemed to find each other and figure out ways to
entertain themselves.

"When I was 5," recalled a builder who grew up in a Philadelphia
suburb, "I had a bike. I'd go to play with a neighbor. I can't remember
having 5-year-olds shuttled to three different communities for three different lessons."

"Everything's so scheduled," agreed a working mother in Fort Myers.
"In order for my daughter to play with another child, we have to make a
date. I just feel like I'm on the road all the time with the van going from
a lesson to a play date to a this to a that. I remember growing up in Chicago
and you walked down the block and you stood in the backyard and you
yelled 'Susie!' and she came out and played with you for a while."

"I lived in a neighborhood where I could walk out the door and always find playmates," said Paul, a 42-year-old computer technician and father of two in Katonah. "I never had preschool or nursery school, or any of that crap that my kids have. When I was growing up we had none of that. We had good friends, and hung out, played ball, rode our bikes, and did what we wanted to do. We had great imaginations."

"I grew up in the Bronx," said Paul's wife, Marilyn, a computer programmer. "I can remember when I was 6 years old walking three houses down after dinner and knocking on a friend's door. My mother didn't have to be protective because everybody was out sitting on their stoops, so you couldn't get into trouble. Here there isn't always a kid to play with. My son is always calling someone and on Tuesday this kid goes to piano, on Wednesday swimming, on Thursday who knows what."

Jack, a teacher who grew up in Bloomington, Indiana, said that after counseling drug addicts in Manhattan for seventeen years he was suffering from culture shock. "I'm up to here with all these women in station wagons and their dogs," said Jack. "They're telling me about their lives. It makes me want to vomit. 'I get up, I take them here, I drive them there, I do this, I do that.' I mean, can't they get on their bikes, pedal their ass over to their friend's, get out a little ball and bat and go play baseball? That's what we did. No adult showed up with shirts."

"If you went back to Bloomington now and asked," wondered Paul, "is the same thing going on now?"

"I did, and it's not," replied Jack. "They do get driven around and they get their asses powdered. Now, is it because their parents are afraid their kids are going to be stolen by rapists? Is it because they've gotten used to having their own asses powdered? I don't know."

I put this question to the fourth graders themselves. How did their calendars get so full? They weren't exactly sure. Most said they enjoyed being involved in activities, but found that the initiative for joining them usually came from their parents. "Mom finds out about things," explained Ashley, "and asks if I want to do them. Like gymnastics. My mom saw me do cartwheels so she asked me if I wanted to do gymnastics and she said I had to make a decision by a certain time. Then she kept saying how much she wanted me to do it, and I felt like I should do it, but I really didn't think I wanted to. Now I love it."

"Sometimes I do get very annoyed when they say, 'Oh, I think you'll like this,' " said Chip of his parents. "Well, two weeks later, after they sign me up for this thing that I don't want to do, they say, 'Oh, Chip, we signed you up for this.' I say 'Why?' They say, 'Well, we thought you'd like it.' "

Jason gave a similar report. His parents would hear about athletic activities, then tell him about them. "I don't know how they do it," he told the group, "but they seem to convince me that if I don't go into them I'll regret it later."

"It's the same with me," said Teddy. "One year I wanted to quit soccer and they kept on pestering me and saying if I quit soccer for one year everyone else would be better than me and I'd have a hard time catching up."

We're all faced with a dilemma. Middle-class kids and parents alike have intensely mixed feelings about the busyness of their lives. Parents compare their kids' activity-driven schedules unfavorably with their own less organized childhoods. Yet the initiative to fill their kids' calendars seems to come at least as much from parents as from children themselves. Why should this be? One reason, obviously, is aspiration inflation. "You feel like you're a bad mother unless your kid is involved in ten types of activities," said the mother of two busy grade-schoolers in Crystal River. "If they're not, they might not get into Harvard." A suburban mother of two in Champaign, Illinois, couldn't recall organized activities such as swimming lessons even being available when she was growing up in a small midwestern community in the 1950s. Now they were, and as a mother she was feeling pressure to get her children involved, to "expose them to new things, give them new challenges. I don't think our parents even thought of that sort of thing."

A second reason parents overschedule their kids' lives is genuine concern for their welfare. Activities provide constructive care in a secure context. Absent parents feel better if their kids are in supervised programs rather than fending for themselves in settings that feel less safe. In many communities this concern becomes self-fulfilling. The more children are involved in activities, the fewer playmates can be found on the street. This makes parents feel more disposed than ever to get their kids involved in activities. If her son was to have a social life at all, noted one Katonah mother, it had to be planned.

The era when kids entertained themselves is easy to recall with nostalgia. But this was a time when at-home mothers gave their children a sense of safe haven. With fewer cars and criminals on the street they didn't worry as much about their children's safety. Drugs were basically a nonissue. And television and video games were not the time sponges for children that they are today. This is yet a third reason that parents pile on activities. What's the alternative? Too often the alternative to organized activities is not that our children will explore the woods or fish in a stream or get up a ballgame or read a book. The alternative is that they will watch Hulk Hogan drive his foot into the stomach of Ultimate Warrior, or play Super Mario Brothers 3 by the hour. Faced with such a choice, is it better to overorganize their time, or underorganize it so they can watch more television, play more video games, or argue strenuously that they ought to be allowed to?

This is the vicious circle parents confront. One reason they encourage their kids to get involved in so many activities is that the alternatives are worse. There's little spontaneous street life. (Even getting up a game takes serious phone skills these days.) In turn, the key reason that there's so little spontaneous street life is that so many kids are involved in organized activities. And so it goes.

A final reason that our kids spend so much time in structured programs is that many prefer it that way. I may wish that my oldest boy spent less time in organized sports and more in pickup games, but he doesn't. And with some reason. Anyone who romanticizes yesterday's pickup games has forgotten how it felt to wait to be chosen, if chosen at all, then to spend most of a game arguing over rules. In well-organized leagues everyone gets to play and more time is spent playing than haggling.

The case is not all for spontaneous over organized activities. But we do pay a price for putting our kids on schedules. That price comes due in the form of kids who internalize time pressure much sooner than their parents did. By taking part in so many organized activities children become aware of how important deadlines are at a very early age. This is why so many wear watches and carry calendars, literally and figuratively. The world they're growing up in virtually demands such attention to time.

I once called the 13-year-old next door who did occasional office chores for me. Would she have a couple of hours to work this week? My neighbor wasn't sure. She was awfully busy. But she didn't want to shut the door. "If I have a break in my schedule," she told me, "I'll call you a couple of days ahead."

One-Minute Parenting

Parents seldom feel comfortable about teaching their children how to crowd their schedules, even as they crowd their own. Yet given today's time pressures, it's the only model many children have to emulate. Asked to depict their parents' schedules, most members of the kids' focus group used the term "busy." Long days, working nights, and extended trips on business were what these children described. "I wish they were less busy," said Molly of her working parents. Why? "Because then I'd have more time with them." "I think he's too rushed," Beth observed about her business executive father. "I don't think it's good for him. Some nights he comes home with headaches from it all." "My mom usually gets up at about six, maybe five-thirty," said Jason. "Usually she leaves for work about seven-thirty. She comes home about six or seven." Do you mind her being gone that long? "Well, not really. I'm so busy I wouldn't be home to see her anyway. I'd probably think they were way too busy if I was home. But since I'm not home I really wouldn't see them a whole lot anyway."

"I think my dad is a little busy," said my own son David. "Sometimes I ask him if he'll have a catch with me, but he has to do some work. Also I think my mom's a little too busy because sometimes she has extra work that she has to bring home to do."

Did the kids feel they were getting enough time with their parents? Some did; most didn't. "I'd like a little more," said Jason. "I think they don't spend enough time," agreed Ashley, "because I don't really ever see them at all because they're always late and by the time they get home, I'm usually in bed."

Teddy thought his parents spent enough time with him, although there was a period when his father, a scientist, was busy writing a grant proposal and "I would ask him to play Frisbee or something and he would say, 'Not now.'"

"Sometimes 'not now' seems to be 'never,'" observed Chip.

"It usually is," agreed Jason.

Jason told us that his father, a teacher, had taken over most of the cooking since his mother became a doctor. "Whenever my dad's not home, my mom orders pizza," said Jason. Did he wish she did more of the cooking? "Yes," Jason replied. Why? "I don't know. I kind of wish she'd cook because that would mean she'd have to be home. Lots of times she's not home till seven o'clock and we eat without her."

When we discussed mealtime, most described hectic occasions with eating done in shifts. Beth (whose mother didn't work outside the home) was an exception. "I like how we always eat together, because we're all busy during the day, people go places and everything. And this is really the only time we're all together." More typical was the report of Ashley, who said her family was only able to eat dinner together about once a week.

The timelocked family feels pressure most at mealtime. What's been called "the arsenic hour"—after work and school, before dinner begins— has become a dreaded part of the day in contemporary American families. What used to be a time to unwind and reconnect for too many has become one more harried slot on the calendar. If anything, mealtimes are more hectic occasions than others. Although modern conveniences such as microwave ovens save cooking time, they speed the tempo of meals and make shift eating easier. Practically speaking, eating together as a family is no longer necessary.

"I think it would be very interesting when you talk to people to find out how many people have a quote traditional family meal at night," said a Dallas mother of two. "I don't think that's true anymore. We really get angry about it. My husband and I will find ourselves mad but without really recognizing and identifying it, when one of the kids has a practice that interferes with us eating dinner together. I know most people don't. They eat in shifts."

When a group of 500 college freshmen (class of '93) were asked to write an essay entitled "Is the traditional family doomed?" most took the affirmative position. The most common supporting argument was that families don't eat dinner together much anymore. They wrote of the family meal eaten together in the past tense, as a regrettable victim of modern time pressures.

Of those responding to my questionnaire, one-quarter said their family ate its main meal together every day of the week (or did before their kids left home). A third ate together five to six times a week, and one-fifth did three to four times a week or less (15% said they ate together once or twice a week, 24% three to four times). A 1986 Roper poll of 2004 families found that of those with children aged 7–17, some 63% said they ate dinner together on a regular basis, down from 72% ten years earlier. But such statistics hide more than they reveal. For they say nothing about the quality of the meal. "The family dinner is an idea that everyone likes," noted psychologist Michael Lewis, who is researching this topic for a book. "But it is often less than wonderful." One study found the average duration of family meals was twenty minutes. In some cases family members came and went during the meal. In 1988 Roper found that half of those polled watched television during dinner, up from a third in 1977. A 1989 Gallup poll found that of those who ate dinner at home weeknights, nearly 40% either watched television, studied, worked, or read as they ate. Only 36% said their evening meal included no such distractions. Barely a third said they found the evening meal to be a relaxing occasion which included conversation.

We should not exaggerate the loss here. Eating together as a family is a fairly modern innovation. The concept of the family meal as a semi-sacred gathering is little more than a century old in this country. But it's a good concept. We should be concerned about its loss; at least until something better takes its place. If we lose the habit of eating entire meals together at a more or less regular time and at a more or less reasonable pace, we'll forgo a basic opportunity to connect with people we care about.

One busy family of five in Fort Myers made a point of having a set time for dinner. Both parents and all three children were expected to be there. "Mealtime for us does serve as the time to talk together," explained Norman, a pharmacist, "see what's going on, argue sometimes. Except for the mealtimes we're sort of in different places. It's not hard to get our kids in tow for meals because we do have a set time for it. They're expected to be there. I think they enjoy that because they all like talking and letting us know what's happening in their lives."

I'll Listen Tomorrow

This report was the exception. Too many families, no matter how hard they try, simply do not have time to eat together in a relaxed way. The decline of mealtime is symptomatic of family life in general. No matter how often we repeat the "quality time" mantra, it's hard to take satisfaction in having so little relaxed time to spend with our children. It's easy to tell if we fall in this category. Just ask yourself how often as a parent you rely on messages such as:

"Not now."

"Maybe later."

"Some other time."

"Can't you see I'm busy?"

In his book, *Childhood's Future,* Richard Louv wrote that time is the element most lacking in contemporary child rearing. Louv's original title was *I'll Play with You Tomorrow.* This is what hundreds of children he interviewed said their parents told them repeatedly. In the course of his research Louv grew skeptical about the notion of quality time. This concept implies that something is being *accomplished* during limited, intense hits of parenting. Yet some of the most important moments in parenting occur when nothing in particular is getting done, when the pace slows down, and real communication becomes possible.

The most telling scene in the movie *Kramer vs. Kramer* is the one in which Dustin Hoffman testifies in family court that he's reduced his workload because raising a child requires so much time simply to "listen." With my older boy especially, I'm painfully aware that the things he has to say take time to get out of his mouth. When such thoughts do finally wander out, they're usually asides during more mundane conversations: a playmate who hurt his feelings, what he doesn't like about school, and what happens to your body after you die, anyway?

And we're parents with only two children. What of those who have more? "I've got four little kids," said a lawyer in New York who left a law firm for the legal department of a large corporation so he could spend more time with his family. "How am I going to give quality time to four kids in two hours? I realized that quality time for me means just forgetting whatever I thought I was going to do. I hear a lot of parents define quality time as, well, now it's eight on a Sunday morning, let's color, or let's read, or let's go to the park. As in, 'It's in my schedule to do that now.' What I realize is that when I'm home it's going to happen and I'm going to go along for the ride."

This is one reason that child rearing poses such a problem for time-locked parents. The tactics required for good parenting are the opposite of those recommended for effective time management. Those qualities that get us ahead in the business or professional world—efficiency, goal-directedness, the ability to work at a brisk pace—are the antithesis of those called for in successful parenting. The highest quality of time spent with children bears a close resemblance to time being "wasted." This could help explain why so many polls find working parents rate their job performance well above their family performance. One reason so many contemporary parents have so much trouble coping with family life is that this requires such a radically different tempo than the one at work.

Family time problems can't be solved in a vacuum. They reflect broader problems in society as a whole. Only when society begins to encourage new values and looser schedules will families be able to alter theirs in any comprehensive way. In the meantime, steps can be taken to get in a better relationship with time—by families and individuals alike.

The next five chapters will discuss some of these steps: ways to break timelock's grip on our lives. The emphasis of these chapters will be on developing a new *approach* to time altogether. Our need is not for yet another time management program. What we need is a new attitude toward time. Achieving this calls for looking at time values in a new light, learning to modulate life's tempo, to seek sanctuary from measured time, and, overall, to put the components of our lives in better balance. Before doing anything else, however, we must first step back from the fray to ask a basic question: "What do I really want from my time?"

Finding the Keys to Timelock

Zen and the Art of Time Management

Live as if you were to live forever; live as if you were to die tomorrow.
—ALGERIAN PROVERB

In twenty-five years' time David Robinson had worked his way up to the presidency of Florida's Edison Community College. Doing so typically called for getting to the office at seven in the morning and leaving at ten at night. On many nights Robinson then stayed up past midnight doing research. On weekends he attended church, taught Sunday school, and directed the choir. After a quarter century of that pace, Robinson suffered a massive heart attack. Technically he had died before medical personnel brought him back to life with CPR procedures. Later, two doctors stood at the foot of Robinson's hospital bed murmuring that if he made it through the next twelve hours, he'd live. Robinson heard. A clock stared at him from the wall in front of his bed. He focused on that clock, thinking, "Okay, twelve hours. I'm going to do it." Robinson ticked off each hour. When twelve of them had passed, he said to himself, "I'm going to live."

David Robinson did live, but was never the same. He didn't want to be. After recovering, the college president made drastic changes in the way he approached his life. The most basic changes weren't physical. He was a nonsmoker who didn't drink and kept his weight down. Rather, Robinson reviewed the way he'd been spending his time. All the nights he worked, the weekends, the doing two or three things at once, the difficulty paying attention to others, the many, many things he'd put off until later. "I can remember saying, 'I'm going to go skiing in another ten years,' " Robinson reflected two years after his heart attack. "Now time is something I don't take for granted. It's very precious to me. I know I don't have the length of time that most people have. I use every day very differently. I use what I call 'precious moments' in each day. I try to find in that day the reason

155

why I was able to live." This might mean stopping to chat with a student on campus. Perhaps lingering over a book he hadn't had time for before. Or eating crabs on the beach with his wife and friends on New Year's Eve. "We are given only this day, this year, and this life," is the way David Robinson described his new attitude toward time. "If we are going to do something we have always wanted to do, we must do it now."

Think of this as present time, time to be present. It's an approach to time one sees almost routinely among those who survive a brush with death. Their interest in the future declines (they realize there may not be one), while absorption in the present soars. Becoming aware that our days are numbered forces us to sniff for honeysuckle like a condemned prisoner whose next morning will be his last, or to listen for leaves hitting the ground with the acuity of a soldier on patrol. We're all about to die. Some get direct evidence, and alter their lives accordingly. They realize that fourth, third, or even second-priority activities consume too much precious time. At the same time this new perspective doesn't necessarily translate into a frantic effort to get everything done while there's still time. To the contrary. If anything, near-death survivors can end up feeling less pressure than before from the fact that seconds are ticking away. "Instead of making me feel that now there's a great urgency about what I must do with my life," said Senator Joseph Biden after surviving two aneurysms, "it had the exact opposite effect. I feel serene."

A 64-year-old cancer survivor named Marvin Barrett found it hard to be bored once he'd been given more life to live. "I could tolerate an extended wait in a doctor's office without a book, or a meandering conversation without fidgeting," noted Barrett. "By the same token, killing time ceased to exist as an option; the senseless switching of TV channels, the changing of tapes, the bleak turning of pages that leave no residue, all were things of the past. Nor was this a deprivation. The time was otherwise and purposefully filled, or perhaps not filled at all."

This response to a near-death experience is quite common. One hears the same message repeatedly from such survivors: Savor each moment of your day. Don't put anything off until tomorrow. There may not be a tomorrow. Yet this sense of urgency does not necessarily lead to a frenzied rush to "do things" while there's still time. Instead, it seems to be accompanied by a sense of serenity, a reluctance to get upset about minor annoyances, "little frets" as one World War II veteran called them. Best of all, so many near-death survivors tell us, nearly everything is minor. Except for life, health, and the people we care about.

There's an irony here. Many of us are racing through life for fear that we might miss something before dying. Yet those who have nearly died commonly lose interest in this race. Rather than attempting to beat death to the finish line, many near-death survivors slow to a saunter, content to stroll for the rest of the event, even to stop now and again if something interesting catches their eye. "You know the old cliche about not smelling the flowers?" said one. "Now I do smell the flowers. Now I'm much more conscious of enjoying things each day, whether it gets me someplace or not."

This is the way journalist Betty Rollin described her post-cancer life. Until she got breast cancer, Rollin put herself in the "frenzied" category. When giving a speech she'd take the last possible plane in and the first one out. The idea of lingering a second longer than necessary appalled her. This wasn't a bad life. "Before cancer," the writer-newscaster told me shortly after her second mastectomy, "I had a very exciting life, a full life. It just didn't have the *quality*. It wasn't even close.

"Like a lot of ambitious people," explained the svelte, dark-haired Rollin, "everything I did was on the way to something else. I was always in a hurry. I was much more *purpose* oriented; more conscious of where things got me." After losing first one, then the other breast to surgery, Rollin made a U-turn in her approach to time. She took an extended leave from TV broadcasting for the more relaxed pace of writing books (including *First You Cry,* about her first operation). When giving a speech she left time to linger before flying out. At home she made time for newfound interests such as cooking, eating meals with friends, and chatting on the phone. "I enjoy that," she said. "In the old days it would have been, 'Can't talk now. Gotta go!' "

This makes it sound as if Rollin was "slowing down," but to her this was only part of the story. "It has more to do with tempo," she explained. "Paying attention: 'Am I having a nice time? Is this where I want to be?' More than making sure every moment is fun, I'm trying to make sure that every moment has *meaning.*" Professionally Rollin found herself less concerned about where her career was headed. She didn't know, and didn't dwell on the issue. "I think about where I am and what I'm doing and whether I like it," Rollin once wrote. "The result is that these days I continually seem to be doing what I like. And probably I'm more successful than when I aimed to please."

This is why Betty Rollin called getting cancer both the worst and best thing that ever happened to her. The worst, obviously, because it almost killed her. "The best because the slight fear that it could all be over at any moment makes you live better."

Present Time/Time to Be Present

After completing a study of breast cancer patients, UCLA psychologist Shelley Taylor was startled to discover how many—well over half—said they were grateful for their life-threatening illness. Confronting death had made them more self-aware, better able to enjoy each moment of a day and to keep things in perspective. "I have no time for game playing anymore," said one. Explained another: "You take a long look at your life and realize that many of the things that you thought were important before are totally insignificant . . . you put things in perspective. You find out that things like relationships are really the most important things you have—the people you know and your family—everything else is just way down the line." Taylor was profoundly impressed by the changes many patients made to improve the quality of their remaining time. Some changes were dramatic. One woman, a bookkeeper, quit her job to pursue a lifelong dream of writing fiction. Others simply made more time for friends and family. "I think what cancer does is it shakes you up and it makes you decide what do you have in life, what is it worth being alive for?" observed Taylor. "And that's when you say, 'my kids, or my spouse, or my family.'"

The day Shelley Taylor was told for about the twentieth time how much a patient valued her children above all else she went out and bought a baby stroller. After fifteen years together, the psychologist and her architect husband had pretty much decided not to have kids. Now she was having serious second thoughts. Patients with families routinely told her that it took getting sick to make them realize that their children and husbands were the most important thing in their lives. "It was interesting to me that they put their children first," said Taylor, "because at the time I only had a husband." Getting the same report from so many subjects made the social scientist feel they couldn't all be wrong. "We've got to have one," she began telling her husband. Within a year they were the parents of a girl and two years later a boy. "They're so important to us," Taylor said of her children. "I just can't imagine not having them."

Shelley Taylor has tried to keep the overall "lessons" of her cancer study prominent in her own life, particularly in her attitude toward time. "It became a personal goal for me and the two women who worked with me to take away what all these women had learned from cancer," she said, "but without getting cancer." This hasn't been easy. "It's something you have to *force* yourself to do," she explained. "It's so easy to get swept up in the garbage."

With luck, most of us won't be facing death anytime soon. But like Shelley Taylor we can learn from those who have. In particular we can learn to take both a more reverent and a more serene attitude toward time. Hospice nurse Joy Ufema said the main thing she'd learned from dying patients was what so many of them told her: "Joy, make sure your life isn't full of things you *should have* done."

We all have a mental list of things we want to do "someday." This could include writing a novel, revisiting the old country, looking up old friends, or telling someone we care about them. Such tasks might be thought of as top priority. But they usually get pushed way down the list while we tend to lower priority errands, chores, and TV-watching. Only after some experience shakes us loose from our routines do we revise our lists and get busy doing the things we've always "meant" to do.

Without the dynamite blast of something like a brush with death, it can feel nearly impossible to break timelock's grip on our lives. Time pressures creep up on us. One task is added to another on our to-do list. Eventually we feel overwhelmed. One management consultant says that a common concept in his business is "TODLIF," short for "to-do-list frustration." This is the feeling one gets after working a long day only to find that one's list of things to do is longer than it was at the day's beginning. Our usual response is to try to reorganize existing activities more efficiently so that we can get them all done, perhaps with a bit of time left over for ourselves. We rarely succeed. Even the most effective time management techniques seldom succeed in breaking timelock's grip.

Why Time Can't Be Managed

"Time management" has nearly sacred status among the timelocked. Understandably. It holds the promise of finally, at last, once and for all giving us the tools to control our own time. Like so many, I pore over books on time management and devour articles on this topic, hungrily searching for the key to "getting organized." I have yet to find it. But how could I not be tempted by *Five Days to an Organized Life* ("Start on Monday—be organized by the weekend!")? Or *How to Get More Done in Less Time*? Time management tomes are like those on weight loss: each one rekindles the fantasy of finally getting it right. Just as it's tempting to assume that being overweight is a result of not having found the right diet, so is it hard to resist the thought that timelock is due to poor time management.

It's not. Conventional time management programs solve some problems but create others. Most such programs are built around a few basic strategies: (1) set goals, (2) make lists, (3) prioritize, (4) do top priority items first, (5) don't procrastinate. These programs seem to assume that we've never heard such suggestions before. But who hasn't? On my questionnaire I asked what tactics respondees had found most useful for organizing their time. With numbing regularity most responded, "Make lists; prioritize." Or, "Prioritize; make lists." Most of us know how we *ought* to be managing time. That's not the problem. Timelock persists and gets worse *despite* the fact that time management concepts are widespread. Some might say *because* of that fact.

With their emphasis on getting more done in less time, too many approaches to managing time are more part of the problem than of the solution. A book promising to add thirty minutes of productivity to each working hour suggested using computers, car phones, music imbedded with subliminal messages, and instructional tapes played at accelerated speed to do so. A magazine article called "High-Tech Cures for the Time Crunch" proposed electronic datebooks, portable phones, laptop computers, and sundry software as the best means to whip one's schedule into shape. "Tight plans and maximum use of time are key to building productivity," advised the article's author. Such an approach may or may not help you get more done in less time, but at what price? Most timelocked schedules need loosening, not tightening.

One veteran of fifteen years as a time management teacher left that calling when she noticed how enthusiastically participants started off, but how dispirited they nearly always ended up. Learning how to manage their time had not brought them the freedom and sense of control they craved. "Although we buy these packages hoping they will show us how to manage time," concluded Diana Hunt, in a book written with Pam Hait, "they can't. Instead of making us more sensitive to our own time-driven needs, they make us more aware of others' time demands. We think we're buying time, but we're getting structure."

The Unused Datebook

What conventional time management too often does is make us more clock-conscious than ever, more wedded to the notion that our schedules can be subdivided, re-organized, and minded like a schoolmarm. Such techniques seldom invite us to reflect, to question the categories themselves, and remain flexible enough to move as the future demands of us. After observing company heads at work, business professor Harvey Mintzberg found that most thrived in chaos, courted interruptions, and had an overall management style so ad hoc as to make a time manager sputter. Based on his own study of chief executives, Harvard's John Kotter concluded that one with a clear sense of purpose for himself and his organization could ignore time management principles and still be effective. "He might wander down the hall on his way to a meeting and never make it to the meeting," observed Kotter. "He gets diverted over here for two minutes, and then talks with someone else for five minutes, and then races across the hall to catch somebody else for another minute, and finally arrives at the scheduled meeting 20 minutes late. The time-management folks would gasp. But what's happening is this: As the stimuli pour at him all day long, his clear sense of where the company is trying to go enables him to be highly efficient in choosing what to react to and what to ignore."

Former ITT head Harold Geneen once complained that efficiency techniques put too much emphasis on terse, tightly organized meetings. "Which is more important," he asked, "to direct a meeting so that it ends on time or to run a meeting so that you don't kill off imagination or miss any opportunities that flash through the air?" Geneen conceded that the price one pays for this approach is that meetings often run late. Running late in general was one of his own shortcomings. But Geneen accepted this as a necessary price for allowing discussions to run their course rather than be cut off prematurely to meet predetermined schedules.

Time management programs are usually based on the premise that there is one best way for everyone to manage time. This is simply not true. To get a little New Age about it, time managers typically try to impose orderly left brain techniques on all kinds of people. For many, such techniques are too out of synch with their inner rhythms. "I took one of those [time management] courses," said a Massachusetts bank head. "The problem is if you are a procrastinator, you never make a list. If you don't want to do something, you won't."

Procrastination, tardiness and disorganization are time management taboos. This is one reason these programs have such limited applicability. Prompt people are usually well organized already. Those who put things off will never be well organized no matter how many seminars they take and datebooks they buy. But this doesn't necessarily affect their ability to get a job done. "I'm a procrastinator," newsman Ted Koppel once admitted. "What can I say? My parents and teachers used to be exasperated by the fact that I would wait until the last minute, and now people are fascinated by it. I need the pressure."

Apparent disorganization can be integral to right brain creativity. At the end of every year America's office wastebaskets are littered with scheduling notebooks—some of them quite expensive—which have a lot of pencil scrawls during the first part of January, fewer toward the end of that month, a few jottings in early February, and none thereafter. Before she founded *Lear's* magazine, Frances Lear admitted that she bought at least three different datebooks a year, and never used any of them past February. Lawyer-literary agent Morton Janklow called himself "the world's leading scrap-paper-note maker. I've had people give me gold memo pads, alligator memo pads, Filofax systems, ermined pads, everything you can think of. I wind up with torn pieces of matchbook covers, paper napkins usually unintelligibly written on while I'm walking down the street."

There is little correlation between the ability to manage time in conventional ways and the ability to manage in general. So-called peak performers are those who can keep the big picture in view, administer others, and delegate work effectively. Being hurried and harried is antithetical to such qualities. I'm continually struck by how relaxed the top people in organizations seem to be. Partly this is because they can afford to be relaxed. They've made it. But even more important is the fact that so many learned early how to husband their energies and get others to work for them so they could step back and get the big picture. As writer Barbara Ehrenreich once observed, genuinely successful people "are not, on the whole, the kind of people who keep glancing shiftily at their watches or making small lists entitled 'To Do.' On the contrary, many of these people appear to be in a daze . . . These truly successful people are childlike, easily distractible, fey sorts, whose usual demeanor resembles that of a recently-fed hobo on a warm evening."

Don't Just Do Something

There are two basic approaches to coming to terms with time. The more prevalent one—the don't-waste-a-minute school—emphasizes squeezing maximum productivity out of each second with better planning, list making, and high-tech tools. The less conventional, but more pertinent approach proposes just the opposite: reducing the volume of one's activities and becoming less concerned about time as such in an effort to better see the big picture, reflect regularly, and stay focused on what really matters. Think of this as the don't-just-do-something school.

What the first approach usually lacks (and best managers have) is a means to keep the *whole* in constant view. The closest most come is in the area of goal setting and prioritizing. But this is usually done in one-year time frames, or less. There is little time, or encouragement to sit back and get a picture of one's entire life, and that of one's organization—not just today, tomorrow, and next year but during the entire foreseeable future. Conventional time management programs teach ways to slot time but not how to continually reassess all slots. In the broadest sense, "What are we actually supposed to be doing?" is the best single time management question. It's been said that if the leaders of Western Union had ever asked themselves that question and realized the answer was *communication,* not telegram transmission, they might be today's AT&T.

None of this means that conventional time management techniques aren't useful. They are, especially at work. I've applied many such suggestions to my own working habits and found them helpful. But there is a limit to their relevance, and a point when the time-managed life becomes counterproductive. "Too often in our rush to achieve and stay on schedule, we experience clarity only after a situation has passed," noted Diana Hunt of the techniques she used to teach. As Hunt added, "Time management programs rarely invite time for introspection. Once we activate the system and plot our time plan, we're urged—in fact, expected—to move ahead according to the schedule. The schedule is all important."

In the Sacramento focus group, one couple described time management techniques they used in their family life. Jerry, who worked in state government, showed his wife and three children how to draw a clock for each day. This clock was to have necessary tasks penciled in: eating, school, work, sleep. What time was left—surprisingly little—then needed to be planned carefully for maximum benefit. "It's a good technique to manage discretionary time," concluded Jerry, "because you have discretionary time and non-discretionary time: the time you sleep, or spend at the office."

Michael, a hospital staff doctor, disagreed. He felt that work time was more discretionary than most people realized, or at least should be treated that way. Michael himself had found that sticking to a schedule made him come home grouchy and snap at his family. "I can either get through at the clinic at five and have an ulcer," he'd concluded, "or I can get finished at six and what the hell. I don't like to do what you're suggesting because when I can't meet the piece of pie, it bothers me."

This is the crux of the issue. It's not that we can't organize our time more efficiently, and perhaps "save" a few minutes here and there. But what price do we pay for doing so? And to what end are we saving time? "I have never yet talked to the man who wanted to save time," observed Will Rogers, "who could tell me what he was going to do with the time he saved." Saving time is of little use if the time saved goes for more of the same (as it usually does). What's the point? Time may be money, but it can't be banked. In theory the money supply is infinite. There are only 168 hours in every week. Once they're gone, they're gone. Any time manager who promises to "expand" our ration of time is playing with words. All such programs can do is show how to squeeze more activity into less time by sticking to schedules, doing several things at once and stepping up the pace. This may or may not improve productivity. It will certainly contribute to one's feeling of being tense, timelocked, and unable to get out from under.

Letty Cottin Pogrebin noted how frustrating it was that she—who tried to get so much out of every minute—never seemed to enjoy her time or use it effectively. By contrast her lawyer husband seemed to have no problem knocking off when his work was done to watch a ballgame or do the crossword puzzle. Time was not a problem for him. It was among her biggest. "Time is my addiction," she admitted. "But the older I get, the less there is and the faster it flies . . . I don't mind getting older, but I hate that time is waning, so I try to transform it into something that can be held and seen and kept. I try to live the present fully, to cherish time before it's gone. It's a losing battle."

The ongoing theme of this book has been that the harder we try to control time, the more time controls us. By the same token, once we stop trying to wrestle time to the ground, its grip on our throats eases. We may not "manage" our schedules better by getting on friendlier terms with time, but we no longer mind as much. Best of all we lose the feeling that time is our enemy. By being obsessed with mastering time we give it far too much prominence in our lives. The less attention we pay to time, the less we feel like its slave. Time is simply not as absolute, clear-cut, and unforgiving a taskmaster as we imagine it to be. Time is neutral; a blank canvas awaiting whatever picture we paint on it. Few of us are in a position to paint an all-new picture. It may not be possible to throw our lives over and flee to Tahiti. But it is possible to put time in better perspective where we are.

To free ourselves from timelock we first need to revise our attitudes to time so that we don't see it as an enemy in the first place. Forgo the delusion that measuring time in precise units and organizing those units efficiently will allow us to make time our servant. Stop trying to "conquer" time. Work with it. Become better friends with time.

"A Spaniard once said that time was a gentleman," wrote French executive Jean-Louis Servan-Schreiber. "Rather than do battle with it, I learned to get it on my side and win its support." To Servan-Schreiber this meant reviewing the day to come each morning, not just in terms of its necessary tasks, but to make sure that those tasks furthered his life as a whole. "Becoming a friend of time," he wrote, "means treating it like a friend by devoting some time to it."

A businessman in Dallas said that the first time he blocks out on any new calendar is time for himself. That entry becomes inviolate, "gospel time that you don't tread on for anything." He thought that this technique was especially necessary for the self-employed who are so susceptible to trying to squeeze more income out of every hour. A San Diego business owner agreed. She and her husband always put time for each other on their calendars "because otherwise it gets invaded by all kinds of other stuff. If we don't set the time aside it disappears on us." Doing this may sound contrived. But for many, scheduling time for themselves is the only way to get any. Servan-Schreiber—who makes regular "appointments with myself" (sometimes just to reflect)—pointed out that if we only put time with others on our calendars, that gives them *de facto* priority in our lives and claims on our time. This is one reason we come to see time as our enemy; we give too much of it away to intruders and lose track of our own needs in the process. Staying current with ourselves calls for scheduling personal time as concretely as a dental appointment. By doing this we can make time's face begin to appear less hostile.

At the outset of this book I noted that few of us have a comfortable relationship with time. As so many near-death survivors discover, this doesn't have to be the case. Changing that relationship is possible. But it requires some fundamental changes in the way we perceive and deal with time. A key tactic of the don't-just-do-something school is to have clients face the prospect of their own demise. This takes different forms. Stephanie Culp, a professional "organizer" in Los Angeles, asks clients to consider what they want mourners to be saying at their funeral. (One woman's answer: "I don't want my children to say, 'My mother was a wonderful businesswoman.' ") An alternative is to envision one's own tombstone, and what might be written there. Meyer Friedman has clients regularly write and review their own obituaries. Doing so can be a bit of a shock. Alfred Nobel once read an obituary of himself written in error. This experience forced dynamite's inventor to consider how much of his life had been devoted to perfecting tools of destruction. He then decided to devote the rest of his life to giving prizes for peace and other contributions to mankind.

One of the best books about time remains Alan Lakein's *How to Get Control of Your Time and Your Life.* Lakein has mercifully little to say about technique. His emphasis is on considering the type of life one wants to lead. The key to Lakein's approach is regularly asking oneself not just "Is this what I should be doing with my time," but "Is this what I should be doing with my *life?*" One of the most basic questions one can ask in getting out from under timelock (as Lakein emphasizes) is, "What would you be doing if you only had six months to live?" Ask yourself that question, then compare the answer with your current life. Those who filled out questionnaires did so. Their answers were revealing. With half a year remaining, the most common preference was to spend time with family, look up old friends, travel, read, and write. Very few were already doing these things. Asked how their actual lives compared to their six-months-to-live scenario, comments included, "It is far from it," "Totally opposite," "Zilch," and "Ha!" Some explanations were, "Spend too much of my life trying to succeed," and "Too busy living for tomorrow."

The futile hope underlying self-imposed time pressure is that by living it fast and cramming it full we'll get more out of life. In fact we get less that way. Slowing down and uncluttering our lives not only allows us to better enjoy our time but to get more done. Why don't more of us do this? The most common explanation is that we can't afford to. When one suggests taking time to reflect, and to savor moments, the obvious response is: "Are you kidding? Get real! Who's got that kind of time?" That's exactly the point. Only by making time to step back can we spot the clutter in our lives. In the process we may come to realize how welcome a distraction that clutter can be. And how addictive it is to be rushed and busy. Thinking about such matters doesn't just take time; it takes courage. Bigger things in life are more frightening to deal with than smaller things. There's more at stake; more to lose. Yet another reason to keep our calendars filled with little tasks is that it's easier to get a grip on little tasks. Preoccupying ourselves with marginal activities is less threatening than tackling ones of consequence. Busyness can keep us from having to reflect, risk intimacy, or face the void. We haven't got the time.

Spending time on low-priority matters also reassures us that death isn't near. If it were, we wouldn't be putzing around running errands, would we? Energy and nerve are required to evaluate which of our tasks are absolutely necessary, and which ones are based on habit, old routines, and obsolete obligations. Without something like a brush with death we rarely get jolted out of such routines. We're never forced to ask ourselves what *really matters.* Living as if time was unlimited, we clutter our lives with trivia, important trivia often, but not tasks central to our existence. As near-death survivors can discover, facing time's end squarely rather than attempting to run around it is the single best way to get on a new footing with time. Until we do that, it's too easy to indulge the fantasy that we've got all the time in the world.

To a greater degree than we realize, time pressures come from within more than from without. How we respond to life's demands has as much to do with our attitudes as the demands themselves. This is not to suggest that timelock is "all in your head." It isn't. Today's time pressures are very real. We live in a time-tense society and must strike the best deal with that society that we can. One way of doing so is by considering our own investment in rush and busyness. Understanding the degree to which time attitudes are a product of values makes it possible to revise those values—individually and as a society—so that we can develop a more humane relationship with time. Sometimes the only way to do this is by stepping back from the fray.

BACK FROM THE FRAY

By the time he was 43, Allen Questrom had spent nearly two decades climbing the ladder of corporate retailing to run Rich's Department Store in Atlanta. Questrom was considered a likely choice to head Rich's parent company—Federated Department Stores. His next step should have been to a Federated vice-chairmanship. Instead, Questrom decided to take a few months off. He needed to step back, he explained, "to reflect about what I had done, what I had accomplished, strengths and weaknesses about myself, and what I wanted to do."

Questrom's peers didn't know what to make of this decision. Even though Allen Questrom was considered one of retailing's brightest lights, the general assumption was that his "sabbatical" was a polite cover for having been fired. How else could you make sense of someone just emptying his desk drawers and taking off?

Midway through his sabbatical Questrom and his wife, Kelli, were skiing in France. They struck up a conversation with another couple whose Boston accents were nearly as thick as his own. Later the two couples had dinner together. When the inevitable "What do you do?" question was raised, Questrom replied, "I'm taking a sabbatical from Federated." Several years of friendship later the other couple admitted to assuming that this meant he'd been fired. They'd felt a little sorry for him.

Questrom laughed as he described this episode from his time off five years earlier. After eight months of travel, clearing his mind of debris, wondering if he might like to try a different line of work, Questrom returned to Federated with a fresh outlook. He'd missed retailing. Department stores had fascinated Allen Questrom since he was a boy in Waltham, Massachusetts. He was eager to get back to them. At the same time, despite his success in managing department stores, the period away made Questrom realize how crucial he wasn't. "You put things in perspective," he explained. "Nothing you're doing is really *that* important. Realizing this takes a lot of the pressure off. You realize that you'll only be here a short time. So you have to operate on the basis of playing a game. Enjoy. But it isn't going to make that much difference. In the end you have to take account, as you might during the thirty seconds before a plane crashes, or on your death bed. That's the perspective I got from the experience.

"When I came back from the sabbatical, I was energized. I changed my style in that I wasn't as driven. I kind of relaxed, and looked at my work from a perspective of 'If I choose to do this, boy, I'd better be having fun at it or change careers.' "

Allen Questrom made these observations in his spacious, uncluttered office at Neiman-Marcus in downtown Dallas. After his sabbatical he'd run Bullock's for Federated in Los Angeles. Following a 1988 takeover by Robert Campeau he'd left that company, despite Campeau's strenuous efforts to keep him. Four months later he became head of the Neiman-Marcus Group.

A six-footer, trim, with full dark hair lightly streaked by gray, Questrom had an easy manner. During an hour-and-a-half conversation he didn't take calls, glance at his watch, or seem to be especially pressed for time while discussing the lasting impact of his sabbatical. Although it obviously didn't derail his career, this hadn't been clear at the time. Walking out of his office for the last time before his leave began, Questrom suffered acute anxiety. "Leaving at the peak of your career," he explained, "you're not sure if there will be a place for you when you get back." But Questrom had vowed to himself that after twenty years in the business he'd take a breather. Even on vacations, Questrom found, he could never quite clear his mind of work thoughts. He was always jotting mental lists of things to do when he got back. Questrom wanted an experience that would erase the blackboard completely. He got it. "The year off was like a vacuum," is the way he described it, "taking out a lot of debris."

The essence of Questrom's management style is to stay close to those working for him, delegate as many tasks as possible, and avoid getting so caught up in details that he loses sight of the broad picture. From this perspective taking time off was not an indulgence but integral to his management style. "When you're on a job too long you get myopic," he explained. "You get so caught up in details you lose track of what's important. By stepping back you get perspective."

"Perspective" is a word Questrom used often to describe the benefits of his sabbatical. "Centeredness" is another. "There's kind of a centeredness you get from doing something like that," he said. "I'm more focused. I spend more time with my wife. And when I do, I try to be totally there, not with my mind in a million different places."

Allen and Kelli Questrom had been married for seventeen years when they took off together. Questrom emphasized repeatedly how much it meant to their marriage to have nothing but time for each other for the better part of a year. "My wife and I really developed a second dimension in our relationship," he said. "It had been good, but now we were spending time together, twenty years later in our lives. We got to know each other at a different time in our lives. People change, they grow apart, in their interests, their goals. This gave us time away from the day-to-day. To travel together, think together, talk together over a glass of wine at the dinner table. Not thinking about what went on today. Only thinking about what's going on right then."

One of the more interesting results of Questrom's sabbatical was the many calls and letters he received from those who had heard about it. Their recurring message was some variation on "Gee, I wish I could do that," and, too often, "I wish I had the guts to do that." Questrom wished more people could have the experience he'd had, get focused, get centered, relax their working style, pay attention to their personal relationships, and realize that they may have it better than they thought. He was aware that the main reason more sabbaticals are not taken is family obligations. (He and Kelli have no children.) "The thing that stuck in my mind was the sadness expressed in some people's letters," he said, "that they wished they could do it, but just couldn't. And in some cases they couldn't because of their families. But I've since seen people who have taken their families and traveled, sold some of their possessions, chosen to be with their family for a year."

Questrom wondered how many of those who felt they couldn't afford to take time off might be victims of their own fears: fears of losing possessions, and of not being able to get back on track at work once they stepped off. "You have a certain power base in a job, and a lot of people feel uncomfortable giving that up," Questrom mused. "The crown passes smoothly, the in-box drops to zero. What would they say when people ask, 'What do you do?' They may fear they'll never get those opportunities again. But the truth of the matter is you *always* have those opportunities. Anything can be replaced, except your wife or kids."

Many have asked Questrom's advice on taking a sabbatical of their own. Those who felt at a career crossroads seemed especially hesitant to do so. " 'Well,' I say, 'Why don't you do it? Life is short. You've got to have career orientation, but your career can't be more important than your life. Career is part of your life, but it's not your life.' " As for possessions, "My feeling is that none of those things make any difference. Whether you have money, don't have money, a home, a car; who cares? People with a lot of money always want something else. They don't always appreciate what they have. Not that I always do. But we don't own boats and we don't own planes and we don't have any of those aspirations. That's not a big issue in my life. I got to the point in my life, I'm fairly well off, money is not a driving force. I never make decisions based on that."

This observation might seem a little disingenuous coming from a man who subsequently signed a $12-million contract to return to the combined Federated and Allied Stores and try to lead that company out of bankruptcy. Financial security certainly makes it easier to take time off. Or is it the other way around? Perhaps a willingness to risk financial loss by doing things like taking sabbaticals is what helps you make money in the first place.

Six months after he returned to Federated and Allied, one could hear echoes of Questrom's sabbatical experience in this observation to a reporter: "I could die tomorrow and the business would continue without me." This is not your typical chief executive's perspective. Would Questrom ever again take another perspective-renewing sabbatical? Absolutely, he said. "I don't know whether it will be five years, four years, three [this was before he signed a five-year Federated-Allied contract], but I'll complete another cycle in my life and maybe it won't be twenty years, maybe it will be ten years before I do it again. Because it was so rewarding that I have absolutely no fear of it.

"As you go through life things go by so fast you don't take time to appreciate the moment. People don't really appreciate what they have. Not that I always do. But I am able to stop. Take five. Whether a long sabbatical or five minutes."

12

Modulating Time

I do rest a lot more than people think. I continue at the right pace; I pace myself well.

—PLACIDO DOMINGO

Studies done at Michigan's Survey Research Center have found that frustrated subjects come disproportionately from two groups: the ones who always feel rushed, and those who have time on their hands. It's the middle group—those who sometimes feel rushed and sometimes have time to spare—who are most likely to be satisfied with their lives overall.

This says something about the best quality of time in our daily lives. It's not so much a question of whether our calendars are more or less filled, our tempo too fast or too slow, but that some sort of *cadence* be achieved. Without deadlines and time pressure, many of us can't function. At the same time, pace and pressure easily get out of hand. The ideal is somewhere in between, combining hectic periods with ones of respite in a satisfying rhythm.

Americans tend not to see much between killing time or filling it up with frantic activity. For most, the latter is more of a problem than the former. Cutting back is easy to talk about but hard to do. We hear a lot about the need to "smell the flowers." Well, okay. But when? Suppose we can't always spare the time? Suppose we're not in a position to slow our life's pace overall, and may not even want to? Smelling the flowers gets old fast. Time pressure has its uses. There is something to be said for full, fast-paced days (at least some of the time). Developing a better relationship with time is not so much a matter of coming to a screeching halt across the board but of *modulating* our time better. This means learning to vary its tempo on a regular basis. Making sure that fast times are balanced with slow times. That days on our calendar that are black with pencil scrawls are followed by ones with lots of white space. Pausing whenever possible. Wasting time. Putting clocks and watches in their place.

Lewis Mumford once said of time-pressed lives, "Though our first

171

reaction to the external pressure of time necessarily takes the form of the slow-down, the eventual effect of liberation will be to find the right measure and tempo for every human activity, and to introduce, at will, appropriate variations: in short, to keep time in life as we do in music, not by obeying the mechanical beat of the metronome—a device only for beginners—but by finding the appropriate tempos from passage to passage, modulating the pace according to human need and purpose." Left to their own devices, this is the way human beings normally manage time. Natural work cycles are discontinuous, flexible, elastic. Down periods alternate with up periods. Leisure is not a separate but an integral part of life. This approach is no longer possible for most of us, nor even necessarily desirable. But a more modulated schedule can be achieved. This takes conscious effort. Without counterweights, the pressure to go faster and be busier achieves a critical mass. In computer terms, speed is the default. Unless we take corrective measures, life will only get more hectic—inhumanly so. When daily life was more constrained by lack of money and technological prowess, this was not a problem. There were plenty of natural brakes around. As we've seen, one brake after another is disappearing. Technological progress will enable us to live increasingly fast-paced lives. But there is no need to do so just because we can. Making haste is not a moral obligation. Timelock isn't the price of admission to modernity. To cope we must reassess our notion of "progress" to make sure that it includes a healthy pace of life. Because limits to technology no longer modulate life's tempo naturally we must find ways to do so for ourselves: apply our own brakes, reduce time clutter, and moderate our pace. We can do this best by making sure that:

- our outer schedules don't get too out of synch with our inner rhythms
- we take as many opportunities as possible to work to the task, not to the clock
- our daily life includes pauses; we make time on a regular basis to shift gears or do nothing
- we have regular access to "hassle-free" zones where time and all of its paraphernalia can't intrude
- we reduce the presence of timekeepers in our lives
- we put brakes on the pace of technological advance by making sure that *in*convenience balances convenience

Synchronizing Outer and Inner Clocks

During a focus group in San Antonio, a retired church worker named Marge observed that time pressure was intense on her family's East Texas farm in the 1920s, but that it was very different from today's version. Then, the pressure ebbed and flowed. Winters were low-key, "a time of relative peace on the farm," said Marge. "But from the beginning of spring until the end of the harvest season, life was very pressured. It just wasn't constant."

Until quite recently, alternating periods of stress and ease were the normal human condition. On farms, planting was followed by waiting for crops to grow, the harvest by festivals and semihibernation. Fishermen or hunters alternated grueling periods spent chasing game with ones at home mending nets, fashioning spears, and recuperating. The year's tempo had a lot of variety. Work was done to the task, not the clock. To this day those who control their own time typically combine periods of hard work with ones of idleness. Peak performers have been found to rely on bursts of extended industry, followed by loafing, recuperation, and brainstorming before they take on a new task. This seems to reflect the organic, preclock pattern. Limitations imposed by darkness, weather, and primitive technology kept our sense of time in harmony with the tempo to which human organisms have adapted. Our internal clocks were set to nature's time long before mechanical ones were invented. During recent centuries external clocks have fought with internal ones. In much of the world external clocks have won in a rout. This is not likely to change any time soon. Nonetheless we can make our lives include more elements of organic time than most do at present.

Whenever possible it makes practical sense to work *with* inner time. We're all more alert at certain times of day than others. In terms of productivity one hour of prime time is worth several of nonprime. Most people's substantial daily output takes place in a relatively short period of time when their energy and ability to concentrate are at a peak. For me that period is from 8:30 A.M. to 1 P.M. I can work during other times of day, and do, but with nothing like my midmorning productivity. Obviously, working during peak periods alone is not possible for most of us. But by paying attention to our most productive times of day we can try to schedule around them, even try to negotiate regular periods at home or out of the office to take full advantage of peak periods. How many hours one does or doesn't work can be less important than synchronizing one's outer schedule with one's inner rhythms whenever possible. "Time management is looking at what type of person you are," Professor Robert Stokes of Villanova University has concluded. "A lot of it depends on your peak hours."

Charles Darwin wrote from eight to nine-thirty every morning, and again from ten-thirty until noon. Herbert Spencer worked three hours daily. John Maynard Keynes developed his most important economic theories during two-hour days. The leisurely approach of such noted figures is not widely known because they seldom advertised it. There is far more prestige in seeming harried and overworked than in being able to get a lot done in limited amounts of time. As a result, history's nonworkaholics have covered up their apparent indolence, sometimes in the most brazen way. "I have, all my life long, been lying till noon," Samuel Johnson once admitted. "Yet

I tell all young men, and tell them with great sincerity, that nobody who does not rise early will ever do any good."

Although he was history's greatest source of "early to bed, early to rise" type aphorisms, Benjamin Franklin himself liked to stay up late playing chess or chatting with friends. He whiled away hours tinkering with kites, bottles, keys, stoves. After introducing the first bathtub to this country in 1790, Franklin spent many hours inside his own, soaking and reading. Later in life he spent the first hour of every day sitting naked in his room with the windows open, enjoying what he called an "air bath." Although Franklin advised us to make productive use even of our leisure time, he himself took long, enjoyable tours of Europe. In this sense he was a fraud, far wiser in his actual approach to time than the one he proposed for the rest of us. We've taken Franklin's advice when we should have followed his example.

Churchill's Choice

Many of history's most effective leaders have had remarkably unorthodox schedules. Although he worked long, hard hours when necessary, Winston Churchill was famous for his eccentric work habits. "Like most men of affairs, he had learned to use his time efficiently . . ." wrote biographer William Manchester. "But he was not what today would be called a workaholic." During most of his political career Churchill took frequent, leisurely baths (". . . it is extraordinary how many crises found him soaking," noted Manchester). Throughout his life he made time to attend horse races, hunt boar, paint pictures, and travel abroad. His family always had priority on Churchill's schedule. And, after picking up the habit in Cuba while covering an 1895 insurrection, Churchill routinely took a daily siesta. Even at the peak of World War II, Churchill insisted on a midafternoon nap. "I regretted having to send myself to bed like a child every afternoon," he later wrote, "but I was rewarded by being able to work through the night until two or even later . . ."

Like Churchill, Anwar Sadat—who developed a habit of contemplation during extended terms in prison—was a renowned nonworkaholic who would sometimes nap for three hours after lunch. Lyndon Johnson napped too, going so far as to pull on pajamas every afternoon at four to "fool the body." History's other nappers included Napoleon, Chou En-lai, Harry Truman, and Thomas Edison. Ronald Reagan was rumored to be a napper, but his aides zealously guarded information on this subject for fear of adding to his reputation for being less than alert. Malcolm Forbes napped on his office couch after lunch, but only after giving his secretary strict instructions to tell anyone who wanted to know that he was "in conference."

Naps have a bad odor in this society. Any adult of good character who lives north of the equator is not supposed to need such an indulgence.

Instead, many of us have perfected the art of "resting our eyes." We learn to doze without being obvious about it. This takes various forms: in a high-back office chair turned to a wall; leaning back, feet on desk, hands in prayerful position as if deep in thought; or (Ronald Reagan's method) by dropping our heads as though deep in thought, then rolling our eyes upward when awakening to suggest they were lowered deliberately.

The struggle to stay awake goes on in most offices throughout the afternoon. General George Marshall once observed that nobody ever had a good idea after 3:00 P.M. Industrial accidents are most likely to occur between 2 and 5 P.M. This is also the period when most errors are made in offices by workers battling to stay alert. Eventually they "win" that battle and resume productive work—about when quitting time nears.

Researchers have found a nearly universal tendency to get sleepy in the early afternoon, regardless of how much sleep one had the night before, or what one ate for lunch. Left to their own devices, subjects in sleep laboratories typically sleep for an extended period at night, then for another hour or two about twelve hours after the mid-period of sleep the night before. Sleep experts now take it for granted that our body clocks are set to nap in the afternoon. Even a brief siesta after lunch is the best single thing one can do to make productive use of the rest of the day. Among sleep researchers there is a near-consensus that naps increase alertness, raise energy levels, and improve mood. So far this finding has been virtually ignored in the world of work. Research is being conducted on the advisability of allowing pilots to take preplanned naps in the cockpit during long flights. Sleep experts foresee such "napping protocols" as an important part of future work routines. In time, perhaps nap breaks will become as common as coffee breaks. They're certainly better for you.

Productive Time Wasting

In the town where I lived for ten years, we had frequent power failures. My reactions to them usually followed a predictable pattern. First came irritation. Damn! Now I won't be able to finish this: piece I'm writing/show I'm watching/reading I'm doing (or all three at once). After I'd scrounged up some candles and given up on getting anything "done" for the duration, I found myself relaxing. At best I'd try to read a book with big type by candlelight. After a while it would occur to me that all background noise had ceased: the refrigerator, air conditioners, and the buzz of a nearby electrical transformer. Tension in my body began to ease. Sometimes I'd stop struggling to read and just lie there and think. Fresh ideas crept into my head. By the time the power came back on, I was usually disappointed.

Others have similar reactions to blackouts, snow days, and sundry natural disasters. Such experiences are a reminder both of how much we

resist "down" time, and how rejuvenating such time can be. Knocking off
on a regular basis is among the most difficult but important time-modulating
skills. The greater our need to take a break, the harder it can be to take
one. Yet there is no better way to get inner clocks in better harmony with
outer ones. In this sense the best single thing one can do to modulate one's
time is nothing at all. Thomas Carlyle, the Scottish historian, used to sit in
perfect silence for half an hour a day. Of his own personal habits, Alan
Lakein noted, "I relax and 'do nothing' rather frequently."

This is easier said than done, Lakein conceded, for compulsively busy
people in particular. One client of his, an aerospace engineer, filled every
second—including weekends—with frenzied activity. This man even made
love with his girlfriend at prescheduled times. Only after Lakein forced him
to sit still and simply muse did the engineer begin to realize his own
emotional investment in staying on the go and making sure he had no time
to reflect. In time he learned to relax, do less, and get greater enjoyment
out of a smaller volume of activities. "When I saw him about three years
later," reported Lakein, "he still had as busy a schedule as ever, but he was
able to balance that activity with relaxing so that he came back to work
Monday morning not pooped out from a strenuous weekend but refreshed."

Stress counselors find that the hardest (but most important) challenge
for many Type A clients is learning how to knock off. Because their sense
of self-worth is so tied to their accomplishments, doing nothing can make
them feel like nothing. In Del Mar, California, stress counselor Lisa Marraro
has tried to get clients not to base their lives on productive activity alone.
This isn't easy. Even taking the time to walk on the beach can be hard for
such clients. "Most people know how to *do* very well," explained Marraro,
"but they don't know how *not* to do. Not doing is essential."

In one case a businesswoman named Mary came to Marraro for treatment of bleeding gums. Her dentist suspected that this was a symptom of
stress. Mary proved to be a classic Type A personality. Her words poured
out in a torrent as she nodded her head and continually sucked in air. Mary
described herself as a hard-driving person who always walked fast and
gulped her food. When eating out with others she'd get impatient and angry
if they lingered too long over their meals. Mary tried to maximize her use
of time by balancing her checkbook while standing in line at the bank and
flipping through magazines at the supermarket checkout. With a variety of
stress-reducing exercises, Marraro helped her client learn to talk less and
listen more. She discouraged Mary from trying to do two things at once.
Marraro advised her to take walks along the beach. Mary did, and was
surprised by the number of work-related ideas she got in those strolls. Her
ability to concentrate improved. Best of all, her gums stopped bleeding.

Allowing ourselves to take five without feeling that we're "wasting
time" is problematic for Americans. We must fight nearly three centuries

of history to do so. Our Puritan ancestors, after all, passed laws against idleness. Doing nothing well, wasting time productively, is a difficult art for us to master. "Americans do not need drink to inspire them to do anything," G. K. Chesterton once observed, "though they do, sometimes . . . need a little for the deeper and more delicate purpose of teaching them to do nothing." At Stanford University, a group of women professors were once asked to sit quietly in a room for twenty-five minutes. Some of them found the experience so unnerving that they left before the time was up. Because he found it so hard to get his own clients to relax, Larry Dossey resorted to biofeedback. Buttons, numbers, and readouts got the job done for time-stressed clients who could not unwind any other way. In time some learned how to relax without a readout. Then they would come back to Dossey and say, "Doc, you old fox. That biofeedback machine wasn't necessary at all, was it?" It wasn't. But it got the job done.

Dossey thinks that one of the most effective remedies for the various forms of time sickness is to be quiet and unoccupied on a regular basis. Among other things this makes it possible to pay attention to important messages one's body is trying to convey, but can't get through the hubbub. (Type As are notorious for ignoring what their bodies are trying to tell them.) But physical health is only one of the rewards for regular indolence. "Most of us could be more productive if we allow ourselves to do nothing from time to time," said Robert Levine. "It's like the value of an 'incubator period.' When you're working on a problem, going to sleep can be more valuable than sticking to it. Sometimes the best way to tackle something is to stop doing it."

Such an approach is hard for many because it apparently "wastes time." But what do we mean by "waste"? Who's to judge? And how can we know in advance which periods of time will be wasted, which put to productive use? Some of the best time one spends can appear useless. Scientists, artists, and creative people of all kinds routinely devote long hours to idling about as ideas slowly germinate. James Michener has always said that the foundation for his success as a novelist was laid in the years he spent floundering before starting to write at age 40. As Michener put it: "It may well be that the years observers describe as 'wasted' will prove to have been the most productive of insights which will keep you going."

Pauses That Refresh

Because modern technology has eliminated so many of life's natural pauses, it is necessary to seek them out, even create some. This is the psychic equivalent of taking vitamins to replace those processed out of our food. The most obvious way to pause is simply to stop whatever one is doing on a regular basis (an executive told me he did this for five minutes of every hour). "I have found," wrote one woman on her questionnaire, "that just a few moments of quiet introspection keeps things in perspective: what is important, what can wait." Before our own evening meal we hold hands in silence for a few seconds, just to slow down, catch our breaths, reconnect. It's remarkable how effective those few seconds can be in improving our ability to pay attention to one another.

One way to create positive interludes in the course of a day is by fashioning them from trash time. We can't control most of life's nagging delays; we can control our response to them. With a simple change of perspective, standing in line, waiting for a delayed flight, even being stuck in traffic can be regarded as "found time." As Richard Collins discovered, line-waiting can be an excellent opportunity to mull over important issues in your life. "I really think that being forced to wait on line is not a curse," said a lawyer in Providence. "That's when I think ahead. Think about the big things in my life, the big decisions. Also the little ones."

As a sort of hobby I collect examples of useful ideas people have come up with while alone in cars, usually while stuck in traffic. Among them are:

- Wayne Dyer thought through the lectures which became his book *Your Erroneous Zones* during traffic james in Detroit.
- Singer-songwriter Larry Gatlin said one of his best country songs was mentally composed during a Los Angeles traffic jam.
- On LA's Ventura Freeway, producer Joe Roth mapped out a plan to form his own film company. This company produced the hit movie *Major League* in 1989.
- Goldie Hawn's partner Nancy Meyers was driving and daydreaming when she got the idea for a film about a woman who joins the Army after her life falls apart. This daydream eventually became the hit film *Private Benjamin.*

Hassle-Free Zones

One of the great attractions of driving has always been that cars were a setting where no one could reach you. The phone never rang when you were behind the wheel. No one could knock on the door and tell you to hurry up. As a result lots of good musing, planning, thinking, or even creative work has been done in cars. Gertrude Stein found inspiration in the sounds of her Ford's gears crunching, its motor revving, and its windshield wipers swishing across wet glass. William Carlos Williams composed poetry as he drove from one patient to another in his career as a doctor. Suppose Williams had been born half a century later and been equipped with a beeper and cellular phone? What if he had been an up-to-the-minute Californian with a phone, computer, modem, printer, and fax machine at his side while driving? Would technology's gain have been poetry's loss?

Many think stocking their cars with high-tech paraphernalia converts down time into up time. This is the cutting edge of never-out-of-touchness. But once life is stripped of locations where we can't be reached, where will daydreaming get done? Creative musing takes place best in settings where we're inaccessible. Arnold Toynbee was inspired to write *A Study of History* while riding on the Orient Express westward from Istanbul. Peter Benchley thought through his novel *The Island* while reclining in a dentist's chair. When Oliver Evans was confined to bed after cutting his leg with a scythe in 1777, he developed the idea for a carding machine that revolutionized the textile industry. Long prison terms inspired major works of literature by Thucydides, Dante, Machiavelli, Lenin, and Nehru, among others. (If they knew what a splendid opportunity they were giving them to scheme, repressive regimes might think twice before imprisoning revolutionaries and removing them from the ringing phones and crying children of everyday life.)

One needn't spend time in prison, a hospital, or a car stuck in traffic to enter a hassle-free zone. Any decent library will do. Or chapel. Or hotel lobby. Or restaurant between meals. I sometimes wander into empty offices of bureaucracies or classrooms at a college in search of isolation. Anywhere that one can't be "reached" qualifies as a hassle-free zone. Taking a walk is a mobile version; also riding a bike, or a horse (the last forms of transportation not susceptible to never-out-of-touchness, so far). Even though some train cars are now equipped with cellular phones, they remain among the best of hassle-free zones. Within a half hour of settling down in a train seat I usually find my pad filled with dozens of scrawled notes. Here I can focus, concentrate. It's not just that the phone isn't ringing, but that one *knows* the phone won't be ringing. During a trip by train, it's possible to let your mind roam. It helps that there are no clocks on the wall. If I can resist the temptation to look at my watch, a train ride can feel virtually time-free.

Going Watchless

At one time Larry Dossey assumed that of all his doctor's tools, his watch was the most indispensable. But when his watch broke a few years ago, Dossey decided to test that hypothesis by not getting it fixed. "To my surprise," he found, "I hardly missed it. The most noticeable difference was the pleasant sensation of the missing weight on my wrist." Timekeepers were all about anyway: in his car, on hospitals' walls, at patients' bedsides. (Most patients not only wore watches but brought clocks to the hospital.) Dossey also discovered that it wasn't necessary to know the time as often as he'd thought it was. At night and on weekends it was even possible to live by nature's rhythms.

One effective way to modulate time is by not wearing a watch whenever possible. Create "watch-free days," or parts of days. Get in the habit of checking the time only when absolutely necessary. It's surprising how seldom that actually is. The more opportunities we have to ignore outer clocks, the better we can live by inner ones. "I do NOT wear a watch to social occasions," reported novelist Jonellen Heckler. "It interferes with 'natural time.' There is a natural end to a conversation or to the evening. I don't want to disrupt this flow."

For the past few years I've tried to wear a wristwatch only on an "as needed" basis. A few years ago I did buy a little key chain watch. This is always there if I need to know the time. Because it is a bit of a nuisance to pull out and check, however, I seldom do so. The fact that my key chain watch also doesn't keep very good time is a minor inconvenience. A general sense of the time is all we usually need anyway.

Watches weigh our wrists down with the time. They interrupt activities more often than is necessary. Timepieces encourage an unhealthy dependency: an addiction to knowing what time it is. Only after going watchless for a while do we realize how habitually—and unnecessarily—we "check the time." In a study of time-telling ability, one psychologist was impressed that those subjects who did not wear watches had a remarkably accurate sense of time. An eighteenth-century Chinese emperor once observed that the members of his court least likely to miss meetings were the ones who didn't own clocks.

Going watchless or semi-watchless does not necessarily make one less responsible about time. The opposite can be true. After eleven years without a timepiece on his person, one lawyer in New York found himself not only more relaxed but more punctual. "When I had a watch, I'd try to cut everything to the minute," he explained. "Now I try to work within blocks of time. I round off fifteen minutes or half an hour and give myself ample time to get somewhere, and I'm rarely late." Another New Yorker, a business owner, had a naked wrist for two weeks while his watch was being repaired. Rather than use a loaner he decided to do without. At first this led him to pester his secretary throughout the day for the time. But this grew less and less necessary over the two weeks, partly because he realized how seldom he actually needed to know what time it was, partly because his inner sense of time grew more accurate. In the process the businessman grew more aware of why he wore a watch in the first place. It wasn't just for the convenience of knowing what time it was but for the immediate gratification of finding out. Glancing at his watch gave him tangible, precise information throughout the day. It enabled him to squeeze more tasks into his schedule. It also made him tense. Going without a watch was relaxing. "I enjoyed it enormously," he concluded. "The novelty, the excitement."

Rather than a nuisance, not wearing a watch can be a challenge. Having to figure out how to keep track of the time adds a little element of risk, a bit of adventure into otherwise ordinary days. Some of the watchless develop elaborate mental maps of public clocks. Others enjoy taking the opportunity to ask strangers for the time. Most become deft at surreptitiously reading other people's watches. Perhaps the most creative approach of all is to learn how to time activities by means other than timepieces. One woman, for example, rediscovered that a perfect soft-boiled egg could be cooked in the time it took her to recite three Hail Marys.

Slow Tech

Balloon-tire bicycles have made a comeback in recent years. Many of their fans are tired of speeding about on anorexic racing bikes. They want to re-experience the casual ride of their childhoods. "It does make you slow down and relax more," said the owner of a vintage Schwinn. "It makes you feel like a kid."

There's something to be said for devices that *aren't* state-of-the-technological-art, that *don't* allow us to go as fast as we please. The tempo scale is so weighted toward pace and pressure that we must create counterpressures. Just as we looked for ways to speed life up in earlier epochs, now we must find ways to slow it down. When it comes to time modulation, brakes are every bit as important as accelerators. The photocopier I now own is 50% slower and twice as relaxed as the one I used to own. Its tempo is closer to mine. My word processor includes a thesaurus that I've never used because I like having to turn away from my computer's screen to pull *Roget's* off the shelf. Doing this requires stretching different muscles and refocusing my eyes. It syncopates the rhythm of my day.

Others have gone even further in turning their backs on state-of-the-art technology to temper the pace of their lives. One author was forced back to her 1936 Smith-Corona typewriter by the breakdown of her word processor. She found that she welcomed the change. "Naturally I'm forced to write more slowly," noted Nancy Willard. "But this has its advantages. When you write slowly, you give the odd associations that hang around the edges of a scene their due. It's like zipping through the countryside in a limousine that suddenly breaks down. I have to get out and walk, and that's when I discover the chicory, the wild grapevine, and the ten different species of wild grasses."

Hunter College English professor Nick Lyons gave this explanation for his continued use of an old Underwood: "I love the machine. I love the sound it makes, the precise speed at which the keys move, a speed to which I've become accustomed; I like its responsiveness to my touch, even the pain it breeds in my shoulder when I've typed for too many hours, which tells me something. I like to correct my words by hand and even to retype a page, whereby I sometimes find more to correct. I like to feel the sensation of typing; I like to know, acutely, that I've put physical work into what I've written. The few words I have to say publicly, or letters to friends, require less speed, not more."

Some writers, including John Barth and Anne Tyler, find that even typewriters are too fast for their composing rhythm. They use fountain pens. Novelist Rumer Godden once went so far as to lament the decline of the quill pen that regularly forced users to "pause to sharpen and shape it, which gave time for thought; most of us know how doing something with our hands releases thought. (It is said that one poet whittled away his whole quill because he was so deep in thought.) Then we had dip pens; at least we had to dip, change nibs. Then came fountain pens which had to be filled; then, of course, typewriters . . . and [now] some authors use computers. They save time and trouble, which is true, but a book *needs* time and trouble . . ."

Even though it's slower and less efficient, I often use a pen to transcribe interviews or to write first drafts. Writing by hand gives me an opportunity to exercise different muscles of my wrist, perhaps even of my brain. Using a pen slows the pace of my writing and thought processes, I hope for the better. It's also more relaxed to write this way. Among other things, pens create no noise. They can be used in many positions, even lying down. Their product looks more personal. Letter writing especially seems more intimate when done by hand. Doing so is one more way to *modulate,* to vary the pace on many levels, and to keep personal tasks from becoming too much like ones at work.

The point is not to eschew conveniences that reduce drudgery and speed the completion of tasks but to make sure such devices don't control the pace of our lives. "The solution to living well lies not in new and better technology," suggested psychologist Bruce Baldwin, "but in the selective disuse of it so that life can be enjoyed in a more emotionally fulfilling way."

High Touch

The owner of Fante's, Philadelphia's most complete source of gourmet cookware, is a low-tech cook herself. A visitor to the kitchen of Mariella Giovanucci-Esposito, 36, found it equipped with few modern conveniences. A microwave oven, automatic coffeemaker and seldom-used blender were the only concessions to gadgetry. (Giovanucci-Esposito also owned a toaster and a Juice-O-Mat that she'd picked up at a flea market.) A food processor was still in its box, unused. An electric can opener that she got as a wedding present had long since been returned to the store. The machine Giovanucci-Esposito used to make pasta for her husband and two girls had to be cranked by hand. On weekends the couple often entertained, preparing meals for up to twenty-five guests with a limited arsenal of hand tools—plastic spatulas, garlic press, vegetable peeler, hand can opener, potato scrubbing brush, corkscrew—that were stuffed into two drawers.

A case can be made for *not* using technological marvels that may or may not speed the completion of mundane tasks. "I for one wish I had not bought a food processor," noted *Megatrends* author John Naisbitt. "I use it infrequently, preferring the high touch of chopping foods by hand, even though it takes longer." After setup and cleanup are factored in, even that isn't clear. "We have a food processor that never comes out of the cupboard," reported a Sacramento doctor. "The amount of time it takes to clean the thing after you chop two carrots just isn't worth it. Get out a knife."

We tend to be so dazzled by high technology and its promise of ease that we can't always compare it objectively to low-tech counterparts. Good examples of the latter are not only cheaper but in some cases less time consuming. Low-tech tools also tend to be more relaxing to use: quieter, slower, dependent on small muscles that we don't use often enough. They're an important means to modulate our pace.

Chef Pierre Franey once called the swivel-action vegetable peeler one of America's most ingenious contributions to gastronomy. Franey also liked a two-wheel hand pastry cutter. Other low-tech kitchen devices which have inspired rhapsody include spin salad dryers, in-pot vegetable steamers, and hand graters, especially those that fit on top of a bowl or pot. "Simple, noiseless, all in one piece," is the way one enthusiast compared her Bluffton Rapid Slaw and Vegetable Cutter to a Cuisinart. She added that it was also easy to clean, and virtually indestructible.

The connection between use of "time-saving" conveniences and an accelerating pace of life is not obvious. But consider sociologist Donald Kraybill's report of his time among the Pennsylvania Amish. This Germanic sect severely limits its members' use of modern conveniences. They do so less on theological grounds than from a pragmatic interest in moderating the tempo of their lives. Although the Amish "may not enjoy all the conveniences of modern life," Kraybill discovered, "they are in control of their technology and intuitively grasp its long-term impact."

"Anyone stepping into Amish society suddenly feels time expand and relax," he reported. "The great irony here is that in Amish society, with fewer labor-saving devices and other technological shortcuts, there is less 'rushing around.' The perception of rushing seems to increase directly with the number of 'time-saving' devices . . ."

GOOD SHABBOS

Zalman Magid is a San Diego psychiatrist. In his practice he's used what he calls "time therapy" to improve the quality of patients' lives. Basically this involved getting them to balance their schedules better among work, leisure, and time to tend to health. Using relaxation techniques, he then tried to help patients make sure that time away from work was genuinely rejuvenating.

In his own life, Magid incorporated a somewhat different version of time therapy. Zalman Magid is an observant Jew. From sundown on Friday until sundown on Saturday he won't drive a car, answer a phone, boil an egg, or turn on a light switch. This is the period of *Shabbos,* or the Sabbath. In addition to attending services at a nearby synagogue, Magid reads, walks, and spends time with his family during this weekly interlude. He gave up playing violin in an orchestra because so many concerts took place during the Sabbath. His three children don't play on soccer teams for the same reason. They must miss favorite television shows during *Shabbos,* and any activities too far to walk to. These are sacrifices. But the payoff is substantial, said Magid. "From the outside, it's a pain in the neck," he admitted. "From the inside it's very different."

During the week, Magid explained in his suburban San Diego office, we're usually rushing here, rushing there. We get consumed by making a living, getting ahead, *doing* things. Little time is left over to *think.* Time seldom gets set aside just to *be,* not to *do. Shabbos* provides that time. "You go through the week," he explained, "this pressure, and that. This has to be done. That has to be done. Then clunk! On Friday at sundown the gate closes." Magid frequently finds he isn't ready to stop as the sun sets on Friday. The transition can be rocky. His faith calls on him to hit the brakes while his mind and body are still racing. By sundown on Saturday, however, he's invariably glad he did. "On the Sabbath," said Magid, "I walk down the street. I notice the grass, the flowers. I'm not rushed. When I'm walking on the Sabbath and I see all the cars whiz by, I say, 'You poor people.' People say to me that keeping the Sabbath is restrictive, a relic of the Dark Ages; it makes you a slave. But I'm free. Free from work, from shopping, doing business, even free from worry. The reality of worry may not change, but there's nothing I can do about it. The Sabbath gives a person a sense of control; the *person's* in control. From the Jewish point of view, God's in control. But *I'm* in control because I know what I'll be doing for that twenty-five hours. As a doctor, I usually feel in control. But if you really think you're in control, try getting stuck in traffic sometime."

From a psychological perspective, Magid found that this required weekly respite from modern technology played a significant stress-reducing role. "Everybody agrees that walking is healthier than driving," he pointed out. "You get in the car, you turn on the radio, you're distracted. When you walk, what do you do? You communicate. I remember taking walks with my own father on the Sabbath, having talks. It gave us a chance to iron things out. We had time. It wasn't just 'I only have five minutes before I have to go to this appointment.' I came to expect that time with him, as well as to read, to expand my horizons.

"I notice with my kids that they open up more on the Sabbath. It's like a little vacation. Not only a physical vacation, but a spiritual one. It's a chance for closeness. A chance to 'see the flowers' in a relationship. Sabbath is a family time. We discuss what went on during the week. We all know that whatever happens during the week, we have Sabbath to discuss things. This gives our life a structure, a stability. We know that every seven days at least we'll be together."

In his work with families, Magid said he'd seen too many parents giving their children ten minutes here, ten minutes there in the guise of "quality time." Some feel they'll spend time with the kids "later." Or they work hard, then spend time with their children on vacation. What children really need, he felt, is time on demand. "If they don't get it," said Magid, "they'll survive, but it's not optimal. As a psychiatrist I know that kids who get time with their parents turn out better.

"Life is getting so much more chaotic. We're constantly flooded with information. And you can't turn it off. Movies. Rock. Seven days a week; no relief. The Sabbath provides twenty-five hours of respite. It's wonderful for parents. In psychological terms, people are in such a rush that they don't have time for relationships. I recently had a discussion with the parents of five kids. Both of them are in a high-powered business (real estate), lots of demands, rushing here, rushing there. But when the Sabbath comes, they become a family unit."

Magid's report would have made less sense to me had I not spent a month in Israel three years before. Even in secular Haifa (where we stayed), life's tempo eased dramatically after sundown on Friday. Most stores were closed on Saturday. Bus service practically shut down. Entertainment was limited. The pace of life slowed to a crawl. One had little choice but to follow suit. Groceries could not be bought. No hardware store sold supplies for home repair projects. My reaction to this mandatory respite was similar to the one I had to power failures back home. At first I resented the coercion involved. Who were they to tell me how to spend my Saturday? But as the pace picked up again on Sunday, I wasn't always ready to get back in step. Israeli Saturdays were like weekly vacations, one day out of seven when the clock barely mattered.

13

Time Sanctuaries

Most men pursue pleasure with such breathless haste that they hurry past it.

—SØREN KIERKEGAARD

Lewis Mumford called the Jewish Sabbath "a social invention of the first magnitude." By requiring that one day a week be completely free of work, he wrote, Jews pioneered the notion of a "creative pause." Ideally the Sabbath is a day devoted to *being* rather than *doing;* a time in which to repair one's relationship with oneself, one's family, and God. In the words of Rabbi Abraham Heschel, it is "a sanctuary in time."

Whether religious or not, we all need such sanctuaries. Easing the grip of timelock calls for taking regular refuge from the pressure of time so that our minds, bodies, and spirits can heal. At best such periods of respite remove us from clock discipline altogether. The most effective time sanctuary returns us to a state in which the light of the day and state of our appetite are more useful time markers than the hands of a clock. A balanced time diet includes regular occasions that don't depend on timekeeping: daily periods when we ignore the clock, a weekly day or two off, an annual vacation and (if we're lucky) longer sabbaticals every decade or so.

Few achieve this ideal. If anything, our lives include fewer time-out periods than ever, especially among those of us who lead secular lives. Most religions require regular pauses for worship. Some also require strict abstinence from use of modern technology on a regular basis (Saturdays for Jews, every day for the Amish). Such requirements have the incidental effect of forcing believers to slow down. Whatever we've gained in freedom and flexibility by forgoing religious faith, we've lost in opportunities to pause, reflect, and reset our inner clocks.

Those of us who have chosen to lead modern lives shorn of religious faith have no less need for time sanctuaries than the devout. Few of us have found them. (These words are being written on a Sunday.) However one feels about God, faith, and strict observance, there is this to be said for old-time religion: It gave structure and predictability to a balanced diet of time. This was true not just in mandatory time-outs, but in forms of worship that transcended time. Larry Dossey thinks one of the great losses we've experienced by forsaking rituals of all kinds is the opportunity they provided to "annul time" on a regular basis.

Annulling Time

We all need regular opportunities to annul time, or at least to have a trial separation. Time away from time. One reason we have fewer and fewer opportunities to enjoy such "timeless" occasions is that we engage in fewer and fewer activities that require this degree of concentration. The essence of rejuvenating time-out is being so involved in an activity that we lose track of time. This could help explain Roper's surprising finding that executives were more likely than others to rely on hobbies to counter stress. (Well over half said they do.) Most hobbies provide an opportunity to work to the task rather than the clock. A Dallas executive described how he once spent an entire weekend building a stereo without going to bed. "I do better if I just stay with something and don't go to lunch, and maybe don't go to dinner," he explained. "I problem solve that way a lot. If I have a problem, I just sit down and don't worry about time and work on the problem."

Anulling time calls for paying undivided attention to a task at hand. Such an experience usually consists of intense, even strenuous activity during which "time stands still," or we "lose track of time." This could happen during worship or meditation; while reading a novel; or while watching a movie or play. Even playing video games can annul time. But it happens best, and is most rejuvenating, during activities with some form of resolution. Making love. Playing baseball. Playing chess. Painting a picture. Composing a poem. Playing a song. Climbing rocks.

During my earlier project on risk taking it became clear to me that one reason many people courted danger was to escape from time. By putting themselves on the line they achieved a degree of concentration so absolute as to virtually erase all awareness of time. From stand-up comics to race car drivers, such risk takers routinely reported entering a state during moments of peril in which they felt calm, focused, and virtually oblivious to time. A motorcycle racer told me that the faster he went, the slower time seemed to move. "In this sense it resembles a dream state," said one chess player of the near-trance he entered during tournaments.

Athletes call this "being in the zone." One of the main ways they know they're in the zone is that time feels infinite. It stretches out toward some unseen horizon. University of Chicago psychologist Mihalyi Csikszentmihalyi has termed this experience one of "flow." In the flow state, absorption in a task at hand is absolute. Time becomes irrelevant. According to Csikszentmihalyi, "freedom from the tyranny of time" is an integral part of flow activities. "When I start on a climb," one rock climber told the psychologist, "it is as if my memory input has been cut off. All I can remember is the last thirty seconds, and all I can think ahead is the next five minutes." Csikszentmihalyi noted of a typical rock climber, "In the flow experience, he loses track of time altogether. Later he may even feel that for the duration of his flowing he was lifted out of time entirely, disattached from internal and external clocks." Not just rock climbers, race car drivers, and professional athletes but chess players, artists, and performers of all kinds routinely entered this timeless zone in the midst of their activity. "When I'm playing piano, it's like I'm in a trance," said a young musician-athlete. "When I'm playing good hockey, it's the same thing."

We've all had occasions when we felt in the flow. A musician in San Diego said that when a concert went well, it seemed to end practically as soon as it started. For a Florida novelist, the test of a good day's writing was that she had no idea where the time went. When my own writing is going well, I lose track of time completely. (When it's going badly I check the clock constantly.) Based on a single fling at rock climbing I can report that when you're 50 feet up a sheer granite wall struggling to find a crack big enough to hold a fingernail, the last thing in the world you want to know is what time it is. In a more soothing way, spending a week rafting the Colorado River was an experience divorced from time. Partly this was because there was nothing to do but what we were doing: paddle. Partly it was because the fear of being swamped by rapids absorbed our attention. Time, in such cases, is beside the point. Sunup, high noon, and sundown are the only pertinent divisions of the day.

Annulling time does not depend on an activity being active or sedentary as much as its being schedule-free. Timeless occasions are ones in which natural markers of time—the position of the sun, the state of your appetite—are more useful than the hands of a clock. This time-free state used to characterize festivals and holidays. Today "festivals" take place at tourist sites, theme parks, or shopping malls—hardly settings that take us out of time. This is especially true as holidays approach. Thanksgiving, Christmas, and New Year's Eve have become nerve-wracking parodies of their former selves, punctuated by workshops on how to deal with "holiday stress." Occasions that used to annul time now drown us in their demands. As a result, we're prone to get wound up at times when we used to unwind. The reverie of a concert or play is now subject to the beeping of digital watches. (Couldn't they be collected at the door as guns once were in western saloons?) Watching clocked sporting events—basketball, football, hockey— reminds us that time is slipping away. Some basketball games now record the final minutes of a period in tenths of seconds, which whirl by on the television screen like a spinning top.

Watching television is, of course, our most popular way to spend spare time. No survey in recent years has found any other leisure activity that even comes close. The average American adult now consumes over thirty hours of television a week. The most common reason given for watching so much television is that it's relaxing. At the same time viewers report low satisfaction for this activity and consider it the first leisure pursuit they would give up if they had to. A major study of TV watching found that the longer viewers spent in front of a television, the more tense, restless, and irritable they felt afterward. An activity meant to be soothing had the opposite effect. A key reason is that television watching does not annul time. It does just the opposite. Television could be the most schedule-bound institution in our society. Its personnel are obsessed with seconds, even fractions of seconds. Their product has its own metronome beat: hours, half hours, and regular commercial breaks of precise duration. Frequent "news breaks" often feature a clock that shows life's minutes disappearing forever. If leisure involves time away from time, watching television has precious little.

The surest way to increase one's sense of leisure is to reduce television intake, if not eliminate it altogether. Other than throwing one's set out the window (as one neighbor did) there are ways to limit television watching. Owning a single set with a small screen and no remote is one way. Making it a little difficult to watch television encourages one to do so only when really motivated. This also discourages leaving the television on as background music, or an accompaniment to other activities. (One reason TV watching is unrelaxing is that we're prone to do something else while "watching" it, thereby reducing our ability to concentrate and annul time.)

Those who eliminate or cut back on their television consumption are usually amazed by the amount of time this seems to put at their disposal; the equivalent of three working days a week, one reformed TV addict reported. We recently gave up cable, eliminating in one fell swoop about 80% of the possible television we could watch (and most of the TV schedule to read). That alone seemed to fill our days with found time. In the absence of cable we're less prone to flip on the TV, just to "see what's on." With less to watch we watch less. Entire evenings go by with the television off. We read more. Sometimes we even talk.

The most creative approach involves competing with the television. One musical family in San Diego did this by becoming a family jazz band with rehearsals in the evening and dates on weekends. After noticing how much of their family's weekends were spent watching television, a Los Angeles mother and father bought a croquet set and some inexpensive prizes, then

created a family tournament. In time even the diehard TV watchers among
their children began to feel left out, turned it off, and joined the tournament.

Semi-Sabbaths

In secular times, it takes determination to keep one's weekend from
getting polluted with chores and obligations. "I try to honor the Sabbath,"
reported a San Diego businesswoman. "My husband and I go to church,
then we usually have lunch and I come home and take a nap and then we
have dinner. For the most part that's how we spend Sunday. I believe if you
can't get it done in six days, it's not going to get done in seven. And if I
work seven days in a row, the eighth day is usually the pits."

Such observance of at least a partial Sabbath was by far the exception.
More typical was a working woman who reported that her Sundays had
become "D-Days" or "do-it-all days," when she tried to reduce the volume
of tasks on her to-do list. A Hilton Hotels survey found that 90% of all
Americans now spend nearly half of their weekend working overtime or
doing chores. For many the weekend can be even more hectic than the work
week; the opposite of a time sanctuary. Two-career couples especially find
that weekend time is absolutely essential to catch on up chores and errands.
One mother of two observed that it's the working parent's secret shame
that Saturday and Sunday are usually the worst two days of their week.

Some salvage weekend time by making a conscious effort to limit errands, or at least to make them less onerous. For many short trips, bikes
or feet actually save time and trouble. But car driving is a hard habit to
break. Cars can make errands a little too easy to run. In the process our
weekends get cluttered with less than crucial travel. There is this to be said
for higher gas prices: They limit our driving by encouraging us to bunch
errands, do some on foot, or skip them altogether. "I'm paying attention
to the runs I make," reported a Los Angeles child care worker as gas prices
rose. "We tend to get lazy and go on five different errands in the course
of a day rather than planning our time usefully. I can get to the grocery store
just as fast by walking."

Some working parents can only keep their weekends from being polluted by doing as many errands and chores as possible during the week. One
mother set aside thirty minutes daily for this purpose. A particularly creative family made Friday "housecleaning night" in which everyone was
assigned tasks. At the end of the evening all gathered to make cookies or
go out for ice cream. This actually became a rather popular event, and freed
weekend time to spend with one another. Another family took the time they
saved by doing chores during the week to plan a family outing every Sunday
afternoon, no excuses. "Not only does this make it happen," explained the

mother, "but it relieves you of the emotional burden of worrying about it all weekend."

Such a calculated approach to salvaging weekend time is better than no approach at all. But it's still tied to the clock. When possible, the best approach of all involves putting on psychological blinders in the vicinity of clocks and watches during time away from work. It also helps to avoid activities that involve deadlines of any kind while cultivating an interest in ones that aren't timed. One of the great virtues of tennis, golf, and baseball compared to basketball, football, and hockey is that they are free of time. Once a baseball game is under way the clock plays no role whatsoever. In theory a single baseball game could be played forever. Chess, too, and cricket. A large part of the appeal, the suspense of such events, is that they take place out of time.

Some have made special efforts to involve themselves directly in timeless activities. This has something to do with the fact that croquet is enjoying a mini-revival. Quiltmaking is being taken up by some who want to take part in an activity that can't be rushed. An advertising man I know took up gliding for that very reason. And a Dallas air traffic manager devoted his weekends to raising cows because, unlike planes, these animals nearly always take their time.

Under ideal circumstances, at least part of our weekends would be reserved for such decelerating activities. Other parts would be devoted to much of nothing. One leisure expert recommended that a day a week be totally unplanned. This can be hard to pull off, due both to lack of time and lack of resolve. Unstructured time can be unnerving. If knowing the time is an anchor of our daily life, annulling time can make us feel adrift. Not having clocks to tell us when to do things can be anxiety-inducing. This is one reason that extended periods away from work are hard for many to deal with. Recalling the many lawyers he's known who either didn't take vacations or routinely cut them short, Supreme Court Chief Justice William Rehnquist once observed that "being a good vacationer takes practice . . ."

Getting Good at Leisure

Dialogue overheard at my dentist's:
Receptionist: Hello, Mrs. Simpson. You look tired.
Mrs. Simpson: Well, we just got back from vacation.

We tend to call free time "leisure time" as if they were synonymous. This is decidedly not so. Time *off* is not the same thing as time *out*. Genuine leisure takes skill, practice, and nerve. As sociologist Sebastian de Grazia has observed about the pursuit of genuine leisure, "Those who have the toughness or psychological security for it are not many."

A San Diego lawyer and mother who halved her working hours after the birth of a second child found that she had trouble taking advantage of her new free time. This lawyer took Tuesday afternoons off without the kids, but was finding that she didn't always know what to do with that time. "You could go see that art exhibit one more time," she explained, "but you happen to hate that type of art. So what do you do? Go shopping? No. You don't want to spend money. I don't have a hobby. So even though I bemoan the fact that there's no free time, I really don't know quite what to do with what I have."

Free time poses a problem for Americans. As a people we've never shown much aptitude for leisure. We're too restless, too work oriented. Even when not working we tend to feel we should be. "Leisure," said Benjamin Franklin, "is time for doing something useful." Heeding Franklin's advice, we crowd our free time—even our vacation time—with work brought from the office, correspondence to tend to, musical instruments to learn, "worthy" books to read. Very little of this happens, of course. But the evidence of deeds undone lies around making us feel guilty for our repose. A semiretired University of Illinois professor noted ironically that because he now had more "elective time," he'd taken on enough commitments to keep his newfound spare time from becoming too leisurely. The retiree wasn't writing the book he'd planned to write, but did feel guilty about not doing so. Therefore he had at least succeeded in preventing himself from enjoying his free time.

The problem of making sure that our lives include rejuvenating time out is both external and internal: external because society provides fewer and fewer sanctuaries from time; internal because we don't know how to take advantage of what sanctuaries are available. Psychiatrists note a "leisure neurosis," or "weekend blues" among patients who can't knock off and grow traumatized when they try. "The fear of free time and leisure . . . belongs to the great fears of our era," noted psychiatrist Joost Meerlo. That is why so many of us schedule our spare time so tightly. As one leisure-phobe admitted, "I protect myself against the unraveling of my ego by making my leisure time as harried as my working time."

Foreign visitors tend to be amused by our inability to relax. Weekends are still semi-sacred even in industrialized countries such as Germany and Denmark. Vacations of a month or more are guaranteed by law in most of western Europe. But 25% of all American workers get no paid vacation at all. The median paid vacation time in this country is 1.7 weeks. When they are polled about whether they'd prefer more vacation or more pay, however, most Americans choose the latter. A San Diego psychologist told me that he didn't even like to take more than two or three days off at a time. "Any longer than that, I get itchy," he explained. "I see vacation not as a place not to work, but a place to work more efficiently."

Pollsters have found that most Americans prefer active vacations with lots to do over ones with looser schedules. In active vacations we usually try to get our money's worth by squeezing in as much as possible: going to as many places, seeing as many sights, and taking as many pictures as we can. Such trips can be educational, stimulating, and memorable. But they're rarely relaxing. Vacations with schedules are usually the opposite of time out. "My husband and I hit Grand Canyon, Bryce, and Zion, and Las Vegas in one week," reported a survivor of one such vacation. "The trip was a paradigm of goal orientation: here for three days, leave at this time in order to get there, go to bed at this hour in order to see that sunrise. Staying at work would have been less stressful."

Becoming a Better Vacationer

In Dallas, a businessman named George said he found the very term "vacation" a misnomer. "You get in a van with a bunch of kids and you haul off somewhere," explained George. "That's a vacation for them, and maybe for my wife, but it's not a vacation for me. Because it's always going, going. When we go on what we call a vacation, it's really not. You race to get ready and you're tired, you drive or fly somewhere, and when you get there you get up early to race and do as much as you can. You never reach the point where you relax and just sleep in or sit down and try to get in touch with yourself."

Andrea, a Dallas psychotherapist, recalled similar vacations in which her family worked themselves into a frenzy getting ready to go, left exhausted, drove great distances, saw everything there was to see, did everything there was to do, and returned home on the verge of collapse. In recent years, and in a second marriage, she'd learned better. "The best vacation we've ever had was when we went to Antigua and there was nothing to do there," said Andrea. "What was good about it was the random schedule that we kept. We'd go to bed whenever, whether it was one or three. Sleep in till whenever we woke up and didn't worry about if we'd slept long enough because if we got sleepy we'd take a nap. We had a real random pattern for about a week, going to the beach whenever we got there, eating when we got hungry. It was the best vacation we've had together. Because we let ourselves respond to our physical needs for sleeping and eating and resting and walking. No place to shop. No monuments to see. No history. Just the sand and the water."

To counter timelock, a vacation must allow one to annul time. This happens best either when one is not obliged to do anything special at any particular time, or when one is engaged in a single thoroughly engrossing activity. Reducing one's sphere of concentration seems to be the key. After an eight-day bike tour of Canada's Channel Islands, one businesswoman reported, "It was really delightful to find my goals reduced from a ten-year plan for corporate ladder-climbing to whether or not I was going to make it to the top of the next hill without getting off my bike and pushing."

One test of a good vacation is how much difficulty the vacationer has reentering the world of clocks and schedules. If we've given our bodies a chance to revert to organic time, they will resist getting back in step with the clock and calendar. One man found that the only time he forgot to pick up his daughter from school on Wednesday, rather than at the bus stop where she met him every other day, was after a vacation "where the weekly cycle was of no relevance to me whatsoever."

The essence of a rejuvenating vacation is freedom from schedules. Only in the absence of clocks and calendars can we fully unwind. Whether it's active or passive is beside the point. At the very least a renewing vacation involves a change of pace, the opportunity to reduce one's tempo.

The wise traveler Kate Simon once gave this prescription for enjoying a trip away from home:

> *Go slow.* If you have time for eight countries, take five. If you're rushed to take five, take three. I don't think anything can be experienced at the speed with which many, many people travel. There's no time, for instance, to wander in a market, which tells you a great deal about a city and a country: the way people conduct themselves, the way they sell to each other, the way they bargain, the products themselves. Sitting in a cafe and listening—and I've always tried to learn enough of a language to be able to eavesdrop—you can learn an awful lot. Also, one of the reasons I didn't drive much was that buses and trains give you companions who indicate, very often, characteristics that are very particular to a community or a city or a country. An Italian train or bus is very rewarding in that way. Go slow, eavesdrop, walk slowly, look, listen, smell.

Time Out

In the midst of this project I spent time with Richard Reiser, a man taking Kate Simon's advice to heart. In years past, Reiser told me, his *modus operandi* had been to do a quick scan while traveling; get a synopsis of the high points. "What's the bottom line?" he wanted to know. "What do I need to take away? Don't tell me anything more than I need to know. Just give me the outline." Now he lingered, asked questions, listened for nuance. In Andersonville, Georgia, Reiser became fascinated by what motivated those who ran the Confederate prison camp there. At Nathan Hale's birthplace in Coventry, Connecticut he pondered the question of whether the executed spy actually did say he regretted having but one life to give to his country, or whether that line actually came from Addison's 1713 play *Cato*.

Reiser had these experiences during an extended leave from the world of clocks and calendars. Intense, engaging, good humored, he described himself as "a classic Type A personality." In 1975 Reiser had started his own advertising agency in southern California and built it into a leading firm specializing in high-tech companies. In the process he gained weight, smoked four packs of cigarettes a day, and read everything he could get his hands on in a frantic effort to keep up. At work his conversations were reduced to terse exchanges of "word bites." After a tense commute home he'd "zero out" in front of the television.

In 1985 Reiser went to a spa to lose weight. In typical fashion he did as many exercises as possible so he could leave sooner. Instead he collapsed. Although the diagnosis was simple exhaustion, Reiser thought he'd had a stroke and was about to die. After recuperating he sold his agency to a larger firm. In 1987 Reiser resigned from it altogether. The next year he bought a small recreational vehicle and began taking extended trips. (His wife of twenty-five years had a business of her own to tend to, and his son had just started college.) During a year-long pilgrimage, Reiser tried to make several changes in the way he approached the time of his life.

Among other things he made it a point not to read newspapers on a regular basis, or to watch TV news. Reiser didn't miss either one. Nor did he feel deprived of information. Important news reached him eventually. And—contrary to his previous conviction—the world seemed to proceed apace whether or not he knew what was going on. After a few months of reduced input, Reiser found his relations with others improving. He paid better attention to what people had to say, and was genuinely interested in what they told him. As a result Reiser found people now seemed nicer, "though obviously the change is in me."

Reiser also found that for the first time in his adult life he didn't mind being alone. "Not being afraid to be by myself is one of the biggest surprises," he said during a layover in Pennsylvania. "Before, when I'd have half an hour alone, I felt lonely. When the tempo slowed down, when there was a break in the tempo and I was alone, I'd be lonely. Now, when I don't have all that other tempo going, when it's not such a break to be by myself, to my great surprise I'm *not* lonely." Overall, concluded Reiser, "the most obvious thing is that I get so much more *out* of a given day. I'm living at a far slower tempo, with a lot less activities, but I get more *out* of the day. More useful information, because it's in-depth. Less *amount* of information, but the information I get is more valid, richer, less superficial. I feel like I actually have more hours to my day, because I'm equipped mentally to take advantage of them."

My own reaction to Reiser's report was mixed. A distant cousin of mine, he'd called on short notice during a busy day of my own. I was glad to see him, interested in his experience, and more than a little envious. At the same time I felt vexed. His schedule was loose; mine was tight. He could be flexible and drop in to pass the time of day. I didn't feel that free. In the "before" and "after" picture Reiser described, I saw more of myself "before." My cousin's example seemed to reflect poorly on my own. He never said this, but the implication seemed to be there. Or was that me doing the implying?

With luck we might get one or more opportunities during a lifetime to take extended time off as Richard Reiser did. There is no better way to repair one's inner clock. Far from being an invitation to sloth, such sabbaticals can be a source of achievement. In their study of more than 400 prominent historical figures, sociologists Victor and Mildred Goertzel found that what they called "a free period in which to think, to plan, to read unrestrainedly" was part of the early development of 10% of those studied. Benefiting from such an experience were John Kennedy, H. G. Wells, Havelock Ellis, Marie Curie, Edna St. Vincent Millay, and Charles Evans Hughes. Winston Churchill had two extended breaks in his life's routine. Matisse took up painting while recovering from an illness.

Although such a free period is beyond the ken of most of us, there are other ways to put our life's time in better balance. Sometimes a change of life-style can get the job done.

A CHANGE OF PACE

In a focus group outside Philadelphia, one couple stood out as unusually timelocked. Arnold Yasinski was a DuPont product manager. He worked long hours and traveled on business several days a week. Cynthia Yasinski was a bank vice-president who had just entered the ranks of senior management. Each spent nearly two hours a day commuting. They made lots of money, owned an elegant suburban home, and had virtually no time for themselves. "There's only so much space available," explained Cindy. "I constantly make lists of all the things I have to do. I have this calendar and it goes on for miles."

Their girls, aged 3 and 6, had a full-time sitter. (An older son was away at college.) When Arnie wasn't out of town and Cindy hadn't gotten stuck in traffic, the Yasinskis would rendezvous at home in the early evening. The girls had usually been fed already by their sitter. After putting them to bed around nine, Cindy and Arnie ate dinner themselves. Because neither felt much like cooking by then, they ate a lot of pizza. Both were concerned about their nutrition. "We'd eat things that were better for us if we had more time," explained Cindy, "or had planned ahead. But when people are pulling on your legs and wanting you to pay attention to them, I don't want to say to the kids, 'I haven't seen you all day, go away. I have to make dinner.' "

Neither was particularly happy about the state of their lives. Arnie felt that living at such a hectic pace "sort of detaches you from your better self. It detaches you from your deeper self. You don't have the time for meditation, and to examine your own emotions and rechannel them. You tend to fly off the handle or overreact to things."

Arnie had dreams of something better, but realized that they'd most likely remain in the dream category. "Sometimes you wonder," he said, "if I wasn't doing this, what would I do? I have this image, sort of wishful, of moving back to New England. That's where I was a lot of my childhood and I somehow think if I lived there I'd be in closer touch with something that I am not in touch with now. Maybe it would be possible to find a less fast-paced life. But I think what I am talking about is a fantasy more than what would really happen."

A few months after making these observations Arnie took a job as vice-president and chief financial officer of a private college in Maine. Once he made this decision, Cindy said she hadn't seen her husband so relaxed in years. She had no objection to leaving her own job and stepping off the fast track. Within two months they sold their Pennsylvania house and moved to a small town in Maine where they rented a more modest home. Cindy took a breather before starting to look for work.

When I caught up with the Yasinskis in Maine they were a few weeks into their new life. Cindy hadn't found work yet. When she did, she had no illusions about matching her Philadelphia salary. In the meantime their total income had been halved. They'd just bought a house that could be paid for with a single salary. Arnie's commuting time was minutes rather than hours, and he rarely left town on business. Arnie could take his daughters to school in the morning and go home for lunch if he chose. Although Cindy had put their youngest daughter in a morning day care center while she looked for work, their child care bill had plummeted. Instead of spending money going to plays, movies, and concerts, they enjoyed a social life consisting primarily of dinner with other couples for the cost of preparing some food now and again.

"The sense of money, the way people use it is so different here," Cindy observed. "When you live around Philadelphia, money's just everywhere. Here it isn't. You don't meet as many people as concerned with their career, climbing the corporate ladder. They aren't commuting, running to catch trains. Many more are doing part-time jobs. So the pace is quite different."

Both natives and newcomers seemed to prefer that pace. At Arnie's college some employees shared jobs. Arnie himself felt he was working at least as hard as he did at DuPont, but didn't mind. Enjoying what you're doing can have that effect. Getting to see his family for extended periods of time every day also took pressure off. The Yasinskis both felt they were eating better, healthier meals for the simple reason that they were no longer gulping takeout food of least resistance. They ate together as a family regularly, something that was seldom possible in Pennsylvania. Combined with the more relaxed pace of life in Maine, such changes at home had given Arnie's life a better sense of balance. As he put it, "I've got the best of both worlds."

Because she had yet to find work, Cindy was less sanguine. If anything she felt out of kilter in the other direction. "Right now," she explained, "the balance has swung way over to spending time with the kids." Cindy had been on two field trips with Sarah's first-grade class, helped tutor reading there, and already knew every one of her daughter's classmates' names. She was also running for exercise every day, something that had been hard to do in downtown Philadelphia. Cindy did find that she missed the stimulation of work, colleagues, and city life. At the same time, she said, "I don't feel in the least that I've given up an interesting life to come to a dull one." With her girls in school and day care, "I have this chunk of time for myself. I have time in exchange for not having money. Also a conscious sense that I need to be watching the dollars."

While enjoying the luxury of time, Cindy was concerned about the effect it might be having on her: "Once you taste this freedom, will you want to go back?" She was looking for a full-time job, but also wondering about working part-time or in a cottage industry or doing free-lance consulting. She'd just had a long conversation with a friend about how appealing it would be to work three days a week. Neither thought that this was likely to be possible. On the other hand, said Cindy, "The thing I worry about is just taking a job so it's the same as if I hadn't moved."

14

Striking a Balance

Own less, do less, and say no.
—GEOFFREY GODBEY

The one thing craved above all else by the timelocked is *balance.* Not too
fast, not too slow. Time enough for family, time enough to work. Neither
time on one's hands nor not enough time. Like gold to a prospector, land
to a castaway, or salvation to a sinner, such balance is what the timelocked
yearn for, yet despair of ever finding.

One of the underlying causes of imbalanced schedules is difficulty cutting back. As time passes we tend to keep adding new tasks without first
pruning old ones. A prerequisite to achieving better balance is giving up the
fantasy of being able to have it all. The defining word for the eighties was
"more." In the nineties the key word is "less." As Riccardo Muti explained
in 1990 when he stepped down after a frantic decade as conductor of the
Philadelphia Orchestra, "I am not doing this in order to do something else.
I am doing it to do something less."

Less Is More

In the midst of this project we moved from a suburban community
outside Philadelphia to a small, rural town in southwest Ohio. This move
included giving up certain things. Our family now had a shorter menu of
activities to choose from. We decided to forgo cable television, let most
magazine subscriptions lapse, and get the local paper instead of the *New
York Times.* Although it hadn't been our intention, reducing our options
eased pressure on our time. With fewer stores to shop at, we spent less
time shopping. With less television to watch, we watched less television.
Without as much to do overall, we took walks, went to softball games, or
just sat around and talked. There was no feeling of missing anything. To

200

the contrary. Without as much to do we didn't feel as though we were missing as much. One thing we didn't miss at all was ultra-organized activities for children. There were few of them in rural Ohio. Kids still prowled the town on their bikes and got up ballgames.

Although it's the path we chose, and the Yasinskis chose, moving is not a prerequisite to changing one's lifestyle in search of balance. As the Alcoholics Anonymous and similar groups emphasize, "geographic cures" aren't always the best ones. The key is not to pull a Gauguin and flee to Tahiti, or even to search for Tahiti at home. Rather it's simply to make sure that unavoidable periods of hectic activity are balanced by ones when we become reacquainted with ourselves and those we care about.

Imbalance is unavoidable at times. When studying for bar exams, say, during seasonal business, or while raising young children, there is little alternative to being pressed for time. The best we can do then is snatch moments of respite whenever possible. Vary the pace and content of our activities. Look forward to upcoming slack periods. And make sure that our calendars are never so full that we can't make time for important matters (our children, say) that didn't get penciled in. Sometimes this is the best we can manage. But it's important to keep the accent on *sometimes.* An ongoing time imbalance implies that there is too much weight on one side of the scale—work usually. This is when corrective measures are called for.

"One of the conclusions that I had to come to in my life," noted Carolyn, a 35-year-old Cincinnati lawyer, "was that there simply isn't enough time to do everything that I would like to do. I have had to adopt a philosophy that allows me to cut things out, and to do that freely, without a lot of pain and guilt. The choices are constantly 'What is it that I am not going to do that I didn't want?' or 'What is really important to me?' It makes me think about my life and what I choose to do in a very different way than I did even ten years ago."

One Kansas family resolved to break the grip of timelock on their lives by comparing lists of activities each member liked and disliked. The results surprised them. The father hated putting in so much overtime at work. His wife didn't enjoy all of her many community activities. Their son said he actually preferred gardening to playing soccer. They all loved family activities such as camping, or just taking walks. As a result, the boy quit soccer, and his parents cut back on their commitments. They now do more walking and camping.

After studying scores of families for her book, *Stress and the Healthy Family,* Dolores Curran found that those who dealt best with stress made a point of reviewing everyone's schedules on a regular basis to make sure that they included time together. "If the schedule looks impossibly full, they find ways of eliminating some activities," noted Curran. "In short, they pay attention to time before time pressures become too great."

It's an unfortunate necessity for busy family members to compare calendars regularly. In many cases this is the only way to make sure they spend time with each other. There are other rewards. Among other things, reviewing schedules this way gives children tangible reassurance that they're on our calendar. It also sets an example for them as teenagers when their own schedules may need pruning for the sake of the family.

The only way to add something new to our schedules without throwing them out of balance is by subtracting something old. This is the single hardest lesson for most of us to learn, and yet the most important: not just to reorganize the same amount of activity (which usually makes us more tense in the process), but to make *choices* about the ways we spend time; eliminate and *not* replace. What makes this process so hard is that it requires us to relinquish dreams; to come to grips with the fact that we may never learn to speak French, or play the guitar, or even do all of the things that we used to do. If beleaguered self-sacrifice is even part of our self-perception, pruning schedules is that much harder. Doing so requires giving up part of our identity. The toughest sacrifice of all can be letting go of the fantasy of being someone who can juggle a record number of balls without dropping one.

But we can't hope to balance our schedules without sacrificing something of value. In the process of pruning, we may find ourselves leading not just less frantic but fuller lives. Trying to increase one's menu of possibilities contributes to over-choice, a key source of timelock. Reducing the range of options makes it possible to narrow one's focus and concentrate better. By engaging in such a process, we may discover that activities we used to treasure have lost value. Many calendars are cluttered with what Meyer Friedman calls "trash events." After going through her own time-locked schedule looking for things to throw out, Jane Brody reduced her volume of "appointments" and traded small amounts of time spent with lots of casual acquaintances for larger blocks of time with a few good friends. "I may be doing fewer things," she reported, "but I am certainly enjoying everything I do a lot more. Oddly enough no one seems to have noticed a decline in my productivity, perhaps because most of what I cut out of my life was time-consuming trivia."

Beyond the Have-It-All Hustle

For years we were subjected to the "have-it-all hustle." Profiles of those who seemed to have achieved fulfilling, chock-full lives at work and home were a media staple. Our own lives looked meager and chaotic by contrast. The problem seemed to lie with our own inadequacies. Once we learned how to manage time better maybe we could have it all too. But it turns out that those we envied may not have had it all themselves. Take Letty Cottin Pogrebin. In 1972 the feminist writer was cited in *Harper's Bazaar* as a woman "able to do it all," one of several contemporaries who "have their lives and their time under control." Sixteen years later Pogrebin confessed that by spending most of her adult life filling her schedule to the brim, all she'd succeeded in doing was exhausting herself. "I can't remember a day in the last twenty years when I was all caught up," moaned Pogrebin.

On closer examination, most of the have-it-all pictures were decidedly blurred. Some turned out to be of those who were childless (Gloria Steinem, for example). Others had grown children (Phil Donahue). Many could afford lots of help. (After delivering her infant by limousine to his nurse at ABC-TV's studios, Joan Lunden advised America's working mothers that "a lot of women could arrange for child care on the job. They just don't think about it.") Other have-it-all types were neglecting major parts of their "balanced" lives, usually their families. Some were going quietly crazy.

In one candid memoir, a recovering superwoman named Elizabeth Whelan described how she'd spent the early part of her career trying to run a professional society; do research at Harvard; write books, articles, and a newspaper column; in addition to raising an infant while maintaining city, country, and suburban homes (from which she spent three hours a day commuting). By the time she was in her early 30s, Whelan's schedule had grown so crowded that she was actually paged in the delivery room while giving birth to her daughter. Five days later she returned to work. "How do you do it?" others would ask her. "I would smile calmly," she said, "looking quite self-assured . . . and say it was as easy as could be." She lied. In fact Whelan was unraveling, communicating with her lawyer husband by memo, keeping her 2-year-old daughter up well past her bedtime just to get time with her, and depending utterly on the typed daily schedule that she kept close at hand. "It was all wrong," Whelan realized at last. "I finally had to acknowledge it. We weren't living. We were existing much the way a computer does when it is plugged in and switched on." After coming to this conclusion, Whelan considered quitting her jobs. But she knew how frustrating being a stay-at-home mom could be. Money was also an issue: "Without two jobs we couldn't have supported our life-style." Whelan was nose-to-nose with the question she didn't want to answer: Was it possible to succeed at being a wife, mother, and career woman? "I finally acknowledged that the activities of my life were more than I or anyone else could handle," she conceded, before adding, "My tentative answer is yes, it is possible. But there are limits." Among them were cutting back to one manageable-sized residence close to work, drastically reducing her professional commitments, and hiring household help to allow more time with her child. Whelan continued to work full-time, but made a point of leaving at five every afternoon. She also limited her business travel to one or two days a month. "The day I faced the necessity for modifying and realigning those life goals made long ago was a most difficult one for me because, in essence, I had discovered my limits," she admitted. "But it was also the day I stopped marching to the beat of a series of other people's drums, and began confidently following the beat of my own. I hope."

To achieve better balance in our lives, principle number one is that we *cannot* have it all. Who would want to? Having it all, or even trying to have it all, is exhausting. This calls for spreading yourself thin, giving nothing proper attention. In the effort to have everything we end up enjoying nothing. The essence of living is choosing. And, having chosen what really matters most to us, ruthlessly giving up the rest. One of the best time-saving suggestions scribbled on a questionnaire was this one from a mother of two: "Not expecting perfection—i.e., your *mother's* standards. Not attempting to 'do it all.' "

In one exaggerated case (but only in degree), a San Diego disabled rights activist named Yolanda discussed the "echo effect" of the polio she'd suffered as a child. This made the 38-year-old Yolanda feel that taking on too many obligations might literally kill her. As a result, she evaluated each task in terms of how much of her life it was worth to her. Something like applying makeup had grown so arduous that Yolanda only did so on very special occasions. "I don't want to be on a respirator in five years," she explained, "so I look at how much energy I am willing to devote to each task and I think about it a lot. What am I willing to say no to? I find myself saying no to a lot more things than I used to say no to. I feel as if I said yes to as much as I would want to say yes to, I wouldn't have enough energy to do anything well. So I'd rather do some things well than everything mediocre. I say no to a lot of things now."

The single most important time-balancing word is *no*. (As in, "No, I don't have time for that.") No can be a hard word to say. It taps a fear of not being liked. A fear of not being respected. A fear of being seen as a negative person, someone who can't manage time. A fear that we'll accomplish less.

One fear many have about cutting back to balance their time is that doing so could make them less productive. This isn't necessarily the case. Hard as it is to grasp when one is caught in the grip of timelock, pruning schedules can actually improve productivity. A management consultant said that the key to getting on top of time is crossing tasks off one's to-do list undone. (One woman executive prefers writing don't-do lists.) Trying to do too much makes it impossible to focus on anything. By cutting back and putting their own schedules in better balance, Allen Questrom, Richard Collins, and many others with whom I talked felt that they had become better, more focused managers.

The Japanese are often cited as a hard-working example for the rest of us. But many of them have gone so far in the direction of unbridled workaholism that concern is widespread about what the Japanese call "karoshi"—a growing number of fatalities attributed to overwork. Even their own government has encouraged Japanese employees to take more time off. Two-career families are rare in Japan, allowing men to work ridiculous schedules at the expense of their home lives. One more thing: Former DayRunner president Robert Dorney noted during many business trips to Japan, that their executives "aren't very well organized. They make up for this deficiency by working extremely hard . . ." A more useful example for us than the Japanese might be those western Europeans, Germans especially, who work hard and have outstanding rates of productivity yet take regular time off, live in a society without much evening or weekend commerce, and are guaranteed at least four weeks of vacation a year.

One upside of the global economy for Americans is that it's putting us in regular contact with capable managers who have a long tradition of balancing work with leisure. Conceivably this could encourage a shift away from our workaholic ethic. "In the future," business professor Robert Kelley of Carnegie-Mellon University has suggested, "the very best managers will be those who keep their work lives under control, while the ones who brag about how much time they've spent at work will be viewed as disorganized."

Money Is Time

The most common explanation for an imbalanced, timelocked life is the need to make ends meet. This is certainly the most valid of reasons, and not always one with a clear alternative. When working long hours is necessary to pay basic bills, balance waits for better times. But in other cases overwork results from wanting to stay on a certain rung of the consumer ladder. Then it's not so much "making ends meet" as "supporting our life-style" that is the rationale for being so out of balance timewise. In such cases it might be well to examine the life-style being supported. Is it worth the cost in time?

It's not as clear as often is feared that pruning one's work schedule is a first step to the poorhouse. As any working couple knows, two salaries rarely double family income. The average two-paycheck family nets only two-fifths more than one with a single wage earner. Cutting back, even quitting one job altogether, won't "halve" one's income; not after commuting costs, child care, business clothing, lunches, eating out, getting takeout, and the general expense of saving time by buying on impulse are deducted. Two-income couples fall easily into patterns of overconsumption and undersaving because they don't have the time to be frugal. Working fewer hours can make it possible to save substantial amounts of money through better planning.

In one two-teacher family south of Los Angeles, the husband left his job to stay home with his children for four years. The first thing Randy gave up was expensive suits; they were no longer needed. He did much of their home's maintenance, making it less necessary to hire help. Time was now available for Randy to make better, money-saving consumer purchases. Garage sales and estate sales became a common source of needed merchandise and a family outing as well (often more fun than buying new, they found). Potluck suppers and picnics replaced pricey restaurant meals. A train trip to see relatives in the Midwest took the place of a more expensive vacation. As a result of reducing their overhead in these ways, the couple found that even though their gross income was reduced, there were months when they were actually better off financially than they'd been with two paychecks.

Seeking balance by cutting back does make it harder to take an active part in the consumer economy. Those who have bought time by adopting a less affluent way of life typically find that expensive restaurant meals are the first thing to go, followed by regular changes of wardrobe. New toys for the kids become the exception (not that big a sacrifice because so many toys are guilt purchases in lieu of time anyway). Using shopping as an antidepressant becomes less necessary because one is usually less depressed. Casual purchases of consumer items are replaced by more carefully considered ones. "We used to buy what we wanted," explained a woman who left work to stay home with her children. "Now I think about needs instead of wants."

Giving up or cutting back on work to balance one's schedule can reduce income. But does it follow that one's standard of living is reduced? When I asked Allen Johnson whether the simpler life they'd tried to fashion since returning from Peru felt like a sacrifice, he said that it was just the opposite: "I think I've raised my standard of living." Assessing the quality of one's life on monetary terms alone is self-denying. Those who have a healthy relationship with time may have the highest living standard of all.

Benjamin Franklin's insight that time is money is central to the American credo. We usually take this insight as an admonition to work harder so that we can earn more money to buy more time. This transaction seldom works as planned. We rarely break even on that deal, let alone turn a profit. Another way to interpret Franklin's aphorism is to turn it around. Not only does time equal money, but money equals time. By reducing our workload we can make a conscious decision to spend money for time. This could turn out to be a real bargain. According to economist Paul Wachtel, Americans recorded an overall satisfaction with their lives in 1957 that has never been surpassed. That was a time when fewer than 10% of our homes had air conditioners, only 4% had dishwashers, and fewer than 15% of all American families owned a second car. According to Wachtel, an average contemporary working week could be cut by a fifth or more and still support a standard of living higher than that which prevailed in our year of greatest satisfaction.

It's nearly impossible to talk about balanced time and dual-income families in the same breath. Two parents trying to work full, conventional schedules usually suffer cruel and unusual punishment. When one parent cuts back, even in part—to become a one, one and a half, even a one and three-quarter career couple—an element of sanity and flexibility is made possible. By doing this families spend a portion of their income on a more humane schedule. What better purchase is there?

A nurse-practitioner in San Diego stopped working after her second son was born, then resumed a part-time career as he approached the age of 2. "I think that for me it's easier to deal with the change in my professional identity and cut corners and budget real carefully," she explained, "than it is to go out and make all the money so that you can go to Disneyland, and splurge here and there. Because there's no way to minimize the guilt that comes from feeling like you're not spending enough time with your children. I look at the relationship I have with my 7½-year-old and realize that when my 7½-year-old was 1½ I wasn't there. I was working full time. I feel very guilty about that and had a lot of unresolved feelings of loss."

One couple in Katonah worked out an interesting balance of work and family commitments. After their second child was born when she was 40, Marilyn took an extended leave from her career as a computer programmer. When this boy was 3 she resumed a half-time schedule. Her husband, Paul, worked four 12-hour days maintaining computers, then was off for four. During much of his four days off Paul was—as he put it—"Mr. Mom." The rest of the time Marilyn minded the kids. This arrangement made it unnecessary for them to arrange ongoing child care. When both were at work they hired a neighbor to look after the kids. Marilyn also hired a sitter and treated Paul to occasional child-free days when she could see he was getting edgy. This couple's schedule wasn't ideal. But it was flexible and allowed them to feel better than most working couples do about the time they gave their family. Neither seemed wracked by the guilt that is usually the working parent's constant companion.

The Parent Track

Guilt about neglecting one's children has traditionally been considered the working mother's problem. In recent years, however, that feeling has become more bisexual. A 1987 *Fortune* poll found that fathers were almost as likely as mothers to be anxious about the impact of work commitments on their family life. In a Stanford study of dual-MBA couples, fathers expressed even more anxiety than mothers about their children. During polls of their 100,000 employees in the United States, conducted between 1985 and 1988, DuPont found a dramatic rise of concern among fathers about issues such as relocation, day care, and vacation time. In a 1989 survey by Robert Half International, 45% of all employed men polled said they would refuse a promotion if it meant giving up time at home. Men are less likely to speak up about such concerns, however, partly for fear of damaging their career prospects, partly because men don't talk about a lot of things.

Companies that shift to flexible scheduling typically find that half of all eligible men who are fathers take advantage. I've known quite a few fathers who stepped off a career path or at least slowed it down to have more time for their families. This was usually an individual decision, not part of any organized effort. Most just accepted the label "lacks ambition" in silence. A *Fortune* survey of 400 working mothers and fathers with children under 12 found that *more* men than women (30% to 25.7%) had actually refused a new job, promotion, or transfer that would have cut into their family time.

Some men take time off altogether to spend with their families. During the past decade AT&T has found a sharp increase in the number of fathers requesting family leave. During his wife's first year of law school Ted Koppel took a nine-month leave from ABC News to care for their four children. In 1990, Peter Lynch, the 46-year-old manager of Fidelity Investment's highly successful Magellan mutual fund, quit to spend time with his family. But such cases are exceptional. More typical is the case of Schuyler, the Seattle management consultant who earned a handsome salary during two decades of jetting about while his wife stayed home to raise their two kids. "I feel they're more her children than my children," said Schuyler. "That bothers me. I would have gladly traded places."

The work-obsessed father who tries to cut back on work late in life so he can spend more time with his grown children is a stock, forlorn, and regret-filled figure in our society. Regrets late in life generally focus on misused time: too much spent on unsatisfying pursuits, too little devoted to what really mattered—families in particular. As a wise man once observed, "No one on his death bed ever said 'I wish I had spent more time on my business.' " I have never known anyone who traded work and income for personal time and wished they hadn't. I have met many who didn't cut back sooner in life and wished they had.

Why didn't they? The big fear, of course, was of not being able to get back on track once they stepped off. What could that move cost, both in career and in cash? Obviously there's a price to be paid. By one economist's estimate a woman who takes off to have a child and get that child through grade school can expect to earn 13% to 19% less over her remaining career than had she stayed on the job. Nonetheless, the overall damage to one's career may not be as serious as often is feared. Supreme Court Justice Sandra Day O'Connor took five years off to raise her children. A survey of 1945 Barnard graduates found that 65 of 70 mothers responding had taken time away from careers to spend with their families. Yet in 1990, as they approached retirement age, most were earning between $25,000 and $50,000 a year. Eleven earned more than that, and three were making over $100,000 (including a teacher and scientist who'd taken 15 years off). Only 5% of those responding wished they'd gone back to work sooner. So, although there is clearly a penalty for stepping off a career track, perhaps the penalty is not as great as we fear. "Before long," said one of the Barnard women, an attorney who took a nine-year family leave, "there's nobody who remembers you weren't always there or were part-time."

We need to find a third way, one which apes neither fifties mommy worship nor eighties career obsession but combines elements of both. The point is not that we should return to a life of mothers at home, fathers at work, and kids playing out on the street. For one thing, the entire economy would collapse if two-career families became one-career *en masse.* Also, decades of two-career life have altered the social fabric. Single-paycheck families of the past lived in a radically different context: one where parents got help from relatives, kids played with each other more spontaneously, and other mothers were home to offer mutual support. Times have changed. Playmates have gone to day care and grandparents to Florida. Other mothers are usually at work. In the current context staying home with children forces parent and child on each other in a way that isn't altogether healthy. As a Dallas psychologist pointed out, when she was between jobs her kids would sometimes ask her to go back to work. "Evidently I'm nicer to be around when I'm working," she explained.

At the same time, two-career parents with young children usually find that they're engaged in at least half a career too many. Serious discussion of this issue has been complicated by oversimplification (e.g., "the mommy track"). Increasing numbers of women and men alike who no longer want to pay the price for trying to have it all are looking for ways to balance their lives. To accommodate such employees, the workplace itself must change. It's easy to forget how recent today's work-family impasse is. Two-career families have only become a commonplace in the last couple of decades. We're still feeling our way. Most workplaces continue to function as if their employees were primarily married men with wives tending the homefront. Family issues have been considered of little concern to employers. Future employers hoping to minimize turnover will no longer be able to indulge that fantasy. "Working couples and single parents face intense pressures trying to juggle their family and work lives," Roper advised its corporate clientele. *"Something* has to give, and it will not be the family."

While studying work-family issues at two New England corporations, researchers from Boston University were surprised to hear children's voices at various worksites. This was particularly apparent on holidays or snow days. At a truck-loading warehouse, the manager told them that thirty to forty children of employees had run around the building at one time. Once this company realized the liability problems they posed, children were banned from the warehouse. According to management, this solved the problem. It didn't. When the researchers added a question about emergency child care to their survey, they found that 41% of all employees polled sometimes took their children to work. "Bringing children to work appears to be an emergency child care option used with increasing frequency by employees," they reported. "Companies may be providing informal child care whether they intend to or not. The alternatives appear to be increased absenteeism of employees, or increased worry among parents about leaving children home alone. Innovative company policies for emergency child care may be a necessity in the future."

Concern about family issues in the workplace has a far longer history in Europe than it does here. Most Western European nations have had programs to assist working parents for the past half century and more. The United States is the only developed nation outside South Africa which does not require employers to grant parental leave. About the time that George Bush vetoed a bill mandating parental leave that had passed both houses of Congress, Spain's parliament extended paid maternity leave from fourteen to sixteen weeks and required four weeks of paid leave for new fathers as well. In addition, Spanish employees of either sex are now permitted by law to take a year of unpaid parental leave without losing their jobs.

This approach to work-family conflicts will become more widespread in the United States. It has to. Society, government, and employers are just beginning to take account of the imbalance in employees' lives. They have no choice. As the labor pool shrinks, employers will be forced to change their work context to attract and retain employees. It's estimated that by the year 2000, women will comprise 65% of all new employees and 75% of mothers with school-age children will work outside the home. With such a workforce, employers won't be able to go on pretending that family issues are no concern of theirs. Employers then will face a choice: Stick to a conventional work ethos and force conscientious parents out of their ranks (perhaps into the arms of more flexible competitors), or change their values to accommodate a new breed of employee who is trying to balance work and family life.

This has begun to happen. A 1987 Labor Department survey found that half of all U.S. workplaces had at least some policies designed to help parents. DuPont has made a companywide commitment to allow employees more latitude for family demands on their time. IBM now offers up to three years of leave for employees who are willing to be on call for part-time assignments during two of those three years. In announcing a new program of flexible work schedules for participating parent-employees, a Johnson & Johnson vice-president explained, "There is extremely heavy competition for good people these days. One of the ways to get and keep them is to help them fulfill their family responsibilities." Johnson & Johnson's program included an extensive referral system for both child and elder care, on-site day care, a year's family-care leave with full benefits, help with the cost of child adoption, and educational programs to sensitize supervisors to their employees' need to balance work and family concerns.

Employers and workers alike will benefit from such innovations. A worried employee is rarely a productive one. Those taking part in flexible work programs are better equipped to focus on the task at hand. A job-sharing team, for example, is probably less concerned about family problems and less tired to boot. As the boss of one such team put it, "I get four hours of a fresh person twice a day." Part-time professionals who want more time with their families can be highly motivated self-starters who get a lot done in limited periods. One San Francisco market researcher who worked a twenty-hour week (divided between twelve hours at the office and eight at home) said she got as much accomplished on her half-days as she used to on full ones because she was so much more motivated to get started and get finished.

Career-and-a-Half Couples

The most time-balanced parents I encountered during my research were those who had reduced their work hours and gross income to achieve a more humane family life. One Dallas mother had quit after eight years as a sales manager and limited her work to one day a week doing accounting. She was among the minority of parents who seemed content with their family's schedule. "When I quit that job, I gave up a whole lot of money," she said of her former career. "But there's a real difference in my life. I'm sure my kids notice. I'm real pleased about how I've got it to balance right now."

The greatest gift we can give our children is the gift of time. They don't necessarily prefer the things we can buy them by working extra hours, if this means the extra hours are credited against our time with them. One Canadian mother decided to stay home with her three children (at least until they reached school age) after she asked them if they'd rather have more toys or more time with her, and they chose the latter. In a study of two-career couples, Patricia Knaub of the University of Nebraska found that because time was so scarce in such families, the children treasured time spent together: traveling, taking walks, talking, celebrating holidays. "One of the most important bits of advice I would give to such families," concluded Knaub, "based on what the children had to say, is to make sure that they plan on a regular basis this kind of time away from household chores, the telephone, and the temptation to work."

One couple in the Fort Myers focus group were Lou and Jonellen Heckler. Until the late 1970s Lou was a television talk show host in North Carolina, Jonellen a free-lance writer. Although their son, Steve, had serious allergy problems, the Hecklers' professional lives were successful. Jonellen sold short stories to major magazines and Lou did well in ratings. Over time, however, a caveat began to appear on his performance evaluations. As he recalled, "They said 'Lou's doing a pretty good job, but he seems to put his family ahead of his work.' I thought, 'Well, yeah. And if that's wrong, then I'm in the wrong pew here. I do put my family ahead of my work.' "

In 1980 Lou left his job and they moved to Fort Myers (with its low pollen count). There Lou began his own business as a professional speaker and Jonellen started writing novels. Money was tight at the outset. But for the first time since Steve was born in 1972 both felt that their work and home lives were in balance. "Early on," said Jonellen (who published three novels after leaving Charlotte), "we decided that we would schedule time with the family and that when it was scheduled it was scheduled and no one could step on it. If anyone said, 'We'd like you to do this or that,' we'd say, 'Sorry, we have a prior commitment.' "

This meant keeping Sunday reserved for one another. To the outside world this was "prior commitment" time because the Hecklers were at church, riding bikes, or just hanging out. Lou especially needed this day because he was spending so much time in his office and on the road. "When you're trying to get a business going," he explained, "you work a lot longer hours. I think during the ten years that we've done this, where we both work inside the home, we have learned to keep cutting back on the work hours and adding more on the leisure. One of the things that has helped is the ability to talk about it a lot with one another. When I was traveling more than I am now we would say to Steve, 'How does this affect you? How do you feel about Dad being gone so many days?' We tried to make it something that was always kinetic, something that could always move and change. If we made my travel ten days a month, which it was at one time, then we could change that. It became eight days a month, and if eight days a month became too many, then we could change it to seven or six until we found a place where we had the blend of having enough money to pay the bills and eat, but also we'd feel comfortable as a family."

Is Home Work the Answer?

One way the Hecklers made their flexible schedules work was through selective use of technology. Their home office is equipped with an answering machine, two computers, one laser printer, a photocopier, and a fax. Some seers say that this is the way more and more of us will work in the future, in "electronic cottages." One member of the Fort Myers group had spent more than ten years working for a Pittsburgh employer by phone, computer, and fax. Her case was unusual. Although modern technology has made it increasingly possible to work from home, most employers' wariness of employees they can't see has kept this alternative from becoming widespread. Is their wariness justified? In fact, a major MIT study found that telecommuters often put in longer hours and were more productive than their better scrutinized colleagues. Without the distractions of actual commuting, office politics, needless meetings, and sundry hassles, most home workers find they got more done than do their office-bound colleagues. There is no reason other than prejudice that many more of us can't do at least part of our work from home. In time, we will.

This will be a mixed blessing. No one who's telecommuted for any length of time can join the romantic chorus of praise for electronic cottages. Working at home can be frustrating, boring, and lonely. The baby cries, a neighbor knocks, stockbrokers call your number cold. The boundaries between work and leisure grow fuzzy when you're on your own. Working flexible hours at home makes it possible to do your job at any time of the day or week. With unfinished work just a few feet away, it's hard to ever feel completely "off." As one member of the San Diego group put it, "My office is out in back and it's always beckoning to me."

Despite such drawbacks, the advantages of working at home, at least part of the time, far outweigh the disadvantages, especially for working parents. No time is wasted commuting, one's schedule is flexible, and your kids see you on a regular basis. (Even if I don't have as much time for them as I'd like, just being able to greet my children when they get home from school and chat for a few minutes does wonders for my comfort level as a parent.) A home worker is available if there's an emergency at school, to stay home with a sick child, or help out with a class field trip. That time can be made up later. Home workers set their own pace. They have the opportunity to work in spurts, the organic way. A Providence lawyer who left his own practice to take a government job said that what he missed most was being able to work when he felt most creative, to keep going late at night if he was so inclined, and to nap in the afternoon.

Taking Your Time

To those who work on their own, the option of working late at night and on weekends is part and parcel of the freedom to knock off on a Wednesday morning. It's not the number of hours they work but being able to arrange them, to modulate their schedules, that home workers find most appealing. The real basis for satisfaction about work time is not the number of hours involved, but how one feels about the tasks. In the Champaign focus group, Illinois Assemblywoman Helen Satterthwaite pointed out that her life in politics was far busier and more hectic than it had been as a housewife and mother. But she was enjoying that life more, said Satterthwaite, because, "At least now the pressures in my life are of my own doing." In a similar vein, the Fort Lauderdale retirees said that what they liked most about their lives was not the free time *per se* but the fact that they chose how to spend their time. "Not only do we have the time to do what we want to do," said retired social worker Patricia Gershwin, "we have the *right* to do what we want to do. That's even nicer."

One ill-appreciated virtue of getting older is that clocks loosen their grip on your life. Older people are expected to slow down and ease the reins of their ambition. If not seen as a defeat, this can provide wonderful opportunities to lead a more balanced life. My own father has often said that retiring from his career as an economist and deciding that he'd accomplished what he could accomplish freed him to enjoy some of his most rewarding years: writing poetry, traveling, taking a more active part in local politics. While attending high school reunions to research an earlier book *(Is There Life After High School?),* I was struck repeatedly by how relaxed the later reunions were: thirtieths, fortieths, fiftieths. Older graduates seemed able to just enjoy each other's company. Younger ones were still so consumed by ambition and competition that they usually spent their reunions being tense and showing off. They were also far more likely to glance at their watches.

Restoring a sense of balance at any age calls for reorienting one's sense of what can be achieved in time remaining. Some things may not get done; certain ambitions may never be realized. It is difficult for goal-oriented people to accept that in the short term, anyway, they cannot accomplish everything they hoped to accomplish. That they can't have it all. One of the hardest nuts to crack is coming to terms with the fact that balancing our life in the present (or trying to, anyway) means accepting that we won't get everything done. We probably won't even finish half-completed projects. So be it. Perhaps life is incomplete by definition. According to Meyer Friedman, "You should not cavil at the fact that perhaps the majority of your activities at any given point in time appear to be in a state of flux; you must begin to take pride in this unfinishedness. It is your reassurance that you are living."

Friedman's admonition could be discouraging. Or it could be just the opposite. I'm finding that it encourages me to accomplish what I can and not worry about the rest. "An artist never really finishes his work," said Paul Valéry, "he merely abandons it." Perhaps the same thing could be said of lives. If so, this thought makes it easier to slow down and cut back. Nothing will be fully completed. Everything won't get done. Oh, well. I no longer kid myself that this is even possible. The payoff for not trying to finish everything is that time which would have been spent trying to do so can be redirected toward pursuits that are more fulfilling. Such redirection usually results in a better sense of completion overall.

We choose to rush and be busy. We can choose to slow down and cut back. This is in our power. But making such a choice is not easy. Among other things, attempting to ease our schedules calls for tacking into the winds of our heritage. Americans have always been subjected to an unusual amount of pressure to waste not a moment. Like most of us, I will always prefer a full schedule and brisk pace. Nonetheless, in the course of writing this book I've come to realize that a more relaxed approach to time is far more attainable than most of us realize.

15

The Timelock Antidote
Handbook

Throughout this book, various means have been suggested to ease the pressure of time. In its final chapter I'd like to gather, highlight, and elaborate on the most useful of those means in a Timelock Antidote Handbook.

1. *Develop a New Sense of Time.* Early in my research, psychologist Martin Seligman made this observation: "It's useful to think of time as not all it's cracked up to be. Time is just something humans invented to organize things. Now it's taken on a life of its own. Time is an abstraction. It stands in for a lot of psychological things." A tense, hostile attitude toward time is so basic to our heritage that it's hard to realize that such an attitude is neither normal nor universal. We invented our approach to time. We can reinvent it. To do so, some basic concepts should be kept in mind.

- Time is neutral, a mirror reflecting whatever emotional hue we project onto it.
- Time can't be controlled; don't try.
- To develop a less hostile relationship with time, approach time in a more relaxed way.
- A more relaxed approach to time will make you more productive, not less so.

2. *Plan Life, Not Time.* Developing a more relaxed attitude toward time calls for paying better attention to your life as a whole rather than to your schedule alone. This is easier to say than to do. Calendars are tangible; lives aren't. Assessing what we really want from life calls for asking ourselves questions at a level we usually avoid. But the alternative—not examining our actual needs—limits us to scheduling time ad hoc. There is more to life than crossing completed tasks off a to-do list. Only after determining what we hope to accomplish overall (as opposed to how much we can get done) can we change direction timewise.

- Reflect regularly on your life as a whole (composing and reviewing your own obituary is one way to do this).
- Evaluate all activities, even the most trivial, by whether they add to that life.
- Remember the lesson of brush-with-death survivors; each day could be our last, but it can't be enjoyed if rushed.
- Weed out ruthlessly whatever does not enhance your day—tasks, errands, TV shows, people.
- Ask yourself repeatedly, "Does what I'm doing contribute to the life I want to lead?"

3. *Manage Time Organically.* A major obstacle to getting on a better footing with time is bad advice from don't-waste-a-moment types. Their principal tool is guilt by example. ("Can't you see how long and hard I'm working? Shouldn't you be doing the same?") This is their problem and must be seen as their problem before the rest of us can cope better with time pressure. There are many ways to do a job well. The usual tactics— list-making, prioritizing, orderly scheduling—are one way. If another approach works better for you, stay with it. When it comes to managing time, the destination is what counts, not the means of transportation.

- Remember that time is uniform only to clocks; our bodies keep irregular time, based on sunlight, season, mood, age, and the uneven patterns of work and leisure that originally set our inner clocks.
- Get to know your body's clock, paying particular attention to peak periods.
- Take advantage of peak periods in scheduling work; if you don't control your work schedule, try to negotiate one that allows you to do so (it's in everyone's interest).
- If your working style is unconventional but gets the job done, be happy (remember Winston Churchill).
- Cut back on sleep only in an emergency.
- Routinely cross items off your to-do list undone.
- *Don't* make use of every minute; this only increases tension while reducing effectiveness.
- Unlearn how to do two things at once; any time saved this way is polluted by a reduced ability to concentrate.
- Remember that trying to get more done in less time usually results in rushed, stressful, sloppy work.

4. *Decelerate.* One of the main obstacles to developing a better sense of time is rushaholism. Hurrying can become its own reward. Once a critical mass of speed is achieved, it's hard to remember that the fastest way of doing things isn't necessarily the best way. Until recently life was filled with unavoidable pauses. As technological progress eliminates one pause after another, it's up to us to create our own.

- Take brief time outs throughout the day.
- Treat delays as found time.
- Do nothing on a regular basis.
- Nap if possible; should inhibition keep you from doing so, confront the inhibition.
- Take an occasional bath.
- When hurried, ask yourself, "Do I really need to rush? What's the worst thing that can happen to me if I don't? Is that worse than what it's costing me to hurry?"
- Distinguish between necessary haste (late for an appointment) and mere impatience (one-hour photo developing).
- Make a conscious effort to not always take the faster path; use stairs at times instead of elevators; walk rather than drive; cut and grate food you used to process.
- Reduce background noise (noise contributes to that hectic feeling and makes it hard to hear important information).
- Listen to your body; it's giving you good advice.

5. *Modulate.* At times we have no alternative to making the best of hectic, pressured schedules. But adjustments that will ease time's pressure can be made even in harried schedules. When it's not possible to cut back or slow down, it still can be possible at least to vary the rhythm of our days.

- No matter how busy you are, always take *some* time off; during hectic periods one free hour can feel like a day in the country.
- When you must work during off days, try to give such days a different texture than ordinary ones—linger over breakfast; work in relaxed settings; knock off early.
- During overly busy periods, keep the end in sight (if there's no end in sight, consider a change of life-style).
- Alternate head work and hand work whenever possible.
- Use a wide range of high- to low-tech tools to syncopate your work tempo and exercise different muscles.
- Work in as many different settings as possible.
- Change position often; try a stand-up desk for some tasks.
- If work rules make it hard to vary your pace, work to change the rules (laws are being passed to this end).

6. *Reduce Awareness of Time.* Because digital timekeepers have grown so cheap and widespread, the exact time is harder than ever to ignore. How often do we really need such information? The fewer reminders we have of measured time, the better equipped we are to make this commodity the inconspicuous servant that it was meant to be.

- Pay attention to how often you check the time; try to reduce such occasions to a minimum.
- Limit the number of timekeepers in your vicinity; make those a little hard to see.
- Before strapping on a watch, ask yourself, "Is this really necessary?"
- Go watchless whenever possible; create "watch-free" days or parts of days.
- When time measurement is necessary, cultivate the ability to do this without mechanical crutches.
- Gauge time with pre-clock tools (e.g., shadows, egg-timers, events).
- Remember that the less often you check the time, the more acute your actual sense of time will become.

7. *Seek Sanctuary from Time.* No matter how hard we try to limit our awareness of time, it intrudes on our consciousness repeatedly. The media especially provide continual reports of the time, along with an up-tempo beat, avalanche of information, and exploded sense of life's options. The result is a sense of overload. One way to make life less hectic is to limit data input while seeking regular opportunities to ignore time altogether.

- Avoid turning on the television to see what's on or as a backdrop to other activities.
- Reduce newspaper and magazine intake; pay fuller attention to fewer pieces of reading matter.
- Before getting a second phone line, call waiting, call forwarding, paging, a fax, or a cellular phone, consider whether your life will be enriched once you're that reachable.
- Create a mental map of hassle-free zones where you can't be reached; retreat to them often.
- "Annul" time regularly with absorbing tasks and hobbies.
- Cultivate an interest in clock-free activities (e.g., chess, baseball, quiltmaking, potting, fly tying).
- Limit activities that require being somewhere at a particular time; deadlines of any kind cause time stress.
- Try to make your week's end at least a semi-Sabbath.
- Become a better vacationer; the less schedule-bound a vacation, the more rejuvenating it will be.

8. *Limit Purchases.* Consumption takes time. Choosing, mastering, and servicing purchases contributes to timelock. Even products sold to ease our burdens often have the opposite effect (the convenience catch). The less we own, the more time we have at our disposal.

- Evaluate purchases in terms of their time-cost, including selection, set-up, and service.
- Avoid products with thick manuals.
- Before buying an appliance to speed completion of tasks, consider whether this is what you really want.
- Bear in mind that a convenience that promises to save time and effort may do just the opposite.
- Remember that low-tech tools can be real time-savers; for many tasks a pencil beats a computer, and a whisk improves on a mixer.
- Before taking advantage of coupons, rebates, or frequent flyer bonuses, calculate whether the time they consume is worth the benefit.
- Consider the cost of travel time (including emotional hassle) when driving in search of bargains.
- Limit errand running; do so by foot or bike whenever possible; if driving is necessary, bunch errands.

9. *Pay Attention to Yourself and Others.* What's the payoff for limiting errands, purchases, and use of conveniences to moderate one's pace? The chief reward is reduced head buzz and improved attention for oneself and others.

- Make sure you are on your own calendar.
- Live according to personal standards, not those of experts, co-workers, your mother or your father.
- Spend more time per person with fewer people.
- Give full attention to those people on a regular basis, without the TV on, a newspaper in hand, or a constant mental review of what else you might be doing.
- Listen.

10. *Upgrade Family Time.* Parenting requires the loose attentiveness that timelock makes difficult. Leading less hectic lives improves our ability to pay attention to our families. Any "sacrifices" made to ease our schedules will be more than paid back in an improved quality of life at home.

- Schedule regular family activities (including meals) when all members are expected to be present.
- Make sure that your kids are on your calendar and know that they are.
- Compare calendars often; look for "trash events" to cross off.

- Trade income for time, an AAA investment in a more balanced life.
- If a two-paycheck family, compare your gross income with the net once work-related expenses, emotional strain, and your time's value have been deducted.
- Consider becoming a career-and-a-half couple.
- If two full incomes are essential, try to make sure that at least one parent's job includes flexible hours.
- If possible, work for a family-friendly employer.
- Consider home work; this is no panacea, but does add flexibility to timelocked schedules.

11. *Achieve More by Doing Less.* In the end, timelock cannot be alleviated and balance achieved by simply reorganizing one's schedule. Something has to give. Usually it's the scheduler. Reducing the volume of our activities makes it possible not only to ease time pressure but to get more out of life overall.

- Before adding a new activity, subtract an old one.
- Practice saying no until you get good at it.
- Accept that you can't have it all, and wouldn't want to.
- Treat career plateaus, tempered ambition, or even a reduced standard of living as a potential time bonanza.
- Approach growing older as an excellent opportunity to ease your pace and do more of what you really want to do.
- Know thyself.

The key to timelock is in our own hands. Pressure from the economy, work, and family demands will always be with us. Inner pressure, including the influence of cultural values, can be harder to deal with. Our culture won't help us cut back. It pays lip service to smelling the flowers, but actual support to getting more done faster. Seeking a better sense of time and a more humane schedule takes *personal* commitment. If enough of us make that commitment, the culture will change.

This has started to happen. Many have come to accept that they can't have at all, and don't even want to try. Instead they are searching for more balanced ways of life. In doing so it's important to keep in mind that the current situation is anomalous; we're making it up as we go along. Our quest for speed and busyness led us into a *cul de sac* in which we lost control of life's tempo. At the same time, a decline of religious and community values deprived us of this counterweight to time's pressures. We've just begun to realize how much we depended on such counterweights to keep our schedules sane. To restore balance, we must apply our own brakes to life's accelerating pace. This does not necessarily mean renouncing technological progress and taking part in a religious revival. It does mean making better choices about what we buy, do, and aspire to do by assessing their cost to us in terms of pace and pressure.

This is not an easy task. Among other things it means accepting that we won't accomplish all that we intended to accomplish. That we can't catch all the movies. That we'll never keep the house our mother kept. And that our career tracks might not be the straight, upward trajectories we'd imagined they would be.

What do we gain in return?

Time.

The most precious possession of all.

Are You Timelocked?

This self-scoring quiz is adapted from the questionnaire used to research *Timelock.* To assess the degree to which time pressure influences your life, answer all questions by circling the number of the best alternative, even if no single answer feels exactly right. Scoring instructions are given at the end.

1. In a typical week, how often do you wear or carry a watch?
   (1) regularly   **(2)** part of the time   **(3)** occasionally
   (4) almost never
2. How many hours do you sleep in an average week night?
   (1) 5 or less   **(2)** 6   **(3)** 7   **(4)** 8 or more
3. When driving, how often do you exceed the speed limit?
   (1) regularly   **(2)** often   **(3)** seldom   **(4)** almost never
4. As you approach a stoplight while driving, if a green light turns to yellow, are you most likely to:
   (1) speed up to get through before it turns to red
   (4) slow down and wait for the next green light

Which Statement Best Describes Your Attitude?

5. **(1)** When I have a train or plane to catch, I like to arrive as close as possible to the scheduled departure time so I won't have to waste time sitting around.
   (4) I always try to leave extra time to get to an airport or train station so I won't have to worry about missing a train or flight.
6. **(1)** At a restaurant, I like my food to arrive as soon as possible after I've ordered.

223

(4) I don't mind waiting a few minutes for the food I've ordered at a restaurant.

7. **(1)** What I like about microwave ovens is that they cut way down on the amount of time it takes to prepare meals.
   (4) I'd rather spend extra time preparing meals than use a microwave oven on a regular basis.

8. **(1)** I often use a remote control device to scan a lot of television channels so I can see what's on.
   (4) To me a remote control device is a convenient tool for turning the television on or off from a distance, adjusting the volume, or occasionally changing channels.

9. **(1)** I like the lively pace of today's television programs.
   (4) I have trouble keeping up with the pace of today's television programs.

10. **(1)** With so many other demands on my time, I find it hard to keep up friendships.
    (4) I try to make time to see my friends on a regular basis.

11. Compared to your life ten years ago, would you say you have more or less leisure time?
    (1) less **(2)** about the same **(3)** a bit more **(4)** a lot more

12. How would you compare the amount of time you spend running errands today with the amount you spent ten years ago?
    (1) more **(2)** about the same **(3)** somewhat less **(4)** a lot less

13. During the past year, how many books would you estimate you've read from beginning to end?
    (1) 0–2 **(2)** 3–5 **(3)** 6–10 **(4)** 11 or more

14. How good are you at glancing at your watch or a clock without anyone else noticing?
    (1) very good **(2)** good **(3)** fair **(4)** not good at all

15. How would you rate your ability to conduct a conversation and appear to be paying attention while thinking about something else at the same time?
    (1) excellent **(2)** good **(3)** fair **(4)** poor

16. How often do you find yourself interrupting the person with whom you're talking?
    (1) regularly **(2)** often **(3)** occasionally **(4)** rarely

17. When talking on the telephone, are you more likely to:
    (1) do paperwork, wash dishes, or do some other chore
    (2) straighten up the surrounding area
    (3) do small personal tasks (e.g., file nails, reset watch)
    (4) do nothing else

18. In an average week, how many evening or weekend hours do you spend working overtime or on work you've brought home?
    (1) 16 or more **(2)** 11–15 **(3)** 6–10 **(4)** 0–5

19. During a typical weekend, do you engage primarily in:
    (1) work for income
    (2) household chores and errands
    (3) leisure activities
    (4) catching up on sleep and relaxing
20. In a typical year, how many weeks of paid vacation do you take?
    (1) 1 or less   (2) 2   (3) 3   (4) 4 or more
21. On the whole, do you find vacations:
    (1) frustrating   (2) tedious   (3) relaxing   (4) rejuvenating
22. How often do you find yourself wishing you had more time to spend with family members or friends?
    (1) constantly   (2) often   (3) occasionally   (4) almost never
23. During a typical day, how often do you feel rushed?
    (1) constantly   (2) often   (3) occasionally   (4) almost never
24. Which statement best describes your usual daily schedule?
    (1) there aren't enough hours in the day to do everything I have to do
    (2) on the whole I have just about enough time to do what I have to do
    (3) I can usually do the things I have to do with time left over
    (4) the day seems to have more hours than I'm able to fill
25. During the past year, would you say that your life has grown:
    (1) busier   (2) about the same   (3) somewhat less busy
    (4) a lot less busy

Scoring: Add up the total of all numbers circled. A score of 25–40 indicates you are *timelocked;* 41–55, *pressed for time;* 56–71, *in balance;* 72–86, *time on hands.*

Bibliography and Notes

Published sources of information follow. Where none is cited, material from interviews, focus group discussions, or questionnaire responses is my source. The following books and essays are referred to in subsequent notes by last name of author and an abbreviated title where necessary.

Bloch, Marc. *Feudal Society* (Chicago: University of Chicago Press, 1961).

Boorstin, Daniel J. *The Americans: The Colonial Experience* (New York: Random House, 1958).

———. *The Americans: The National Experience* (New York: Random House, 1965).

———. *The Americans: The Democratic Experience* (New York: Random House, 1973).

———. *The Discoverers* (New York: Random House, 1983).

Brown, Richard D. *Modernization: The Transformation of American Life, 1600–1865* (New York: McGraw-Hill, 1976).

Bush, Donald J. *The Streamlined Decade* (New York: George Braziller, 1975).

Celehar, Jane H. *Kitchens and Gadgets* (Lombard, IL: Wallace-Homestead, 1982).

———. *Kitchens and Kitchenware* (Lombard, IL: Wallace-Homestead, 1985).

Cipolla, Carlo M. *Clocks and Culture, 1300–1700* (New York: Walker, 1967).

Consumer Reports. *I'll Buy That!* (Mount Vernon, NY: Consumer Reports Press, 1986).

Cowan, Ruth Schwartz. *More Work for Mother* (New York: Basic Books, 1983).

Davidson, Marshall. *Life in America*, vols. 1 and 2 (Boston: Houghton Mifflin, 1951).

de Grazia, Sebastian. *Of Time, Work and Leisure* (New York: Twentieth Century Fund, 1962).

———. "The Problems and Promise of Leisure." In Brigitte Berger, ed., *Readings in Sociology* (New York: Basic Books, 1974).

de Romilly, Jacqueline. *Time in Greek Tragedy* (Ithaca: Cornell University Press, 1968).

Dodds, John W. *American Memoir* (New York: Popular Library, 1959, 1961).

———. *Everyday Life in Twentieth Century America* (New York: Putnam's, 1965).

Dossey, Larry. *Space, Time and Medicine* (Boston: New Science Library, 1982).

Edlund, Matthew. *Psychological Time and Mental Illness* (New York: Gardner Press, 1987).

Elkins, John. "Out of Time." *The American Way,* December 15, 1987, 16–19.

Epstein, Steven A. "Business Cycles and the Sense of Time in Medieval Genoa." *Business History Review* 62 (1988): 238–260.

Fisher, Marvin. *Workshop in the Wilderness* (New York: Oxford University Press, 1967).

Forty, Adrian. *Objects of Desire* (New York: Pantheon Books, 1986).

Fraser, J. T. *Time, the Familiar Stranger* (Amherst: University of Massachusetts Press, 1987; Redmond, WA: Tempus Books, 1988).

———, ed. *Voices of Time* (New York: George Braziller, 1966).

———, F. C. Haber, and G. H. Muller, eds. *The Study of Time I* (Berlin: Springer-Verlag, 1972).

———, and N. Lawrence, eds. *The Study of Time II* (Berlin: Springer-Verlag, 1975).

———, N. Lawrence, and D. Park, eds. *The Study of Time III* (Berlin: Springer-Verlag, 1978).

Friedman, Meyer, and Ray H. Rosenman. *Type A Behavior and Your Heart* (New York: Alfred A. Knopf, 1974).

———, and Diane Ulmer. *Treating Type A Behavior and Your Heart* (New York: Alfred A. Knopf, 1984).

Furnas, J.C. *The Americans* (New York: Putnam's, 1969).

———. *Great Times* (New York: Putnam's, 1974).

———. *Stormy Weather* (New York: Putnam's, 1977).

Gibbs, Nancy. "How America Has Run Out of Time." *Time,* April 24, 1989, 58–67.

Giedion, Siegfried. *Mechanization Takes Command* (Oxford: Oxford University Press, 1948; New York: W. W. Norton, 1969).

Gutman, Herbert G. "Work, Culture and Society in Industrializing America, 1815–1919." *American Historical Review* 78 (1973): 531–587.

Hall, Edward T. *The Silent Language* (Garden City, NY: Doubleday, 1959; New York: Fawcett, 1967).

———. *The Dance of Life* (Garden City, NY: Anchor Press/Doubleday, 1983).

Hine, Thomas. *Populuxe* (New York: Alfred A. Knopf, 1986).

Hunt, Diana, and Pam Hait. *The Tao of Time* (New York: Henry Holt, 1990).

Kasson, John F. *Civilizing the Machine* (New York: Grossman Publishers, 1976).

Kern, Stephen. *The Culture of Time and Space* (Cambridge: Harvard University Press, 1983).

Lakein, Alan. *How to Get Control of Your Time and Your Life* (New York: Peter Wyden, 1973; New York: Signet, 1974).

Landes, David. *Revolution in Time* (Cambridge: Harvard University Press, 1983).

Langdon, Philip. *Orange Roofs, Golden Arches* (New York: Alfred A. Knopf, 1986).

Lauer, Robert H. *Temporal Man* (New York: Praeger, 1981).

Lears, T.J. Jackson. *No Place of Grace* (New York: Pantheon Books, 1981).

Le Goff, Jacques. *Time, Work, and Culture in the Middle Ages* (Chicago: University of Chicago Press, 1980).

Levenstein, Harvey A. *Revolution at the Table* (New York: Oxford University Press, 1988).

Lewis, Peter. *The Fifties* (New York: Lippincott, 1978).

Liebs, Chester H. *From Main Street to Miracle Mile* (Boston: Little, Brown, 1985).

Lifshey, Earl. *The Housewares Story* (Chicago: National Housewares Manufacturers Association, 1973).

Linder, Staffan. *The Harried Leisure Class* (New York: Columbia University Press, 1970).

Macey, Samuel L. *Clocks and the Cosmos* (Hamden, CT: Archon Books, 1980).

Marchand, Roland. *Advertising the American Dream* (Berkeley: University of California Press, 1985).

Marquis, Alice G. *Hopes and Ashes* (New York: Free Press, 1986).

Marx, Leo. *The Machine in the Garden* (New York: Oxford University Press, 1964).

Meikle, Jeffrey. *Twentieth Century Limited* (Philadelphia: Temple University Press, 1979).

Meyerhoff, Hans. *Time in Literature* (Berkeley: University of California Press, 1955).

Mumford, Lewis. *Technics and Civilization* (New York: Harcourt, Brace, 1934).

———. *The Conduct of Life* (New York: Harcourt, Brace & World, 1951).

O'Neill, William. *American High: The Years of Confidence, 1945–1960* (New York: Free Press, 1986).

Palmer, Brooks. *The Romance of Time* (New Haven: Clock Manufacturers Association of America, 1954).

Quinones, Ricardo J. *The Renaissance Discovery of Time* (Cambridge: Harvard University Press, 1972).

Ridgely, Julia. "Changing Work, Changing Times." *Alumni Magazine Consortium,* November 1987, I–VIII.

Rifkin, Jeremy. *Time Wars* (New York: Henry Holt, 1987).

Robinson, John P. "Television and Leisure Time: Yesterday, Today and (Maybe) Tomorrow." *Public Opinion Quarterly* 33 (Summer 1969): 210–222.

———. In Eli Rubinstein et al., eds., *Television and Social Behavior* (Rockville, MD: National Institute of Mental Health, 1972), 410–431.

———. *How Americans Use Time* (New York: Praeger, 1977).

———. " 'Massification' and Democratization of the Leisure Class." *Annals of the American Academy of Political and Social Science* 435 (1978): 206–225.

———. "Television and Leisure Time: A New Scenario." *Journal of Communication* 31 (1981): 120–130.

———. "Changes in Time Use: An Historical Overview." In F. T. Juster and F. P. Stafford, eds., *Time, Goods and Well-Being* (Ann Arbor: Institute for Social Research, University of Michigan, 1985), 289–311.

———. "Time Diary Evidence About the Social Psychology of Everyday Life." In Joseph McGrath, ed., *The Social Psychology of Time* (Newbury Park, CA: Sage, 1988), 134–148.

————. "Who's Doing the Housework?" *American Demographics,* December 1988, 24–28.

————. "When the Going Gets Tough." *American Demographics,* February 1989, 50.

————. "Time for Work." *American Demographics,* April 1989, 68.

————. "Time's Up." *American Demographics,* July 1989, 33–35,

————. "Caring for Kids." *American Demographics,* July 1989, 52.

————. "Americans on the Road." *American Demographics,* September 1989, 10.

————. "Up Close and Personal." *American Demographics,* November 1989, 10–11.

————. "The Time Squeeze." *American Demographics,* February 1990, 30–33.

————, Vladimir G. Andreyenkov, and Vasily D. Patrushev. *The Rhythm of Everyday Life* (Boulder, CO: Westview Press, 1989).

————, and Philip E. Converse. "Social Change Reflected in the Use of Time." In Angus Campbell and Philip E. Converse, eds., *The Human Meaning of Social Change* (New York: Russell Sage, 1972), 17–86.

————, and Jonathan Gershuny. "Historical Changes in the Household Division of Labor." *Demography,* 25 (November 1988): 537–552.

Rodgers, Daniel T. *The Work Ethic in Industrial America 1850–1920* (Chicago: University of Chicago Press, 1978).

Rybczynski, Witold. *Home* (New York: Viking, 1986).

Samuelson, Robert J. "Rediscovering the Rat Race." *Newsweek,* May 15, 1989, 57.

Schivelbusch, Wolfgang. *The Railway Journey* (Berkeley: University of California Press, 1986).

————. *Disenchanted Night* (Berkeley: University of California Press, 1988).

Schudson, Michael. *Advertising, the Uneasy Persuasion* (New York: Basic Books, 1984).

Schwartz, Tony. "The Acceleration Syndrome." *Vanity Fair,* October 1988, 144–149, 180–188.

Servan-Schreiber, Jean-Louis. *The Art of Time* (Reading, MA: Addison-Wesley, 1988).

Stains, Lawrence R. "Beat the Clock." *Philadelphia,* December 1986, 208–214.

Strasser, Susan. *Never Done* (New York: Pantheon Books, 1982).

Suplee, Curt. "Driven to Distraction." *Vogue,* November 1984, 206–209.

Thomas, Keith. "Work and Leisure." *Past and Present* (old series) No. 29 (December 1964): 50–66.

Thompson, E.P. "Time, Work-Discipline, and Industrial Capitalism." *Past and Present* 38 (1967): 56–97.

Thrift, Nigel. "Owners' Time and Own Time: The Making of a Capitalist Time Consciousness, 1300–1880." In Allan Pred, ed., *Space, Time and Geography* (Lund, Sweden: CWK Gleerup, 1981), 57–84.

Tichi, Cecilia. *Shifting Gears* (Chapel Hill: University of North Carolina Press, 1987).

Tivnan, Edward. "Healing Time Sickness." *American Health,* March 1989, 76–82.

Whitrow, G. J. "Reflections on the History of the Concept of Time." In J. T. Fraser, ed., *The Study of Time I* (Berlin: Springer-Verlag, 1972), 1–11.

Wright, Lawrence. *Clockwork Man* (New York: Horizon Press, 1968).

Young, Michael. *The Metronomic Society* (Cambridge: Harvard University Press, 1988).
Zerubavel, Eviatar. *The Seven Day Circle* (New York: Free Press, 1985).

Trish Hall's ongoing coverage of social trends for the *New York Times* was a continual source of help. So was Ann Kolson's October 26, 1989, feature on time for the *Philadelphia Inquirer,* and *USA Today*'s series on the "The Time Crunch," August 17–21, 1987.

Newspaper titles are abbreviated as follows: the *Dayton Daily News,* DDN; the *Los Angles Times,* LAT; the *New York Times,* NYT; the *Philadelphia Inquirer,* PI; *USA Today,* USAT; and the *Wall Street Journal,* WSJ.

Author's Note

Berry, Robinson, "Market to the Perception," *American Demographics,* February 1990, 32.

1   Desperately Seeking Time

5 Harris survey, NYT 1/2/88, 5/19/90; PI 10/26/89. Harris's numbers about declining hours of leisure were questioned by other pollsters during private conversations with the author. For a detailed assessment of Harris's methodology, see John Robinson, "The Polls—A Review," *Public Opinion Quarterly* 53 (Fall 1989): 397–414.

Harris quote, *Time,* April 24, 1989, 58.

7 nonvoters, ABC Evening News, November 6, 1990.

pets to pound, NYT, 3/29/90.

appointment calendars, *Dallas Times-Herald,* 12/8/89.

9 court reporter, NYT, 10/19/76.

Kingston Trio, Champaign-Urbana (IL) *News-Gazette,* 7/5/83.

"speed of transactions," George Stalk, Jr., "Time—The Next Source of Competitive Advantage," *Harvard Business Review,* July–August 1988, 41–51; "Time is Money," *The Economist,* October 8, 1988, 68–69; Brian Dumaine, "How Managers Can Succeed Through Speed," *Fortune,* January 13, 1989, 54–59; Rudyard L. Istvan, "The Most Powerful Competitive Weapon of All—Time," *Boardroom Reports,* September 1, 1990, 1, 6; Alvin Toffler, *Powershift* (New York: Bantam, 1990).

Bank of New York, NYT, 4/24/90.

Compaq, Cable News Network, October 24, 1989.

Toshiba, WPGR radio, Philadelphia, April 6, 1990.

10 Roper executive, NYT, 5/12/88.

Robinson data, "The Time Squeeze," 30, 33.

Robinson's perspective: personal interview; Robinson and Gershuny, "Historical Changes in the Household Division of Labor"; Robinson, "Time for Work," 68; Robinson, "Time's Up," 33–35; Ann Kolson, PI, 10/26/89.

2   A Brief History of Timekeeping

14 Mumford, *Technics and Civilization*, 14.

Follini, NYT, 5/17/89, 5/24/89; *Time,* June 5, 1989, 66–67; *People Weekly,* June 12, 1989, 52–53; Martin G. Ralph, "The Rhythm Maker," *The Sciences,* November–December 1989, 40.

15 primitive units of time, Martin P. Nilsson, *Primitive Time-Reckoning* (Oxford: Oxford University Press, 1920), 24–25, 42.

"pissing while," Thompson, 58; *Oxford English Dictionary,* 2nd ed. (1989), vol. xi, 907.

16 Evans-Pritchard, *The Nuer* (Oxford: Clarendon Press, 1940), 101–103.
"belly chimes," Macey, 204.
Ovid, Quinones, 13.

17 holidays, de Grazia, *Of Time, Work and Leisure,* 89.
work patterns, *ibid.,* 315; Young, 47.
Thompson, 73.
Plautus, Landes, 15–16; Daniel Boorstin, *Discoverers,* 28; Wright, 29.

18 water clocks, hourglasses, Fraser, *Time, the Familiar Stranger,* 49–51.
Bloch, 74.
different means of telling time, Fraser, *Time, the Familiar Stranger,* 84; Le Goff, 49; Landes, 94.

19 debut of clock, Cipolla, 39, says according to "general consensus," the first mechanical clock appeared in the second half of the thirteenth century. Landes, 53, says "Not until the fourteenth century do we get our first unmistakeable reports of mechanical clocks."
Landes, 16.
Town Council of Lyon, Cipolla, 42; Wright, 62.
"o'clock," Macey, 185–193; Cipolla, 104–105.

20 Frenchman, Landes, 82.
Welshman's complaint, a combination of translations in Cipolla, 104, and Wright, 68.
Petrarch, Quinones, 17, 146–169, 494

21 "spede," *Oxford English Dictionary,* 2nd ed. (1989), vol. xvi, 184.
memento mori, Landes, 91; "Curious Time-Measurers," *Leisure Hour,* 28 (1879): 710–712, 744–748.
Italian poet, Cipolla, 310–311.
Young develops at length the metronome-like beat of mechanically timed life, as does Mumford, *Technics and Civilization.* See also Thompson, Thrift, and Thomas.

22 Franklin tweaks Europeans, Davidson, vol. 2, 3.
Franklin, "Advice," *Autobiography and Other Writings,* Russell B. Nye, ed. (Boston: Houghton Mifflin, 1958), 166–167.

23 time discipline, Thompson; Thrift; Landes, 228–229; Gutman argues that American workers never really fell in step with this discipline.
clergymen, Le Goff, 46–47.
English minister, Thompson, 83.
school historian, Thrift, 65.

Cipolla, 103.
Landes, 230.

The Time Traveler

25–29 Levine reported his Brazilian research with Laurie J. West and Harry T. Reis, "Perceptions of Time and Punctuality in the United States and Brazil," *Journal of Personality and Social Psychology,* 38 (1980), 541–550. He discussed his Brazilian experience and subsequent travels in "It Wasn't the Time of My Life," *Discover,* December 1985, 66–71, and in an undated manuscript titled *Travels with Time.* He reported his pace-of-life research with Kathy Bartlett in "Pace of Life, Punctuality, and Coronary Heart Disease in Six Countries," *Journal of Cross-Cultural Psychology,* 15 (1984), 233–255; with Ellen Wolff in "Social Time: The Heartbeat of Culture," *Psychology Today,* March 1985, 29–35; and in Joseph McGrath, ed., *The Social Psychology of Time: New Perspectives* (Newbury Park, CA: Sage, 1988), 39–62

26 chart, *Psychology Today,* March 1985, 35.

3 The American Tempo

30 Adams, *The American: The Making of a New Man* (New York: Scribner's, 1943), 380.

Chevalier, Fisher, 65; Michael Chevalier, *Society, Manners, and Politics in the United States: Letters on North America by Michael Chevalier,* John William Ward, ed. (Gloucester, MA: Peter Smith, 1967), 270.

Grund, in Douglas T. Miller, *Then Was the Future* (New York: Alfred A. Knopf, 1973), 1.

Marryat, in Jack Larkin, "The Secret Life of a Developing Country (Ours)," *American Heritage,* September–October 1988, 46.

visitors from abroad, Otto L. Bettmann, *The Good Old Days—They Were Terrible!* (New York: Random House, 1974), 123–124; Davidson, vol. 2, 138.

31 Lenau, Albert Bernhardt Faust, *The German Element in the United States,* vol. 2 (New York: Steuben Society of America, 1927), 346.

Chevalier, *Society, Manners, and Politics,* 77, 270.

Jefferson, Davidson, vol. 1, 284.

32 Bremer, *Homes of the New World: Impressions of America* (New York: Harper & Brothers, 1853), 539–540.

steamboat casualties, John G. Burke, "Bursting Boilers and the Federal Power," in Melvin Kranzberg and William H. Davenport, *Technology and Culture* (New York: Schocken Books, 1972), 109.

Emerson, Kasson, 129.

Marryat, *A Diary in America, with Remarks on Its Institutions,* Sydney Jackman, ed. (New York: Alfred A. Knopf, 1962), 369–371.

33 Schivelbusch, *Railway Journey,* discusses at length the visual and spiritual

effects of travel by rail; see also John R. Stilgoe, *Metropolitan Corridor* (New Haven: Yale University Press, 1983).

Emerson, Kasson, 116.

Lieber, Schivelbusch, *Railway Journey,* 59.

Thoreau, *Walden* (New York, Mentor, 1942), 83.

1853 crash, Carlene Stephens, " 'The Most Reliable Time': William Bond, the New England Railroads, and Time Awareness in 19th Century America," *Technology and Culture,* 30 (1989), 1–24.

34 Bremer, *Homes of the New World,* 539.

1881 guide, George Gray, "When We Had 87 Varieties of Time," *The Reader's Digest Reader* (Garden City, NY: Doubleday, Doran, 1940), 91. See also Robert W. Shoemaker, "The Day Time Got on Track," *Chicago,* November 1988, 176–177, 245; Schivelbusch, *Railway Journey,* 44; Kern, 12; and Landes, 285–286.

Sentinel writer, Ian R. Bartky, "The Adoption of Standard Time," *Technology and Culture,* 30 (1989) 25–56, 52; William H. Earle, "November 18, 1883: The Day That Noon Showed Up on Time," *Smithsonian,* November 1983, 202.

35 "on time," Lears, 10.

clocks, watches, Brown, 135; Davidson, vol. 1, 504.

Beard, *American Nervousness: Its Causes and Consequences* (New York: Putnam's, 1881), 103, 138, 103–104.

alarm clocks, Daniel Bell, *Time,* September 8, 1975, 55.

Taylor, Boorstin, *Americans: The Democratic Experience,* 363–370; Davidson, vol. 1, 562.

time clocks, *Scientific American,* August 12, 1893, 101.

36 such tributes disappeared, S.G.F. Brandon, "The Deification of Time," in Fraser, *Voices of Time,* 475.

Rosenfeld, Gutman, 547.

AT&T ad, *Literary Digest,* April 16, 1910.

On domestic science, see, for example, Bertha J. Austin, *Domestic Science* (Chicago: Lyons & Carnahan), 1914.

Levenstein discusses turn-of-the-century eating customs at length in *Revolution at the Table.* See also Liebs, Langdon, and Stuart Berg Flexner, *Listening to America* (New York: Simon & Schuster, 1982), 131–138, 469–471.

37 *Chicago* magazine, Levenstein, 186.

Carnegie, *Triumphant Democracy* (Garden City, NY: Doubleday, Doran, 1933), 1.

"jas," Jules Abel, *In the Time of Silent Cal* (New York: Putnam's, 1969), 199.

bicycling, Richard F. Snow, "The Great Bicycle Delirium," *American Heritage,* June 1975, 61–72; Furnas, *Americans,* 809–812.

1895 race, Maurice Duke in M. Thomas Inge, ed., *Handbook of American Popular Culture,* vol. 1 (Westport, CT: Greenwood Press, 1982), 30.

Ford, Florida train, George Gray, "Speed," *Atlantic Monthly,* March 1930, 324–325.

magazine writer, Kate Masterson, "The Tyranny of Speed," *Lippincott's,* July 1912, 117–118.

38 study of postwar trends, *Recent Social Trends in the United States,* Report of the President's Research Committee on Social Trends (New York: McGraw-Hill, 1933), 172.

Muncie mother, student, Robert and Helen Lynd, *Middletown* (New York: Harcourt, Brace & World, 1929), 151.

cinema speed, Werner Adrian, *Speed: Cinema of Motion* (New York: Bounty Books, 1975), 82.

S.L. Rothafel, "Speed and Business," *The Magazine of Business,* May 1928, 565–567, 676.

company president, R.H. Beaumont, "We Watch Time More Closely than Money," *System,* June 1921, 793.

39 cut inch off, A. V. Levering, "Making Time by Saving It," *System,* March 1920, 497.

writers such as, Tichi discusses the era's up-tempo writing style at length.
1927 adman, Marchand, 3–4.

prerolled cigarettes, Schudson, 198–199.

NYT, 9/24/25, 24.

wristwatches, Landes, 334; Boorstin, *Americans: The Democratic Experience,* 362.

Meikle, 8.

40 DuPont ad, *Literary Digest,* August 12, 1922.

"typical citizen," Marchand, 3.

40–41 Tichi ads, 237–239.

41 1928 writer, Millicent Yackey, "What's Next in Foods?", *Ladies' Home Journal,* November 1928, 98.

advertising man, Marchand, 42.

Quaker Oats, *Saturday Evening Post,* November 12, 1927.

Muncie, Robert and Helen Lynd, *Middletown,* 153–154.

42 proposed scheduling, Alice Bradley, "Where Does Your Time Go? A Schedule That Will Really Work," *Woman's Home Companion,* June 1922, 42, 108.

efficiency expert, Giedion, in Celehar, *Kitchens and Gadgets,* 8.

"life on the jump," Hildegarde Hawthorne, "Saving Time," *St. Nicholas,* January 1922, 268.

"time snobs," "French Alarm at American Speed," *Literary Digest,* August 24, 1929, 19.

Norman Bel Geddes, *Horizons* (Boston: Little, Brown, 1932), 24.

streamlining, Bush, Forty, Giedion, Langdon, Marquis, Meikle.

"Speed!" Harold Ward, "Towards a New Era of Speed," *Travel,* April 1934, 10.

43 "cunningly devised," Morris Massey, *The People Puzzle* (Reston, VA: Reston Publishing, 1979), 70.

White Castle, Langdon, 29–38; Joseph Monninger, "Fast Food," *American Heritage,* April 1988, 68–75; WSJ, 3/22/85.

Kraft's macaroni and cheese ad, *TV Guide,* February 14, 1987.

convenience foods, James Trager, ed., *The People's Chronology* (New York: Holt, Rinehart and Winston, 1979), 950; Boy-Ar-Dee, label to Beef Ravioli in 1989 can says, "Since 1939, Chef Boy-Ar-Dee has been serving American families with steaming platters of good, nutritious pasta dishes packed in cans."

Rombauer, *Newsweek,* September 4, 1989, 63.

GIs' food preferences, Paul Dickson, *Chow* (New York: New American Library, 1978), 279.

Nescafé, "Swiss Family Nestlé," *Fortune,* February 1946, 104+; passage cited from "Nestlé and Soluble Coffee," undated manuscript from Nestlé files.

Camel ads, Marchand, 341 (from *Orlando Morning Sentinel,* 3/24/36); *American Home,* December 1938.

44 Westinghouse pavilion, NYT, 3/2/89; "The World of Tomorrow," 1984, part of "The American Experience" series, rebroadcast October 6, 1989, Channel 39 (PBS-TV, Allentown, PA).

World's Fair, Marquis, 187–231; Meikle, 153–155, 189–210; Bush, 138–170; Joseph J. Corn and Brian Horrigan, *Yesterday's Tomorrows* (New York: Summit Books, 1984); Helen A. Harrison, ed., *Dawn of a New Day: The New York World's Fair/1939–1940* (New York: New York University Press, 1980); Queens Museum, *Remembering the Future: The New York World's Fair from 1939 to 1964* (New York: Rizzoli, 1989); Barbara Cohen, Steven Heller, and Seymour Chwast, *Trylon and Perisphere: The 1939 New York World's Fair* (New York: Harry Abrams, 1989); Larry Zim and Mel Lerner, *The World of Tomorrow* (New York: Harper & Row, 1989).

Sarnoff, Harrison, *Dawn of a New Day,* 54.

McSpeed

45–47 on McDonald's genesis: personal communication from Richard McDonald, November 26, 1990; John Love, *McDonald's: Behind the Arches* (New York: Bantam Books, 1986), quoted from page 19. Kroc on McDonald's, Love, *Ibid.,* 208. See also Max Boas and Steve Chain, *Big Mac* (New York: Dutton, 1976); Ray Kroc, *Grinding It Out* (Chicago: Contemporary, 1977; Berkeley, 1978); Langdon, 81–90; Liebs, 212–213; *Time,* September 17, 1973, 84–92; Monninger, "Fast Food," 70–71.

4 Fast Times

48 Huxley, Young, 162.

Dunkin' Donuts architect, James Simon Kunen, "Slow Down," *New Times,* September 6, 1974, 6.

Langdon, 102.

49 1956 compilation, Ray Josephs, "Nine timesaving secrets," *Better Homes and Gardens,* April 1956, 132.

Ogden Nash, *I'm a Stranger Here Myself* (Boston: Little, Brown, 1943), 31.

49 MacLeish, "In Praise of Porches," *Reader's Digest*, July 1975, 70.

50 Oroville woman, Pamela West, "The Rise and Fall of the American Porch," *Landscape*, 20 (Spring 1976): 42–47, 47.

Levitt official, Champaign-Urbana (IL) *Courier*, 9/3/74.

"kitchen eating," "A place to eat in your kitchen," *Better Homes and Gardens*, August 1955, 45.

AMERICAN KITCHEN, *American Home*, February 1950.

blender makers, "The Sociology of the Blender," *New Times*, April 29, 1977, 25.

Hine, 124–125.

Plymouth ad, *Ladies' Home Journal*, December 1957.

51 "family with two cars," Lewis, 18.

Robinson quote, "Changes in Time Use," 293.

statistics, Robinson and Converse, "Social Change."

women's driving time, Robinson and Converse, "Social Change," 52.

52 one homemaker, Marguerite Dodd, *America's Homemaking Book* (New York: Scribner's, 1957, 1968), 4.

another woman, Leota Harris Keir, "Put Your Schedule on a Diet," *American Home*, October 1954, 101–102.

Swanson, Strasser, 276; Len Albin, "When the Revolution Came, You Got Designer Dinners in 10 Minutes," *TV Guide*, March 16, 1985, 44–45; *Business Week*, August 7, 1989, 34. Chef Boy-Ar-Dee, *Life*, May 5, 1957.

Sure-Jell, *Better Homes and Gardens*, August 1955.

Campbell's & Junket, *Ladies' Home Journal*, December 1957.

French's, *Sunset*, May 1972.

Safeway executive, LAT, 10/1/72.

postwar working women, William Henry Chafe, *The American Woman* (New York: Oxford University Press, 1974), 180.

toilet-cleaning ad, *Woman's Day*, June 1945, 72.

working women statistics, Robinson and Converse, "Social Change," 83; *Time*, July 26, 1971, 56; O'Neill, 43; William V. Thomas, "Two-Income Families," *Editorial Research Reports*, July 13, 1979, 503.

54 Robinson about television, *How Americans Use Time*, 178.

early television, O'Neill, 77–83.

early commercials, Jonathan Price, *The Best Thing on TV: Commercials* (New York: Penguin Books, 1978), 2.

"Our culture is learning," *Ibid.*, 1.

as 1970s began, *Ibid.*, 6–8; Ron Powers, Suplee, 208; *Advertising Age*, May 9, 1983, 2; Leo Bogart and Charles Lehman, "The Case of the 30-Second Commercial," *Journal of Advertising Research*, 23 (1983): 11–19.

mid-1970s study, *Newsweek*, June 6, 1977, 74.

55 ads halved again, WSJ, 1/19/84.

Zenith, Michael Burg, "The Remotest Idea," *Channels*, September 1988, 55.

Hewitt, Larry King, *USAT*, 10/13/86.

Tartikoff, Tony Schwartz, "The Acceleration Syndrome," *Vanity Fair*, October 1988, 182.

   remote users, Peter Ainslie, "Confronting a Nation of Grazers," *Channels,*
      September 1988, 54; Michael Couzens, "The Undoing of Nielsen," *Madison
      Avenue,* January 1987, 16; *Public Pulse,* November 1988, 8; September
      1989, 4; *Advertising Age,* November 28, 1988, S4.
56 18 year-old, Adam Snyder, "In Search of Greener Pastures," *Channels,* Sep-
      tember 1988, 58.
   Shapiro and Bombach, "Eating Habits Force Change in Marketing," *Advertis-
      ing Age,* October 30, 1978, 27, 65–66, 68.
   eating out, *ibid.,* 65.
   family meals, *ibid.,* 27, 65.
   Shapiro and Bombach, "Heavy Grazers Pace Consumers," *Advertising Age,*
      November 12, 1984, 80, 82.
   coffee sales, *Advertising Age,* December 15, 1986, 28; WSJ, 3/19/86; NYT,
      1/20/88.
   "hot drinks," *Advertising Age,* August 16, 1982, 34.
57 *Cosmopolitan,* 1958, Hine, 125.

5 Why Time Is So Scarce

61 Collins, Sandy Denny-Irving Music, BMI & Winckler Music, BMI.
   Roper's poll, *Public Pulse,* July 1988, 2.
   USAT, 8/17/87.
   home size, *Yellow Springs News* (Ohio), 1/17/90; NYT, 6/14/90.
62 Goodman, PI, 8/9/89.
   Goldstein, PI, 3/25/90; interviewed by Clark DeLeon on WCAU Radio (Phila-
      delphia), March 30, 1990.
64 mutual funds, *Consumer Reports,* May 1990, 330.
   Toffler, *Future Shock* (New York: Random House, 1970), 239.
   "brand clutter," *Public Pulse,* August 1989, 1–3.
65 breakfast cereal, Flexner, *Listening to America,* 133.
   supermarket and new product data: Schudson, 62; NYT, 11/16/79; 5/29/90.
   Goslin, NYT, 2/14/90.
   meet more people, Gary Lockwood, "48 Hours," CBS-TV, March 8, 1990.
66 Robinson, "When the Going Gets Tough," 50.
   San Jose Yellow Pages, USAT, 3/17/89.
   Melbin, *Night as Frontier* (New York: Free Press, 1987), 132.
   over 30 million, *Ibid.,* 27, citing a May 1980 survey which said that the figure
      at that time was 29 million.
   Schwab ad, WCAU Radio (Philadelphia), May 9, 1990; NYT, 9/3/88.
67 New York Stock Exchange, NYT, 6/14/90.
   Melbin, *Night as Frontier,* 5.
   Roper, *Public Pulse,* September 1986, 4; December 1988, 7.
   two Michigan State University economists, Daniel Hammermesh and Jeff Bid-
      dle, NYT, 8/2/89.
   Robinson and Converse, "Social Change," 56.
68 one-handed food, Trish Hall, NYT, 4/15/87.

Sidney Mintz, "American Eating Habits and Food Choices," *Journal of Gastronomy,* Fall 1986, 21.

70 answering machine ownership, DDN, 1/7/91.

New York actor, NYT, 4/28/79.

traveling businessman, WSJ, 11/15/84.

Detroit lawyer, NYT, 10/11/89.

71 Washington lawyer, NYT, 12/9/87.

future cellular phones, Stephen Fried, "The Beep Goes On," *Philadelphia,* February 1989, 85–87, 117–119; Hugo Dixon, *World Press Review,* October 1989, 36, 38; NYT, 5/10/90; USAT, 8/13/90; "Real Life," NBC-TV, January 5, 1991.

72 Becker, "A Theory of the Allocation of Time," *Economic Journal,* 75, 493–517, 1965. Linder elaborates on Becker's basic point at length in *The Harried Leisure Class.*

74 Kapot, David Churbuck, "Prepare for E-mail attack," *Forbes,* January 23, 1989, 82.

The Affluent Society

75–78 Allen Johnson discusses his personal experience in Peru in "In Search of the Affluent Society," *Human Nature,* September 1978, 50–59, from which some of his comments are excerpted. His more technical reports are in "Time Allocation in a Machiguenga Community," *Ethnology,* 14 (1975): 301–310; "Reductionism in Cultural Ecology: The Amazon Case," *Current Anthropology,* 23 (1982): 413–428; and with Orna Johnson and Michael Baksh, "The Colors of Emotions in Machiguenga," *American Anthropologist,* 88 (1986): 674–681.

6 The Convenience Catch

79 Caldwell, *Reader's Digest,* May 1949, 7.

Lawn mowers are discussed by Donald and Eleanor Laird in *How to Get Along with Automation* (New York: McGraw-Hill, 1964), 255–259.

80 Xerography, Ralph Keyes, "America's Favorite Reproduction System," *New Times,* January 9, 1976, 34–40; "Home, Home on the Xerox," *New York,* November 17, 1980, 60–61.

81 Davidson, vol. 1, 493.

eggbeater, Cowan, 53.

82 college student, DDN, 9/16/90.

83 Panasonic, *People Weekly,* January 16, 1989.

Dustbuster, *People Weekly,* November 16, 1987.

survey of studies, Christine E. Bose, Philip L. Bereano, Mary Malloy, "The Social Construction of Housework," *Technology and Culture,* 25 (June 1984): 53–82, 74.

Michigan studies, Robinson interview; Robinson, "Time Diary Evidence," 145.

Vanek, "Time Spent in Housework," *Scientific American,* November 1974,

116–120; "Household Technology and Social Status: Rising Living Standards and Residence Differences in Housework," *Technology and Culture,* 19 (1978): 361–375.

84 Strasser, 268.

85 Lever-operated sink stopper cited as a time-consuming labor-saver by Ruth Baldwin in a letter to *Smithsonian,* July 1975, 12.

Talese and Rooney, Ralph Keyes, "Classics," *GQ,* January 1989, 146.

86 GE Center, PI, 5/7/89.

Bush, Connie Koenenn, LAT, 5/11/90; "Real Life," NBC-TV, July 17, 1990.

New York woman, Ellen Azorin, *New York,* October 31, 1988, 30.

87 Donald Norman, *The Psychology of Everyday Things* (New York: Basic Books, 1988), 1.

Norman, DDN, 9/16/90; *People Weekly,* January 9, 1989, 91–94.

88 Norman quote, *People Weekly,* January 9, 1989, 91.

Koffler, "How Do We Confuse Thee? Let Us Count the Ways," *Forbes,* March 21, 1988, 157.

Digital founder, Norman, *Psychology of Everyday Things,* 1.

89 Kafka, PI, 11/29/87; 11/1/89.

90 research on home computers, LAT, 5/11/90.

Fallows, "Help! I'm the Captive of My Home Computer! (And I Love It!)," *TV Guide,* December 18, 1982, 26–29; "Living With a Computer," *Atlantic,* July 1982, 84–91.

7 The Speed Trap

94 Wynn, *Reader's Digest,* May 1933, 107.

96 one study, PI, 9/6/89.

98 Ellul, Servan-Schreiber, 55.

100 Warhol, *People Weekly,* December 16, 1985, 208.

fast food getting faster, Dena Kleiman, NYT, 12/6/89.

101 "The PC," Alfred Poor, "What's Inside," *PC Magazine,* February 14, 1989, 4.

Seybold, Cheryl Spencer, "Speed! Speed! Speed!," *Personal Computing,* January 1987, 74.

one computer user, Art Kleiner, "The Ambivalent Miseries of Personal Computing," *Whole Earth Review,* January 1985, 6–7. Jeremy Rifkin develops this point at length in *Time Wars.*

102 as many as ten million users, DDN, 10/15/90.

clothing factory, WSJ, 6/3/85.

103 sound bites, Kiku Adatto, "The Incredible Shrinking Sound Bite," *The New Republic,* May 28, 1990, 20–23.

time compression, "Cheers 'n' Jeers," *TV Guide,* March 4, 1989, 38.

Meyer, NYT, 1/22/89.

Ailes, with Jon Kraushar, *You Are the Message* (Homewood, IL: Dow Jones-Irwin, 1988), 12–13.

Mander, "Six Grave Doubts About Computers," *Whole Earth Review,* January 1985, 18.

104 German physiologist, *Science News Letter,* July 31, 1965, 78.
    another experiment, *Newsweek,* September 19, 1955, 72.
    Milliman, "The Sweet Sound of Profits," *Restaurant Management,* July 1988,
    53–54; see also "The Influence of Background Music on the Behavior of
    Restaurant Patrons," *Journal of Consumer Research,* September 1986, 286–
    289.

8 The Hurried Body

109 Spanish proverb, DDN, 3/26/91.
110 Peace Corps volunteers, James P. Spradley, "Culture and Stress: A Quantita-
    tive Analysis," *American Anthropologist,* 74, 518–529, 526.
    Republican official, PI, 4/23/79.
    Dossey, 49.
112 accountants, Friedman and Rosenman, 59; Redford Williams, *The Trusting
    Heart: Great News About Type A Behavior* (New York: Random House,
    1989), 24.
    Ornish, LAT, 11/15/88; "Heart Disease in Retreat," *Psychology Today,* Janu-
    ary–February 1989, 46–48; NYT, 11/14/89; "A New Menu to Heal the
    Heart," *Newsweek,* July 30, 1990, 58–59; Joanne Silberner, "Reversing Heart
    Disease," *U.S. News & World Report,* August 6, 1990, 55–61; *Dr. Dean
    Ornish's Program for Reversing Heart Disease* (New York: Random House,
    1990).
113 Department of Labor study and subsequent data, NYT, 6/24/90; 11/16/89.
114 Bevin, *People Weekly,* May 7, 1990, 127, 130, 133.
    sleep deprivation, NYT, 5/15/90; DDN, 1/7/91.
    Maas, PI, 3/26/90.
    sleep and "Type A" behavior, "Newsline," *Psychology Today,* June 1979, 29,
    31.
    research at Friedman Institute, Friedman and Ulmer, 10.
115 pages from calendars, Marilyn Machlowitz, "A New Take on Type A," *New
    York Times Magazine/Business World,* May 3, 1987, 42.
    Friedman and Ulmer, 56.
116 Levine, "Pace of Life Around the World," *Psychology Today,* October 1989,
    45–46.
    "in our own culture," *Ibid.,* 46.
    Williams, *Trusting Heart,* 152.
117 Wright, "The Type A Behavior Pattern and Coronary Disease," *American
    Psychologist,* January 1988, 4.
    Friedman said, Meyer Friedman, "Type A Behavior: A Frequently Misdiag-
    nosed and Rarely Treated Medical Disorder," *American Heart Journal,* 115
    (April 1988): 930–936, 934.
    reduce risk by half or more, Meyer Friedman, "Effect of Modifying Type A
    Behavior After Myocardial Infarction on Recurrence Rate," *The Mount
    Sinai Journal of Medicine,* 51 (January 1987): 47–55.

9   Rushaholics Anonymous

123 O'Keefe, *American Heritage,* September–October 1988, 47.
     Brody, NYT, 10/22/80.
126 1987 study, Lynette Unger, "Effect of Actual and Perceived Availability of
     Time on Volunteerism," *Perceptual and Motor Skills,* 65, 524–526, 1987.
127 Harris, "The Theory of the Busy Class," *Money,* April 1987, 205.
     "too busy to talk," Irene Borger, "Active Lives '85," *Vogue,* August 1985, 294.
128 Lawrence Wright, "Time on My Hands," *The Inc. Life,* Spring 1990, 13.
     T. E. Lawrence, Paul Morand, "The Only New Vice," *Harper's,* October 1934,
     618.
129 Linda Snyder, "Cosmo Tells All," *Cosmopolitan,* August 1984, 176.
     chronic speeders, Ola Svenson, "Risks of Road Transportation in a Psychologi-
     cal Perspective," *Accident Analysis and Prevention,* 10 (1978): 267–280,
     271.
     Wright, "The Type A Behavior Pattern," 8.
     stress addiction, Ralph Keyes, *Chancing It* (Boston: Little, Brown, 1985),
     128–49; "The Fear of Living Dangerously," *GQ,* December 1990, 178, 182.
130 Pogrebin, "Prisoner of Time," *Ms.,* October 1988, 20.
131 Baldwin, "Stress and Technology," *USAir,* November 1989, 38.
     Ailes, *You Are the Message,* 13–14.
132 Judith Martin, *Miss Manners' Guide for the Turn-of-the-Millenium* (New York:
     Pharos Books, 1989), 85.
     singles services, "People Resources," NYT, 3/14/89.
     "Short Talks," *Learning Annex Catalog,* Philadelphia, January 1989.
     Modern Romance, NYT, 3/13/81.
133 Howard, "Whatever Happened to Downtime?" *Lear's,* October 1988, 77.
     disponibilité, Martin E. Marty, *Friendship* (Allen, TX: Argus Communications,
     1980), 91, citing Gabriel Marcel.

10   The Timelocked Family

139 Bombeck, newspaper column, 12/23/79.
141 "If my daughter," Sylvia Rabiner, "Hurry up or we'll be late," *Working Mother,*
     September 1981, 160.
148 "arsenic hour," Louise Lague, "Getting Through the Night," *Working Parents,*
     April–May 1987, 26.
     500 freshmen, Margaret Robinson, PI, 2/27/90.
149 1986 Roper poll, NYT, 5/12/88.
     Lewis, Carin Rubenstein, NYT, 5/12/88.
     Twenty-minute meals, John Elkins, 18.
     1988 Roper poll, NYT, 2/14/90.
     1989 Gallup poll, PI, 11/8/89.
150 Richard Louv, *Childhood's Future* (Boston: Houghton Mifflin, 1990).

11   Zen and the Art of Time Management

155 Algerian proverb, Pierre Bourdieu, "The Attitude of the Algerian Peasant Toward Time," in J. Pitt Rivers, ed., *Mediterranean Countrymen* (Paris: Mouton, 1963), 63.

Robinson, in addition to discussing his experience during the Fort Myers focus group, wrote about it in *Wellness Brief* (American Association of Community and Junior Colleges), undated.

156 Biden, *People Weekly*, October 3, 1988, 43.

Barrett, "Death Trip," *Lear's*, November 1989, 118.

157 Rollin, *New York Times Magazine*, April 6, 1980, 37; Ralph Keyes, "The Best Thing That Ever Happened to Me," *McCall's*, September 1985, 15, 19.

157–158 Taylor, LAT, 3/6/84; "Adjustment to Threatening Events," *American Psychologist*, November 1983, 1161–1173, 1163; Ralph Keyes, *McCall's*, September 1985, 15, 19.

158 Ufema, *People Weekly*, January 19, 1981, 69.

159 "TODLIF," R. James Steffen, *U.S. News and World Report*, January 25, 1982, 51–53.

160 A book promising, Jay Conrad Levinson, *The Ninety-Minute Hour* (New York: Dutton, 1990).

magazine article, Roxane Farmanfarmaian, "High-Tech Cures for the Time Crunch," *Psychology Today*, March 1989, 46–48.

Hunt, with Pam Hait, xiii, 29.

Mintzberg, *The Nature of Managerial Work* (New York: Harper & Row, 1973).

Kotter, Ford S. Worthy, "How CEOs Manage Their Time," *Fortune*, January 18, 1988, 88.

161 Geneen, "In Praise of Cluttered Desks," *Fortune*, October 15, 1984, 98.

New Age, Marjory Roberts, "Eight Ways to Rethink Your Work Style," *Psychology Today*, March 1989, 42–44.

Massachusetts bank head, *Bottomline*, July 1987, 48.

Koppel, *People Weekly*, December 27, 1983, 89.

Lear, Lisa Belkin, NYT, 10/5/85.

Janklow, Shu Shu Foo, "Dossier," *Manhattan, Inc.*, December 1988, 18.

162 Ehrenreich, NYT, 2/21/85.

Hunt, 31.

163 Will Rogers, *The Harper Book of American Quotations* (New York: Harper & Row, 1988), 234.

Pogrebin, "Prisoner of Time," *Ms.*, October 1988, 20.

164 Servan-Schreiber, 110.

Ibid., 119.

165 Culp, Gibbs, 67.

Nobel, *PACE* (Piedmont Airlines), May–June 1984, 5.

Back from the Fray

167–169 Questrom, WSJ, 4/21/86; NYT, 2/3/90; "Can Allen Questrom Clean Up Campeau's Mess?" *Business Week,* February 19, 1990, 40; Nancy Marx Better, "Questrom's Quest," *Manhattan, Inc.,* July 1990, 39–47.
170 six months after, DDN, 10/28/90.

12   Modulating Time

171 Domingo, DDN, 11/4/90.
Center studies, Angus Campbell, *The Sense of Well-Being in America* (New York: McGraw-Hill, 1981), 125; Robinson and Converse, "Social Change," 65; Robinson, *How Americans Use Time,* 171.
Mumford, *Conduct of Life,* 261–262.
173 Stokes, Ridgely, VIII.
Darwin and Spencer, Donald Laird, "The Thieves of Time," *New Outlook,* November, 1934, 37.
Keynes, Servan-Schreiber, 121.
Johnson, Israel Shenker, "A Samuel Johnson Celebration Recalls His Wit and Wisdom," *Smithsonian,* December, 1984, 68.
174 Franklin, "He Gave Light as Soon as He Rose . . .," *Early American Life,* June 1978, 17; Eric Sloane, *The Cracker Barrel* (New York: Funk & Wagnalls, 1967), 56; "Americana Page," *Hobbies,* November 1953, 100–101; Lifshey, 198; Thomas Fleming, *The Man Who Dared the Lightning* (New York: William Morrow, 1971), 73; Daniel Freeman Hawke, *Franklin* (New York: Harper & Row, 1976), 257.
Churchill, William Manchester, *The Last Lion,* vol. 1, (Boston: Little, Brown, 1983), 377, 418; vol. 2, 24, 552; Winston Churchill, *The Gathering Storm* (Boston: Houghton Mifflin, 1948), 421.
Sadat, *Time,* October 19, 1981, 31; Johnson, NYT, 11/10/89; Reagan, Forbes, other nappers, WSJ, 6/2/83.
175 Reagan's method, Maureen Dowd, NYT, 11/10/89.
Marshall, Judith Chase Churchill, "The Time of Your Life," *Woman's Home Companion,* March 1949, 8.
industrial accidents, Georgia Canty, "Sleep and Peak Performance, Is Napping the Answer?" *Quill* (Pennsylvania Hospital, Philadelphia), Winter 1990, 6; office errors, Judith Chase Churchill, "Time of Your Life"; WSJ, 6/2/83.
sleep research, *Quill,* Winter 1990, 6; Daniel Goleman, NYT, 9/12/89; Edmund L. Andrews, NYT, 4/22/90.
176 Carlyle, *National Enquirer,* 5/9/71.
Lakein, 160, 53–54.
Marraro, Mary Hardie, *San Diego Business Journal,* June 5–11, 1989; Katy Benson, *Del Mar Surfcomber,* 1/25/89.
"Mary," Liz Swain, *Del Mar Citizen,* 1/25/89.
177 Chesterton, NYT, 6/28/31.
Stanford, WSJ, 4/21/86.
Michener, "On Wasting Time," *Reader's Digest,* October 1974, 193–196.

178 Dyer, *People Weekly,* January 10, 1977, 63–64.

Gatlin, WXTV Radio (Philadelphia), June 17, 1984.

Roth, NYT, 4/25/89.

Meyers, PI, 3/15/80.

Stein, Janet Hobhouse, *Everybody Who Was Anybody: A Biography of Gertrude Stein* (New York: Putnam's, 1975), 131.

Williams, Tichi, 245–246.

179 Toynbee, Peter Chew, *The Inner World of the Middle-Aged Man* (New York: Macmillan, 1976), 227.

Benchley, *New York Times Book Review,* July 8, 1979.

Evans, John Chamberlain, *The Enterprising Americans* (New York: Harper & Row, 1963), 51.

long prison terms, de Grazia, *Of Time, Work and Leisure,* 338.

Dossey, 26–27.

180 psychologist, Aaron Lowin, Joseph H. Hottes, Bruce E. Sandler, and Marc Bornstein, "The Pace of Life and Sensitivity to Time in Urban and Rural Settings: A Preliminary Study," *Journal of Social Psychology,* 83 (1971): 247–253, 252–253.

Chinese emperor, Landes, 50–51.

New York lawyer, Enid Nemy, NYT, 1/26/83.

181 egg-cooking woman, Sally Cunneen, "Measuring My Days," *Christian Century,* October 2, 1985, 878.

vintage Schwinn, Ralph Keyes, "Classics," *GQ,* January 1989, 148.

Nancy Willard, "Telling Time," *Prairie Schooner,* Spring 1988, 13.

Nick Lyons, "My Old Underwood Standard: A Loving Tribute to an Upright Machine," *Author's Guild Bulletin,* Winter 1985, 8.

182 Rumer Godden, "The Will to Write," *The Writer,* May 1985, 15.

Baldwin, "Stress and Technology," 41.

Fante's owner, Maria Gallagher, *Philadelphia Daily News,* 11/9/88.

183 Naisbitt, *Megatrends* (New York: Warner Books, 1982, 1984), 50–51.

Bluffton Rapid Slaw, Sue Gorisek, "Industrial Arts," *Ohio Magazine,* February 1988, 61.

Donald B. Kraybill, *The Riddle of Amish Culture* (Baltimore: Johns Hopkins University Press, 1989), 43–44.

13   Time Sanctuaries

186 Kierkegaard, *Reader's Digest,* January 1990, 144.

Mumford, *The Conduct of Life,* 258.

Heschel, *The Sabbath* (New York: Farrar, Straus & Giroux, 1951), 29.

187 hobbies, *Public Pulse,* February 1988, 6.

187–188 Mihalyi Csikszentmihalyi, *Flow* (New York: Harper & Row, 1990), 67; *Beyond Boredom and Anxiety* (San Francisco: Jossey-Bass, 1975), 40, 87.

the musician-athlete, Derek Geary, is discussed in *People Weekly,* April 24, 1989, 112.

189 reformed TV addict, USAT, 8/20/87.

Los Angeles family, Dexter Faulkner, "Get Your Family off the Couch," *Plain Truth,* July 1990, 29.

190 "D-Days," Anne Taylor Fleming, "A Case of Guilts," *Special Report: On Living,* February–April 1989, 65.

mother of two, Louise Lague, "The Weekend Quandary," *Working Parents,* June–July 1985, 22.

Los Angeles child care worker, USAT, 8/31/90.

creative family, Linda Hamilton Clinton, "Working Mothers with Infants & Toddlers: How They Manage," *Working Mother,* September 1981, 144.

another family, Louise Lague, *Working Parents,* June–July 1985, 23.

191 one leisure expert, Michael Marsden, Bowling Green State University.

Rehnquist, *Vital Speeches of the Day,* July 1, 1987, 50.

191–192 de Grazia, "Problems and Promise of Leisure," 341.

192 Franklin, *Autobiography and Other Writings,* 170.

leisure-phobe, Lawrence Wright, "Time on My Hands," 14.

Meerlo, "The Time Sense in Psychiatry," Fraser, *Voices of Time,* 241.

European leisure, John Elkins, 16, 18; Liz Lufkin, "Body Management," *Working Woman,* April 1990, 112; Suzanne Gordon, "Work, Work, Work," *The Boston Globe Magazine,* August 20, 1989, 41.

American vacation data, *Public Pulse,* August 1987, 6; March 1986, 5; July 1988, 2.

193 "My husband and I," Judith Stone, "Beware the Shattered Idyll," *Savvy,* January 1981, 48.

194 eight-day bike tour, *ibid.,* 49.

man who forgot daughter, Eviatar Zerubavel, 137.

Simon, *Contemporary Authors,* vol. 127, 1986, 413.

196 Victor and Helen Goertzel, *Cradles of Eminence* (London: Constable, 1962), 254–255.

14   Striking a Balance

200 Godbey, Mary Ellin Barrett, "Balance, The New Buzzword," *USA Today Weekend,* October 21–23, 1988, 5.

Muti, PI, 3/30/90.

201 Kansas family, Richard Louv, *San Diego Union,* 6/19/88.

Dolores Curran, *Stress and the Healthy Family* (Minneapolis: Winston Press, 1985), excerpted in *Redbook,* June 1985, 88.

202 Brody, NYT, 10/22/80.

203 Pogrebin, Susan Edmiston, "Organizing Your Time," *Harper's Bazaar,* September 1972, 10; Pogrebin, "Prisoner of Time," *Ms.,* October 1988, 20.

Lunden, *People Weekly,* November 3, 1980.

Whelan, "Confessions of a 'Superwoman,' " *Across the Board,* December 1980, 17, 20–25.

204 management consultant, Jack Falvey, WSJ, 9/17/84.

woman executive, USAT, 8/20/87.

205 "karoshi," DDN, 1/6/91.

   Dorney, "Making Time to Manage," *Harvard Business Review,* January–February 1988, 39.

   Kelley, WSJ, 6/13/89.

   overconsumption, Jan M. Rosen, NYT, 5/19/90.

206 two-teacher family, Deborah Gemmill, "Strrretch That Pay Check," *American Baby,* May 1990, 85–86.

   woman who left work, Margaret Day, "From Two Incomes Down to One," *Better Homes and Gardens,* October 1987, 36.

   Wachtel, "Are You Better Off Now Than You Were in 1957?" *Utne Reader,* July–August 1988, 58.

207–208 *Fortune,* Fern Schumer Chapman, "Executive Guilt: Who's Taking Care of the Children?" February 16, 1987, 30.

208 Stanford study, *ibid.*

   DuPont surveys, NYT, 3/8/89; *Newsweek,* March 18, 1989, 45.

   Half survey, Sam Allis, "What Do Men Really Want?" *Time* Special Issue, "Women: The Road Ahead," Fall 1990, 81.

   half of all eligible men, Joseph F. McKenna, "The Daddy Track," *Industry Week,* March 5, 1990, 14.

   Fortune survey, "Executive Guilt," 30, 35.

   Koppel, *Newsweek,* February 16, 1981, 75; PI, 5/29/87.

   Lynch, DDN, 7/12/90.

   wise man, Arnold Zack, in Paul Tsongas, *Heading Home* (New York: Alfred A. Knopf, 1984), 160.

   one economist's estimate, Barbara Basler, "Putting a Career on Hold," *New York Times Magazine,* December 7, 1986, 160.

209 O'Connor, John Leo, "Reality Check for Harassed Parents," *U.S. News and World Report,* April 3, 1989.

   Barnard graduates, Carol Kleiman, DDN, 7/30/90.

   Roper, *Public Pulse,* December 1988, 3.

210 Boston University study, Dianne S. Burden and Bradley Googins, *Balancing Job and Homelife Study* (Boston University School of Social Work, 1987), 23, 25.

   U.S. and South Africa, Nina Darnton, "Mommy vs. Mommy," *Newsweek,* June 4, 1990, 67.

   Spain's parliament, NYT, 5/30/89.

   1987 Labor Department survey, Robert Samuelson, "The Daddy Track," *Newsweek,* April 3, 1989, 47.

   IBM, *U.S. News & World Report,* October 31, 1988, 13; *Business Week,* March 20, 1989, 128.

   DuPont, NYT, 3/8/89.

211 Johnson & Johnson, NYT, 1/28/90.

   job-share boss, NYT, 10/12/89.

   San Francisco market researcher, LAT, 8/22/89.

   Canadian mother, "Commitments to Family," *MacLean's,* January 5, 1987, 74.

Knaub, in Anita Shreve, *Remaking Motherhood* (New York: Viking, 1987), 164.

213 MIT study, "Memos," *Industry Week,* March 20, 1989, 8.

214 Friedman, 1974, 205.

215 Valery, Robert I. Fitzhenry, ed., *The Barnes & Noble Book of Quotations* (New York: Harper & Row, 1987), 39.

Index